NATO AND THE RUSSIAN WAR IN UKRAINE

JANNE HAALAND MATLARY
ROB JOHNSON *(Editors)*

NATO and the Russian War in Ukraine

Strategic Integration and Military Interoperability

HURST & COMPANY, LONDON

First published in the United Kingdom in 2024 by
C. Hurst & Co. (Publishers) Ltd.,
New Wing, Somerset House, Strand, London, WC2R 1LA
© Janne Haaland Matlary, Rob Johnson and the Contributors, 2024
All rights reserved.

Distributed in the United States, Canada and Latin America by
Oxford University Press, 198 Madison Avenue, New York, NY 10016,
United States of America.

The right of Janne Haaland Matlary, Rob Johnson and the
Contributors to be identified as the authors of this publication
is asserted by them in accordance with the Copyright, Designs and
Patents Act, 1988.

A Cataloguing-in-Publication data record for this book
is available from the British Library.

ISBN: 9781911723141

www.hurstpublishers.com

Printed in Great Britain by Bell & Bain Ltd, Glasgow

This book is dedicated to Professor Christopher Coker: stoic philosopher, bon vivant, and aficionado of literature, but, above all, an exemplary scholar and true friend.

CONTENTS

Foreword by General Sir James Everard ix
Acknowledgements xiii
List of Contributors xv
List of Abbreviations xix

1. Introduction 1
   Janne Haaland Matlary & Rob Johnson

PART ONE
MILITARY INTEGRATION IN NATO

2. Multidomain Integration and Multidomain Operations 21
   Rob Johnson
3. The NATO 2022 Strategic Concept: Guiding, Aligning, Binding? 41
   Tim Sweijs & Tara de Klerk
4. Maritime-Strategic Integration and Interoperability in NATO: The Case of Standing NATO Maritime Group 1 (SNMG1) 71
   Steinar Torset & Amund Lundesgaard

PART TWO
THE WAR IN UKRAINE
STRATEGIC SHOCK, STRATEGIC CHANGE?

5. Return to a bleak past? The Russian Invasion of Ukraine and the International System 99
   Beatrice Heuser

6. The United States and Europe: Reforging the NATO Alliance 117
   Andrew A. Michta

7. The Threat Posed by Russia and China After the Ukraine War 133
   Kori Schake

PART THREE
THE IMPACT OF THE WAR
ENHANCED MILITARY INTEGRATION?

8. *Zeitenwende* or Business as Usual? German Defence Policy Following Russia's Invasion of Ukraine 153
   Robin Allers & Håkon Lunde Saxi

9. Finland's Approach to Military Cooperation and Integration: From Alignment to Alliance 175
   Tuomas Iso-Markku & Matti Pesu

10. NATO and the Ukraine Defense Contact Group: Frontline States and Followers 197
    Janne Haaland Matlary

Notes 223
Index 263

FOREWORD BY
GENERAL SIR JAMES EVERARD

Timing is everything, and this book could not be more timely, relevant or important given the truth of its central hypothesis—that in response to Russia's war in Ukraine, strategic and military integration in Europe continues to be enhanced, with NATO at the point of the spear.

NATO is already stronger than it was before Russia's illegal and unprovoked invasion of Ukraine. NATO is growing in terms of combat power. Yet a second, less overt message, is that after 'three decades of strategic slumber' there is a mountain to climb to navigate the threat posed by a resurgent Russia, China's rise and the shifting geopolitical landscape. This book clearly shows that, together, there is a better chance of exploiting opportunities and reaching the summit, not just as NATO, but as a collective of 'frontline states and followers'.

The 2022 Strategic Concept is short on detail, but that is for a reason. As you build consensus, ambiguity is often the way out of a dark wood; it is a strength and not a weakness. The Strategic Concept was the product of the most intense period of consultation about NATO's requirements since 9/11. The transformation of Euro-Atlantic strategy and common purpose that it generated was the most significant since 1991 and the most important since 1949. Having opened a window of opportunity in Madrid to modernise NATO for a new era of collective defence, the Vilnius Summit went further by supporting the Strategic Concept with a new specific military concept—the Concept for Deterrence and Defence of the Euro-Atlantic Area (DDA). DDA represents the return to an over-arching force employment strategy—in peace, crisis and war—and placed deterrence and defence back at the heart of alliance action. DDA includes Regional Plans—now in place—that integrate national and NATO plans and take account of 'the geostrategic reconfiguration of NATO's Northeastern flank'. NATO leaders also made a commitment to provide a larger pool of high-readiness forces across different domains—land, maritime, air and cyber—to be pre-assigned to specific plans for the defence of allies.

And they needed to, because the alliance was not ready for a '*eine Zeitenwende* in the history of our continent' and a return to the political and military challenges of collective defence. It was not just that 'Europeans have got used to a comfortable life' and failed to prioritise defence spending but that NATO leaders have faced a rolling barrage of difficult and distracting strategic shocks this millennium. Bottom line? If allies keep to their promises—and the evidence to date is that they are and will—delivering DDA will still take years of sustained effort to deliver in full. However, the momentum is undeniable.

I write this several hundred metres underground in the Joint Warfare Centre In-Rock Facility, where NATO is conducting the largest command post exercise in its history, connecting all points of command across the NATO area under Supreme Headquarters Allied Powers Europe (SHAPE) in its role as a warfighting headquarters. Simultaneously, as part of a wider programme of operational experimentation, NATO is testing and developing the cross-domain aspects of DDA, with success despite shortfalls in connectivity (to be addressed over time). We are also learning that sometimes a single domain 'hammer' is all you need.

I admire all the scholars who have contributed to this book, and the ideas and arguments they put forward. Every chapter is an education and I recommend this book highly; it should be pored over and scrutinised. After all, as Rob Rieman, the author of *To Fight Against the Age: On Fascism and Humanism*, told us, 'Clio, the muse of history, offers us the gift of historical (and contemporary) awareness—but one has to read books to get to know her and benefit from her gifts'.

Sir James Everard
Former Deputy Supreme Allied Command Europe (DSACEUR),
NATO

ACKNOWLEDGEMENTS

We would like to thank the Norwegian Ministry of Defence for their generous grant, which supported the research, and colleagues at workshops in Oslo and Oxford for useful comments at the drafting stage of this book.

Oxford/Oslo
JHM and RJ, Autumn 2023

LIST OF CONTRIBUTORS

Robin Allers is Associate Professor at the Norwegian Institute for Defence Studies and the Norwegian Defence University College. He holds a PhD in History from the University of Hamburg. His research focuses on European security policy and Norway's security and defence relations with close allies such as Germany.

Beatrice Heuser holds the Chair of International Relations, University of Glasgow. She is currently seconded to the General Staff College of the Bundeswehr as head of the strategy section. She is the author of *The Evolution of Strategy* (CUP 2010), *War: A Genealogy of Western Ideas and Practices* (OUP 2022) and many other works on war and strategy. She has worked in NATO Headquarters and has taught at universities in France and Germany and currently has an affiliation with the Free University of Brussels.

Tuomas Iso-Markku is a Senior Research Fellow at the Finnish Institute of International Affairs. His research deals with the EU's role in security and defence matters, European security and defence cooperation, EU–NATO relations, German politics, Finnish EU policy, Finnish foreign security and defence policy

LIST OF CONTRIBUTORS

as well as party politics in Europe. Iso-Markku's publications include both academic and policy-oriented contributions.

Rob Johnson is Director of the Secretary of State's Office of Net Assessment and Challenge and Director of the Changing Character of War Research Centre, Pembroke College, Oxford.

Tara de Klerk works as an Assistant Analyst at the Hague Centre for Strategic Studies, where she specialises in transatlantic relations, hybrid warfare and transnational crime. She holds degrees in Crisis and Security Management Studies (MA, Leiden University, 2023) and European Social and Political Studies with a focus on International Relations (BA, University College London, 2022).

Amund Lundesgaard is Associate Professor at the Norwegian Defence University College. Academically, his expertise lies in maritime and naval strategy and operations as well as emerging operational concepts in the US and NATO. He has also contributed to national and multinational force structure and concept development efforts. He holds a PhD in History from the University of Oslo.

Janne Haaland Matlary is Professor at the Department of Political Science, University of Oslo, and the Norwegian Command and Staff College. Her most recent books are *Verden blir ikke den samme* (Kagge, Oslo, 2023) and *Military Strategy for the 21st Century. The Challenge to NATO* (Hurst 2021) edited with Rob Johnson. She was Deputy Foreign Minister 1997–2000 and is a columnist in various papers.

Andrew A. Michta is Director and Senior Fellow, Scowcroft Strategy Initiative at the Atlantic Council's Scowcroft Center for Strategy and Security and the former Dean of the College of

LIST OF CONTRIBUTORS

International and Security Studies at the George C. Marshall European Center for Security Studies. He holds a PhD in International Relations from Johns Hopkins University. His areas of expertise are international security, NATO and European politics and security, with a special focus on Central Europe and the Baltic states.

Matti Pesu is a Leading Researcher at the Finnish Institute of International Affairs. His areas of expertise include Finnish national security, the Northern European security landscape and transatlantic relations. He has published extensively on his topics of interest, and his writing has appeared in publications such as *Diplomacy and Statecraft*, *War on the Rocks* and *The National Interest*.

Håkon Lunde Saxi is Professor at the Norwegian Defence University College in Oslo. He holds a PhD in Political Science. His research deals with Nordic, British and German defence policy and military strategy. His latest book (in Norwegian) is *War in Europe: The Norwegian Armed Forces in the Balkans, 1992–2005* (Bergen: Fagbokforlaget, 2023).

Kori Schake is a senior fellow and the director of foreign and defence policy studies at the American Enterprise Institute. She served in the US State Department and Department of Defense as well as in the National Security Council at the White House. Dr Schake is the author of *America vs the West: Can the Liberal World Order Be Preserved?* (2018); *Safe Passage: The Transition from British to American Hegemony* (2017) and *Managing American Hegemony: Essays on Power in a Time of Dominance* (2009). She was also co-editor, along with former Secretary of Defense Jim Mattis, of *Warriors & Citizens: American Views of Our Military* (2016). She is a regular contributor to policy journals and the media.

xvii

LIST OF CONTRIBUTORS

Tim Sweijs is the Director of Research at The Hague Centre for Strategic Studies and a Senior Research Fellow at the Netherlands' War Studies Research Centre. He recently published a book on state threat behaviour and interstate crisis escalation over the past century titled *The Use and Utility of Ultimata in Coercive Diplomacy* (Palgrave Macmillan 2023) and the edited volume titled *Beyond Ukraine: Debating the Future of War* (Hurst 2024); he is currently completing a book project as *Rethinking Force Development in An Age of Disruption: Defence Planning for Small and Middle Powers* (Routledge 2024).

Steinar Torset is a Captain (Navy) and Section Head of Military Strategy and Joint Operations at the Norwegian Defence University College in Oslo. He has varied experience from service in national and international staffs. He has served in the Norwegian Joint HQ as well as in the UK Maritime Battle Staff and Combined Joint Operations from the Sea Centre of Excellence, Norfolk, Virginia, as part of an international staff attached to US Fleet Forces Command. He has experience in maritime international operations in UNIFIL, EUNAVFOR Atalanta and Combined Maritime Forces/CTF 150.

LIST OF ABBREVIATIONS

AI	artificial intelligence
A2AD	anti-access area denial
AUKUS	Australia, United Kingdom, United States
C2	command and control
CBRN	Chemical, biological, radiological and nuclear weapons
CDU/CSU	German Christian Democratic Party
CSDP	Common Foreign and Security Policy
DARPA	Defense Advanced Research Projects Agency
DDA	Deterrence and Defence of the Euro-Atlantic Area
E12	European Intervention Initiative
FNC	Framework Nations Concept
GDP	gross domestic product
GPS	global positioning system
JADC2	Joint All-Domain Command and Control
JEF	Joint Expeditionary Force
EU	European Union

LIST OF ABBREVIATIONS

FDP	Free Democratic Party of Germany
ISAF	International Security Assistance Force
MDI	multidomain integration
MDO	multidomain operations
NATO	North Atlantic Treaty Organization
NFM	New Force Model
NORDEFCO	Nordic Defence Cooperation
NRF	NATO Response Force
NRF/M NATO	Response Force/Maritime
PfP	Partnership for Peace
RBIO	Rules-Based International Order
SACEUR	Supreme Allied Commander Europe
SDP	German Social Democratic Party
SNMG1	Standing NATO Maritime Group 1
SNMCMG1	Standing NATO Mine Countermeasures Group 1
UDCG	Ukraine Defense Contact Group
UN	United Nations
USAF	US Air Force

1

INTRODUCTION

Janne Haaland Matlary & Robert Johnson

It is no exaggeration to state that the illegal and unprovoked full-scale Russian invasion of Ukraine transformed Europe and gave renewed purpose to the North Atlantic Treaty Organisation (NATO).

This is the first account of the challenges and the solutions for so-called multi-domain and strategic integration in the defence sector in Europe, focusing on how NATO is the 'hub' for such integration and how Russia's war may impact on the alliance structure. It shows, thematically and through national cases, how interoperability and strategic integration are conceived, debated, problematised and resolved. It is written with specific reference to the influence of the Russian invasion of Ukraine, asking: to what extent has Russia's war driven effective and permanent NATO integration?

We understand the term 'integration' to go beyond cooperation. Integration suggests states are more deeply 'connected', creating dependence on each other and thus forging a lasting commitment. This creates challenges for defence integration because matters of sovereignty and political preference make themselves felt. Before the full-scale war in Ukraine in 2022, there was a rich debate about strategic integration and military interoperability, about the conditions for defence integration and the role that the alliance plays in national defence policies among member states. The existence of bi-, tri- and mini-lateral cooperation, or integration in regional groupings, was thought to give potential alternatives to the alliance, but the war of 2022 demonstrated there was not much evidence for that.

Coalitions of states with common interests are increasingly common. However, they do not 'compete' with formal multilateral organizations; rather, they complement them. This is the major point made by Bence Nemeth in his book *How to Achieve Defence Cooperation in Europe: The Subregional Approach*.[1] He points out that there exists a web of formats and that, together, they in fact complement formal organizations. He writes: 'NATO and the EU continue to provide crucial structural context in which bi- and mini-lateral cooperation can happen'.[2] In a survey of more than seventy such coalitions, he finds that: 'their proliferation is unprecedented in European history' and that they are driven by several factors: the economic need to generate so-called 'critical mass' for key capabilities; deep historical and cultural ties that foster trust through long-standing NATO membership; and an interest in spearheading action and influencing NATO or the EU in a particular direction.[3]

There are striking examples of coalitions, such as the Joint Expeditionary Force (JEF), led by the UK. It was the JEF that invited Sweden and Finland to become full members before they joined NATO.[4] They had not applied for NATO membership at the time of joining JEF, but this coalition certainly assisted the process of joining the alliance. In another example, AUKUS is the trilateral alliance on submarine procurement between the US, UK and Australia, which will enhance the nuclear capabilities

INTRODUCTION

of the UK for the Euro-Atlantic area. In addition, there are various bilateral agreements between Finland and Sweden, with the US, the UK, as well as Norway. Moreover, the Lancaster House agreement between the UK and France has been in existence from 2010. Finally, the Nordic Defence Cooperation (NORDEFCO) represents a specific regional focus but has the effect of strengthening the capability and interoperability of northern allies as a homogeneous group.

Right after Finland joined NATO in April 2023, the four Nordic air forces signed an agreement to integrate in the air domain, through common basing, training and exercising but also, critically, in the form of operational planning. This allows for a seamless system of air defence and acts as a real force multiplier.[5] It is an excellent example of military integration within NATO. Crucially, it represented a significant strengthening of the alliance: when all the Nordic countries became members, integration was achieved and thus the allies presented a common front—in operational as well as geographical terms. Interoperability, common standards and procedures and intelligence sharing are vital in any military alliance. Once states share these features, they are free to integrate far more effectively, provided, of course, that they share strategic interest and an appreciation of a common threat. We can therefore expect a far deeper defence integration in the Nordic region in the years ahead. Trust and levels of historical cooperation are high, the region is a natural 'security community', where its governments are willing to go further in creating mutual interdependence. A strongly integrated Nordic defence region will also benefit the UK, the leading state in the Northern European theatre, and, in turn, this is advantageous for the US which can partner with a strong and reliable coalition.

Most of these examples of coalitions are in the category of strategic enterprises—AUKUS came about because Australia needed to be able to deter China's threatening submarine activity and therefore abandoned the contract for diesel-engine submarines with France—much to the consternation and anger of Paris. NORDEFCO was conceived as a way to save money while not endangering the various arrangements with NATO that the Nordic countries had at the time. With Sweden and Finland in NATO and Nordic military integration in the face of Russia's clear aggression, NORDEFCO assumed greater strategic importance. The Lancaster House Agreement between France and Britain is clearly a strategic relationship between two of the major military powers of Europe, both with global reach, nuclear deterrence capacity and veto membership of the UN Security Council. The British 'refresh' strategy (2023) acknowledges France as the key partner in its region.[6] Naturally, there is also a potential financial saving in these cases, as training, procurement and maintenance benefit from military integration and cooperation. However, the cost factor itself, although a strong and unavoidable driver of military integration, is not sufficient to achieve this unless there is common strategic outlook.

The imperative to save money was certainly not the motive that drove the coalition to give weapons assistance to Ukraine. States in this grouping have contributed weapons and financial assistance and they have depleted their own armaments, munitions and equipment stocks. Their motives have been to enable a neutral, sovereign nation to defend itself as a point of principle, but the fact that this has occurred on the periphery of Europe against a self-evident threat to Europe by Russia has added to its importance. There is a sense in which assisting Ukraine is a way to reduce Russia's aggressive power without risking a full scale, escalatory war. If these strategic interests explain the coalition, it may be of a more lasting nature than an ad hoc coalition. However, we observe groups of states within the alliance contrasting with a more proactive coalition, each taking

INTRODUCTION

different positions, a point this volume highlights. Nevertheless, on balance, Russia is a strategic challenge with a record of hostile actions against the West. It has forged a more integrated NATO alliance precisely because Russia was willing to take a massive risk and invade another country. Russia's political intention to displace Western leadership with a new 'multipolar order', its enhanced military capacity and its blatant war of aggression in Europe has spurred the West's robust response.

A major assumption of this volume is that NATO membership enables deep defence integration, despite a tendency for the member states to pursue separate national interests, equipment programmes and defence postures, an idea that lingered long after the years of a 'peace dividend' after the Cold War. It is not surprising that, with more than 30 member states, NATO is a large entity with varying national interests, and the sheer size of the alliance means that it will likely develop further 'regional clusters'. This was already evident before the war with regard to Northern Europe. However, once there is a shared strategic interest, given sudden sharp relief by the Kremlin's war against Ukraine, there is a much stronger incentive for integration, and sovereignty issues assumed less importance.

There is a risk that, if the war in Ukraine reduces in intensity, the cost factor will reassert itself. A steady and long-term approach to procurement has been the means to keep defence costs down. By contrast, the urgent demand for munition stocks drove up the price. Artillery ammunition has increased fourfold since the war started, as the chairman of NATO's Military Committee, Admiral Rob Bauer, recently told media in Oslo.[7] The cost is much higher, but the higher demand is likely to remain for some time due to the need to refill depleted stocks and because Russia must be deterred in a new way, as NATO's new strategic concept of 2022 makes clear. The UK, for example, is completing the modernisation of its entire nuclear fleet and increasing its stockpiles of warheads, while Poland and Sweden are increasing the scale of their conventional armed forces by a significant degree.

In sum, the drivers for more integration can be assumed to be stronger after the intensified phase of Russia's war against Ukraine, despite the cost. Even though procurement is more expensive, there is a demand to spend more on defence across all the NATO member states. We can therefore conclude that, of all the factors driving greater integration, it is the dramatic change in strategic interest, initiated by the war, that has made it easier politically to take action and contribute to deterring Russia. Thus, our hypothesis is that the war has had a positive impact on strategic and military integration in Europe. As one humourist put it, Putin has been NATO's best recruiting sergeant.

It is still too early to evaluate the full impact of the war. This book was written during 2023 when the war was raging and no clear outcome was in sight. The advantage is that we can provide analysis of the alliance's early response; the disadvantage is that we cannot forecast the end of the conflict or its lasting impact. Nevertheless, we have opted to offer this early analysis of the effect on the alliance, rather than commentating on the war itself, as many other analysts have chosen to do. The war will be, by its nature, a dynamic and unpredictable phenomenon, but the NATO alliance has greater stability and longevity, which gives us the chance to convey observations with greater certainty. Our method is therefore exemplification and not a comprehensive coverage of the conflict. We provide examples of key types of strategic and military integration and the relationship this has to NATO.

* * *

In Part One, Military Integration in NATO, we present the latest thinking in major states, such as the US and UK as well as

INTRODUCTION

NATO as a whole, on military integration beyond joint doctrine, the so-called multi-domain integration. As Rob Johnson points out in his chapter, NATO has developed its templates for multidomain operations (MDO) as well as for the even more complex alliance-wide multi-domain integration (MDI), which would integrate non-military tools along with military ones in one single strategy. These are concepts yet to be refined and operationalised, but they point the way forward for allies that want to develop deeper levels of integration than those common to all members. However, the importance of this work implies that NATO is ever more relevant to all its members, as they increasingly depend on the conceptual and operational framing that NATO does in this field. As Johnson points out, the US is, as usual, in the lead, underlining the strong dependence that allies have on Washington. European 'clusters' of states will therefore continue to depend very much on US developments.

Tim Sweijs and Tara de Klerk provide an analysis of the NATO Strategic Concept (2022), asking whether it facilitates cooperation and integration while facing up to the challenges of the alliance. The authors observe that 'NATO has returned to a state of "persistent confrontation" that is likely to endure at least for the coming decade' as Russia's revisionism traces 'a historical pattern of rivalries'. In their assessment of the guiding, binding and aligning power of the Concept, they examine whether NATO's Strategic Concept 'offers allies a template for cohesive action' that will facilitate integration and coordination. Overall, they consider the Concept a 'useful beacon' that comes with 'strong implementation guidelines' and thereby 'helps guide and shape national defence efforts while binding a diverse coalition of allies'. The Concept's 'regional concentration and assignment of troops to defend specific allies is testament to this approach (multi-domain operations)'. Sweijs and de Klerk caution, however, that the Concept's ultimate impact on driving integration will depend on a sustained and prolonged effort of individual members.

The changes observed or wrought by the Russian war against Ukraine are not merely diplomatic and political: they are also operational and tactical. Ukraine was widely expected to crumble under the mass of Russian military power, but it made a defence in depth, resisted Russian attempts to seize Kyiv in an airborne *coup de main* and lost only one major urban centre in Kherson. Its tactics were determined, devolved, with dispersed infantry and armoured manoeuvre, while Russian forces seemed to expect only minor resistance. The Russians were forced to consolidate, pulling back to occupied zones in Donbass. NATO member states studied the conflict carefully, observing how Ukraine had to receive multiple types of weapons, munitions, equipment and vehicles since NATO had no standard types. Ukrainians adopted Western systems very rapidly though, calling into question the long training schedule preferred by NATO. The scale of munitions consumption also surprised the allies. Ukraine was using vast stocks every week, even though it was firing only a fifth of that which Russia possessed.

The war in Ukraine therefore highlighted several integration difficulties for NATO. The dilemma of varied commitments, investments and defence spending matched the variety of arms and equipment NATO was using. Moreover, while Europeans focused on the Russian land forces threat, it was actually in naval, air and strategic rocket forces that Russia was still intact. It is also in these areas that NATO is well integrated and has been so for a long time. In the naval domain, the chapter by Steinar Torset and Amund Lundesgaard presents an in-depth analysis of the level of maritime integration in NATO. They use the case of the Standing NATO Maritime Group 1 (SNMG1), which is nevertheless just one part of NATO's integration in the maritime domain. Using an innovative method for measuring

INTRODUCTION

activity and interoperability, they find that the force is a 'hub' for integration which 'is crucial in showing alliance solidarity and it is central in preparing the alliance as a collective for conventional maritime warfare'.

Our findings are that there are some areas that are already well developed in integration and some areas of discordance. The charter of the NATO alliance remains unambiguous: there is one command structure, and there are three independent nuclear powers in the alliance. At sea and in the air, NATO forces are entirely interoperable. US and French aircraft can fly onto and from British aircraft carriers, and US, Canadian and European allies often contribute to NATO flotillas in the high North Atlantic, in the Baltic and in the Mediterranean. Yet in terms of land forces, much more can be done in integration.

**

In Part Two, The War in Ukraine: Strategic Shock, Strategic Change?, we look at the impact of the war on strategic interests and strategic-level integration in Europe in particular. If military integration at lower levels is hampered by the lack of common strategic outlook, common strategic interests must 'solve' this problem as it presents the West with a clear-cut, unambiguous threat: Russia the aggressor. As we saw, this has major implications for NATO planning, as evidenced in the new strategic concept, but does it lead to more integration among states in Europe?

Two American contributions make an assessment: as Kori Schake points out in her long list of strategic implications for Russia, Moscow should realise that the West does not tolerate attacks on civilians and civilian infrastructure and that such crimes matter a great deal for the West. Values and security interests work in the same direction and reinforce each other. Moreover, Western resolve has been firm; there was no split or weakening in the support for the Ukrainians. The war united the West, contrary to Russian assumptions, and this in turn has strengthened NATO.

Yet the West needs to prepare for war. Schake states: 'We have not been serious about the prospect of war', and there is a major task of preparation ahead. There is not the necessary production capacity, and there is a need for strategic culture that emphasises readiness and preparedness. The war has strategic implications contrary to Russia's aims, but the implications of these require that Europeans in particular have be able to mount a credible defence and, hence, deterrence. It is a change of both funding and strategic mindset.

Andrew Michta discusses 'three decades of strategic slumber' in Europe and calls for 'burden-transferring' rather than 'burden-sharing'. There is a need for Europe to lead and to fund their own defence to a much greater degree. The US will continue to 'pivot to Asia' and will most likely provide the 'nuclear umbrella' for NATO in Europe, but perhaps not major conventional forces in the future. Thus, the war is a 'wake-up call' for the Europeans: they will have to deter Russia in their own continent. Yet we notice that the supply of weapons to Ukraine was initiated and led by the US, and it is the US that provides 90% of the aid. Michta argues that it is the Northern and Central European states that are most committed to aiding Ukraine, and it is these states that have a strategic culture most closely aligned to the US. Thus, the US will seek closer integration with these allies, and, among these member states, the UK and Poland stand out.

A European perspective is provided by Beatrice Heuser's analysis, which points in the same direction: the war may have united Europe, but that does not mean that Europe is ready to deal with the consequences. 'No war comes at a good time', she notes drily, 'but the Ukraine war definitely not'. Before the conflict, Europe was in an economic crisis and defence

INTRODUCTION

spending was low. However, the stakes in this war are high. Under threat are the principles of the UN Charter and the concomitant 'rules-based order'. Europe has long insisted it is committed to these principles and values. Yet, strikingly, the leadership in dealing with the war has been provided by the US, not Europe.

In sum, there is not much to laud in terms of European leadership in a war on its own borders: Europe followed the US. While one may praise the fact that there has been unity of effort in aiding Ukraine so far, this is a war that affects Europe directly; as such, one would expect its strategic leadership in it.

At the strategic level, then, Russia has undoubtedly failed, but that does not mean that Europe has yet succeeded. We do not see clear European leadership in this situation although strategic interests are shared. But to 'walk the walk' is harder than to 'talk the talk'. Several European states are still below the 'threshold' of 2% GDP spending on defence, and there is little evidence of consolidation of the European armaments industry for a war-time effort. When one assesses the sheer volume of resources that have been needed to check and hold the Russian armed forces, and the rates of expenditure, it leaves some serious questions for the NATO member states.

So, on the defence policy and military operational level, do we see any specific impact of the war at a national level?

* * *

In Part Three, The Impact of the War: Enhanced Military Integration?, we look for effects that are caused by the war at national domestic level and among states. Here, we examine the major changes that have taken place in Finland and Sweden, and in Germany, as well as in the ad hoc weapons coalition that supplies Ukraine. These are all major new developments where European states assume new roles.

The accession of Finland and Sweden makes Northern European defence more robust, but the North is also more important strategically, given the new long border between NATO and Russia and the renewed importance of the High North as a region of increasing strategic confrontation between Russia and the United States. Northern Europe is more united, strategically, and integrated as a result of the war. The Northern European states have joined forces around British leadership, while the Nordic air forces have adopted an agreement for fully joint operational planning, basing and training. This is a good example of how a clear, common strategic interest—deterring Russia—now allows for close operational integration. The same common strategic sense is also evident in Central Europe, with the exception of Hungary (which believes it can chart a middle course). Poland emerged as the new leader of the NATO member states in that region, along with the Baltic states, Slovakia and the Czech Republic. They have been the most welcoming of Ukrainian refugees, eager to modernise their militaries and keen to enhance their readiness to fight if required. These states have furthermore integrated among themselves as a result of the war, both in terms of coordination of weapons supply to Ukraine but also within NATO in the organisation's new emphasis on deterrence by denial. They have done so within NATO, not as an alternative structure to the alliance. Put simply, it was purely the shock of the Russian invasion of Ukraine, on such a large scale, that prompted them to seek closer cooperation as a matter of urgency.

The North-European 'cluster' of states cooperates closely with the Central Europeans. One example of this is the so-called Tallinn Pledge, where the then UK defence minister Ben Wallace encouraged his Northern and Baltic colleagues to support F-16 pilot training and the donation of these fighter planes to Ukraine. The Baltic states were brought much closer

INTRODUCTION

to Nordic cooperation through Swedish and Finnish NATO membership. The fact that Russia has shown the political will to launch a conventional attack on a European state despite the very great risk it implied is the critical new element that created the urgency to respond and which made deep military integration an imperative. The perception is that their adversary is serious and presents the same danger to all European states. They therefore need not worry about sovereignty issues and differing political interests in accepting a deeper level of integration.

A major effect of the war of Europe was that Finland and Sweden applied to join NATO. As the chapter by Iso-Markku and Pesu shows, the strategic shock of the invasion of neutral Ukraine led Finland to apply for membership in record time. Here we can observe that the extensive military integration with NATO, with the US, the UK and the other Nordic countries, especially Sweden, did not suffice for Finland. There was also now a need for the nuclear security guarantee that only NATO membership offers. The authors point out that both Finland and Sweden have integrated with NATO and other NATO states to an unprecedented degree in the years leading up to their application, but the public had not wanted membership until the war broke out. This level of integration made accession natural and easy to agree on, but the causal factor was the lack of full protection that previous bilateral and trilateral agreements entailed. There was a desire for more cooperation, but, more importantly, there was suddenly an existential need for an alliance with nuclear deterrence.

The case of Finnish and Swedish membership and the full gamut of cooperative agreements preceding this and continuing illustrates the major point of this book: NATO is a 'hub' for clusters of deeper integration formats among members, but these schemes do not replace membership or compete with the NATO alliance itself. Only membership within NATO provides access to and participation in the common operational and planning structures, and only membership provides protection by the so-called 'nuclear umbrella' and the ultimate deterrent effect that this entails. It is a point that has led to Ukraine's appeal to join the alliance at the earliest possible opportunity.

NATO membership is therefore more often than not the necessary, but not sufficient, condition for deep strategic and military integration among member states.

The German *Zeitenwende* is also solidifying Germany's role and place in NATO. Not only is the country charting a new course entirely with regard to Russia, but it is also firmly underlining its transatlantic security commitment. The idea of the EU as a possible alternative to the alliance has been weakened significantly by the war as NATO and the EU now appear to play complementary roles: NATO as the military alliance and the EU as the economic and political organisation for Europe. Germany is developing its defence role and has pledged to spend much more on defence, but, as the authors of the chapter on Germany in this volume, Håkon Lunde Saxi and Robin Allers, point out, while the German chancellor has promised a major role in defending the Eastern flank of NATO, 'even with more funding and an active defence minister it will be a huge task to reverse decades of spending cuts and to reform the bureaucratized procurement system'. However, Germany's political, demographic and economic weight is such that it will matter a great deal for NATO once the *Zeitenwende* becomes a real *Wende*. If so, Germany could become the driving force in European defence that its allies have long called for, playing a leading role in integration of deterrence and defence capacities in this region.

As Matlary's chapter shows, although more than 50 states contribute to the weapons coalition to aid Ukraine, there are groupings of states with different approaches. The 'front-line'

INTRODUCTION

states that most strongly want Ukraine to prevail militarily consist of the US, UK, the Poles, the Finns and the Balts. They form a leading coalition within the group. They are also the most likely to continue their cooperation after the war, as they are clear that they see Russia as an adversary that has to be deterred for many years to come. These states also share geography—close to Russia and the extremely important High North and North Atlantic. Thus, while the large 'aid' coalition comprises almost every state in Europe, there are differences in threat perception and strategic thinking and the balance of cost and commitment.

Interests, Integration and Cooperation

The inspiration for this volume was the developments, issues and themes that have preoccupied NATO allies since the end of the Cold War and how the war in Ukraine has impacted on them. These include: the sense that the interoperability of NATO in the 1980s had somehow atrophied; the evolution of differences in national interests in the 1990s; the re-rolling from conventional warfare to 'out of area operations' (particularly peace enforcement and counterinsurgency); the development of hybrid (sub-threshold coercion) in 2011–14; and, not least, the shock of the illegal and unwarranted Russian invasion of Ukraine in 2022. The volume was also driven by discussions about the promise of multi-domain warfare and the associated imperative that there would be inter-allied integration. This was raised as a collective security question but also through the interests and concerns of individual countries.

The challenges for NATO can sometimes appear weighty. The alliance is faced with the prospect of an aggressive Russian neighbour armed with nuclear, chemical and large conventional forces. The Kremlin made clear in December 2021 that it regarded itself as in a struggle with the West, not just Ukraine.

Moscow's alignment with Beijing, deeply opposed to the United States, suggests that NATO would face the prospect of seeing its primary actor, America, divided between two strategic theatres. Washington has long called for the European allies to do more for their own defence, and the Russian invasion of Ukraine appeared to make that imperative. In addition, NATO member states like France and the United Kingdom also have global interests and see their role as one which retains an expeditionary focus. This leaves the smaller northern, eastern and southern European states with the prospect of greater defence spending at the time of an energy crisis created by the Russian attack and their own negligent dependence on Moscow's supplies. In short, the war drives major changes in NATO, as an alliance, but also in terms of the strategic interests and approaches of its member states.

The hypothesis, in line with the literature on the subject, is that NATO and bi-, tri- and multilateral cooperation and integration are mutually reinforcing. The alliance provides a system for military standards and templates for interoperability, whereas member states are the ones that own and decide on almost all military assets. But NATO interoperability is the 'gold standard'. Even before joining NATO, Sweden and Finland strove to be NATO-interoperable, as does every partner state. As we have seen, Finland's way to full membership was greatly aided by its persistent adaptation to NATO standards and not least its eager and full participation in groups like JEF and NORDEFCO as well as its bilateral relationship with the US and the UK.

We have also seen that a major change occurred with the Russian attack on Ukraine. Both Finland and Sweden rushed to seek membership in NATO. Partnership and coalitions were not enough; they also needed the 'nuclear umbrella' provided by article 5 in the NATO treaty. NATO has been strengthened as an alliance as a result of the war, not only regarding these two states, but also Ukraine's strong wish to become a member.

INTRODUCTION

Coalition-based security assistance and even security guarantees will not suffice.

The strategic impact on NATO is that it has produced a new strategic concept that provides policy on how to deter Russia. The military plans for NATO are naturally classified, but it is known that they call for major increases in troop deployments along the whole border with Russia and that states in NATO will provide earmarked troops to north, central and south regions. This will impose much more direction on regional cooperation and integration than before, and we can expect regional integration to be much deeper than before now that the strategic interest of deterring Russia is crystal-clear to states in the north of Europe and hopefully beyond. The provision of a plan for regional deterrence that NATO now has is the template for such integration.

There is a problem of varying degrees of agreement on the importance of this strategic interest among NATO member states, however. Although all states signed on to the strategic concept, there are groups in NATO that we call the 'frontline' states and others we call pragmatists, the latter being less concerned about Russia as a threat and often situated far from the country. We can therefore expect NATO to remain the institutional basis for military integration, but not for political-strategic integration of 30 or 32 members. There will continue to be groups of states that share strategic interest to such an extent that they are willing to integrate more deeply than others. North and Central Europe come to mind.

The cost factor will also increase in importance. As mentioned, the cost of procurement has risen considerably during the war as demand soars and stocks must be replenished. This happens at a time with zero growth in Europe, high inflation and economic hardship in general. It is not realistic that defence budgets will increase enough to pay for larger defence sectors while aid to

Ukraine must continue. States will have to cooperate also for this reason, and only those that share strategic interests will see the need to make the sacrifices that such integration implies. If one has a choice of not doing much, that is probably the chosen position, but if one's country really needs to deter Russia, there is not that choice.

In a way, it is very fortunate that NATO now provides plans that will act as a template for further integration, and certainly that Finland and Sweden will be able to fully partake in NATO planning as members. This is particularly true for land forces which are not well integrated yet, unlike the sea, special forces and air domains.

PART ONE

MILITARY INTEGRATION IN NATO

2

MULTIDOMAIN INTEGRATION AND MULTIDOMAIN OPERATIONS

Rob Johnson

The Russian war against Ukraine, a conflict still underway at the time of writing, fostered a spirit of unity and integration across NATO, but it exposed some discordance and gaps in the interoperability of its armed forces. While the conduct of operations occupied the attention of NATO member states, defence planners had to consider whether they should increase the scale and stocks of existing forces, or if they should accelerate modernisation programmes through investment in advanced systems and new platforms. At the heart of this discussion was the degree to which NATO could integrate at the tactical and strategic level.

The perennial dilemma for these defence planners was to ascertain as accurately as possible how wars in the future would be fought. The question that dominated discussion was: to what extent did the war in Ukraine indicate the future character of war? By the early 2020s, there was a debate between the advocates of a futuristic digitised battlespace, where everything is integrated, and the sceptics who looked at past wars and the follies of former futurists. These were, of course, polar positions, but the advocates of modernisation argued that the only effective approach was to construct a truly integrated system across all domains of land, sea, air, space and the informational-electronic environment. The sceptics maintained that things always go wrong, and the complexity of multidomain operations could be its undoing. Moreover, the critics stated that the new systems were so expensive that they could only be produced in very small numbers, when cheap quantities, 'mass', had 'a quality all of its own'.

This chapter examines how NATO plans integration and the dilemmas associated with the introduction of a highly connected approach to military operations. The concept of multidomain operations (MDOs) sets out a doctrine on how to fight, whereas multidomain integration (MDI) implies the close cooperation of policy, strategy, investment and modernisation, but ensuring an even development across the alliance is a major challenge.

The dysfunctional nature of the Russian invasion of Ukraine in 2022 exposed all the difficulties of 'combined arms operations', and of the challenges of keeping highly mechanised forces sustained and supplied in the field. For the highly mobile and manoeuvrable operations that NATO member states have in mind, this problem is magnified. The solution, and watchword, for Western states in this regard is 'integration', where all elements work towards a common objective, and assets from all domains are brought together to achieve a greater effect than the sum of their parts.

The integration of command, sensors, formations, vessels, aircraft, munitions and logistics is a common aspiration, and many in NATO look back favourably at the 1980s, when interoperability was a major driving force. After the Cold War, the absence of a common threat and the varied demands of national budgets meant that member states' systems diversified, and, in some cases, atrophied. NATO support to the International Security Assistance Force (ISAF) in Afghanistan highlighted the need for better coordination, but it was the emergence of the threat from Russia that pushed member states back towards a unified approach. The challenge, however, was that, while the United States forged ahead with its development of MDOs, its alliance partners were unsure how, and if, they could fully integrate into such a system. The United States made it clear that it favoured alliance and coalition strategy, and some American analysts estimated that the US could not do without its allies, but it was uncertain how so many varieties of allied military systems could be incorporated. In operations, the solution was to train together, create combined planning and command and aim for realistic levels of interoperability, all enabled by new emerging technologies. Strategically, the dilemmas of ensuring cooperation were subject to political agendas.

Defining Multidomain Operations and Multidomain Integration

In an MDO, sensors in the air, at sea and on the ground, and electronic sensors on most networks, are part of a comprehensive communications grid, where, in some cases, systems have the ability to 'talk' directly to weapons, logistics and other assets. Where an automated drone detects a concealed target, it will communicate with, say, a ground weapon system, and with the approval of the appropriate human operator, only the order to attack may be needed. Strategic decrypts are transferred directly into operations. Special forces are deployed in the enemy's rear (known as the 'deep manoeuvre' in an 'operational deep fires area') to locate strategically valuable targets. Air assets are formed in layers above the target areas, sensing and striking with great rapidity, while electronic warfare interdiction is underway, and sea and amphibious operations, like other areas of the surface battlespace, are preceded by uncrewed robotised systems. The result is that Western forces will be established inside the defended zones of an adversary and break down resistance comprehensively. At sea, while anti-submarine warfare systems are expected to be highly effective, enabling a maritime logistics bridge ensures sustainment of land operations.

The common features of contemporary and historical examples of allied MDI can be summed up in three parts: one, communications; two, appropriate data management; and three, decision-making. In this respect, MDI is more than 'operations'. The idea is that the term 'integration' in MDI applies to higher levels of direction and the full range of the levers of national power.

In economic leverage, political warfare, information campaigns and cyber, these three elements apply. At the political-strategic level, MDI requires seamless communications, specifically knowledge of each other's departments and priorities. It demands appropriate data management. It requires a precise, concise and accurate feed for the achievement of national or alliance objectives. It is also a question of decisions, that is, clarity in setting the objective and mission and a willingness to cooperate and support each decision across all instruments of power.

The three criteria of communications, appropriate data management and decision-making are required at the tactical level in MDO, and at the strategic level in MDI, at the interface between the armed forces and government. In the latter case, they must be applied to enabling resources, such as the regeneration of military force, munitions supply, war production, transportation and logistics.

The US view is that MDOs require joint, all-domain command and control (C2). Given the sheer scale of this, it is thought that artificial intelligence will be vital to maintain control of all the communications and data available and prevent human commanders being overloaded. Advanced networking technologies would also be vital to ensure the flow of data. It is envisaged that a battle-management system is utilised, offering a single control point for all domains. Moreover, this single battle-management facility enables the convergence of effects on a target from one or more domains in a synchronised way. The entire system is underpinned by a gigantic singular sensing grid, with the whole battlespace digitised down to the smallest granular detail.

The guidance document on MDOs, the Joint Warfare Concept, lays out six component parts. The first is that MDOs depend on the gathering of ubiquitous data to structure, direct and coordinate forces. The second is that those forces rely on 'information advantage', provided by a harvesting of observed, cyber and space datasets. Where data are incomplete, artificial intelligence will, it is assumed, fill the gaps. The third component is 'expanded manoeuvre', a term used to describe filling space and time ahead of an enemy's decision cycle, or, in a simpler definition, being able to anticipate the actions and direction of the adversary and placing one's own forces to take advantage of them. The fourth component is complementary and known as 'functional battle'. This is where friendly units are dispersed to survive and only aggregate to conduct attacks. The fifth element is the 'centralisation of all fires'. The sixth is the 'centralisation of all logistics', a necessary factor for efficiency and to ensure that units can fight their way out of their bases to the battle zones.

According to the Defense Advanced Research Projects Agency (DARPA), MDOs consist of three complementary principles: lethality, surprise and continuous speed. The claim that lethality is a key component of MDOs should come as no surprise since it is the purpose of military operations. However, the emphasis is offered because, as DARPA maintains, new weapons offer a better option than continuously trying to 'protect'. The hardening or enhanced defence of vehicles, ships, airframes and networks just reaches a point of diminishing return. The sheer costs of an individual craft or system just becomes prohibitive and counter-productive. It offers a better return on investment to generate vast numbers of cheaper, expendable offensive products rather than a few armoured or defensive ones.

The second element is surprise, by being able to operate from any domain, along multiple axes and in unexpected combinations. The criticism has been that trying to synchronise assets in the battlespace was itself an indication of how siloed assets really were. Targeting an enemy unit that appears in the battlespace, say, in the land domain, has demanded communications back to a central targeting cell, manual processing and prioritisation, the issue of instructions to, say, an air domain force, and the further allocation of the appropriate call sign and weapon system, all before ordnance is released. The slowness of the process and the likelihood of friction make the system unviable. MDO instead suggests that a surprise attack is possible because the combined sensor-shooter platforms simply 'talk' to each other, across domains. The battlespace is divided into a single sensor array and network, and computing assesses, in seconds, the most suitable weapon system, regardless of which domain it belongs to. There is no human intervention, except, perhaps, to make the final decision on the release of the relevant weapon or not.

This indicates the importance of the final element: continuous speed. Unlike the 'battle rhythm' of the past, with its episodes of intensity and its pauses, the promise of MDO is a continuous and unrelenting tempo. It suggests a constant acquisition, development and adaptation to situations and targets and the execution of operations. The literature on MDO emphasises its ability to create multiple dilemmas for the enemy, but it also suggests that the adversary would be overwhelmed and exhausted by relentless pressure, losses and unexpected developments.

MDO is often couched in specific vocabulary: 'cross domain manoeuvre forces provide situational understanding and precision fires to protect friendly assets' or 'analyses will reveal critical vulnerabilities in the cyber seam that may be exploited to provide the joint force commander with fleeting advantages and narrow windows of opportunity' and similar. But in essence, the process is to position oneself 'for advantage' before a conflict; to destroy the enemy's anti-access, area denial (A2AD) defences; to link the various sensors and strike platforms to destroy the enemy in depth; and then build momentum in this regard until resistance is defeated. All of this is achieved, as noted earlier, by digitising everything in the battlespace, as a single network. Units can be called upon, as required, regardless of their parent organisation, to achieve their part of the mission. One analyst describes the arrangement as a mosaic, where each tile is arranged and then reassigned. The analogy is problematic, not least as it fails to capture the speed at which the situation and arrangement change. A better analogy might be streams. It is fluidity which marks the quality of MDO and MDI.

The advantage imagined of the MDO is to be achieved by software and not just the hardware of defence. The emphasis is on cloud computing (which requires disciplined data management), a greater density of sensors, multiple lines for communications through a thicket of networked systems, and powerful AI data processing that can handle millions of interactions in seconds to produce the complex flight patterns of swarms, for missile delivery, survivable intelligence, surveillance and reconnaissance sensors or drone attacks from multiple angles and axes.

In the defensive posture, enhancements in software and AI suggest a form of encryption that quantum-enabled decryption could not keep up with. The logic of such a system would be that no human would have access to it, since the human is the slowest link. Secure communications hubs would be human-free, although commanders will be keen to retain control of the final decision to release ordnance.

The difficulty here is that the old geographical categories of 'deep', 'close' and 'rear' operational areas have been replaced with an almost limitless battlespace spread over seven areas. These are: a strategic support area (in one's home nation or that of an ally), an operational support area, a tactical support area (behind the battlefronts), a close fighting zone, a deep manoeuvre area in the adversary's area of control, an operational deep fires zone and a strategic deep fires region (largely in the adversary's home territory or networks). The mantra is to compete (or assert), then to penetrate, disintegrate, exploit (seize opportunities) and then turn to a new phase of assertiveness or competition.

Imagining a singular network is understandable. Combatants want singularity and unity. Yet diversity and specialisation are the usual outcomes of technological transformation. There is therefore a tension in the MDO concept between aspirations and the likely methods that leaders will actually use in the information and synthetic age.

The Origins of Multidomain Concept

A lack of familiarity with MDOs and anxiety about whether they could actually work in practice created scepticism about the viability of the concept. The anxieties are to be expected, but may be exaggerated. In conceptual terms, the strategic-operational wargames one observes around operations replicate historical campaigns, such as North-West Europe in 1944, from D-Day to the crossing of the Rhine. The Normandy amphibious landings were MDOs that had to break into an 'anti-access, area denial' zone. The Nazi regime used uncrewed autonomous systems (V1 and V2) to bombard the allied rear area of the United Kingdom. But the allies' own air operations reduced the capacity of the Wehrmacht to wage war, and all worked to the common objective of Hitler's defeat. Historical analogies like these can be used to test the idea of MDO, short of the technological detail. The point is that, aside from the advanced technology, MDOs are not as novel as is sometimes assumed.

There were essentially three steps, each a response to a particular threat, that led to MDO and MDI. The first step was a response to the greater conventional mass that Soviet forces could bring to bear on the continent of Europe during the Cold War. If the Soviets had rolled across West Germany, the United States wanted to be able to thwart an attack without having to resort to nuclear weapons. The solution was to introduce the concept of the 'AirLand Battle'.[1] The close cooperation, and integration, of air and land forces would mean that Soviet formations would be identified and broken up, while, in their rear, air forces would wreak havoc with Soviet logistics. The requirements of this approach led to a greater dependence on technology – in surveillance, targeting and precision missile strikes. Collectively, the development was subsequently titled the 'second offset strategy'.

In the First Gulf War of 1990–91, the Airland battle was used with tremendous success against Iraqi forces. Not only was there the anticipated close cooperation of arms, but there was an efficient communications grid, satellite navigation for each vehicle, precision-guided munitions and high levels of training, education and familiarity with the equipment and systems employed. The advent of 'blue force tracker' and GPS (global positioning system) as new technologies in this conflict gave an indicator of how fast operations could be conducted.

Strategically, space surveillance, air intelligence, surveillance and reconnaissance, along with battle damage assessment and measures of effect, and air operations had to be coordinated to determine the precise moment to commence and conclude land operations so as to preserve a political coalition in the Arab world. As Iraqi forces were located and defeated, data was fed rapidly, almost in real time, across these domains and shared with the relevant authorities in the rear. Given the multinational nature of the Coalition force, this was a significant achievement. It suggests that, while new technology attracts considerable attention, and gives the impression of a 'revolution in military affairs', the principles of MDO are, in fact, well established.

The second step emerged in the early 2000s. Concerns about the technological enhancement of Russian and Chinese armed forces gave the impression that a 'third offset' was required to maintain advantage. Work commenced in robotics, uncrewed air systems, electronic operations (including cyber) and AI. However, the issue was that hostile states could employ integrated air and littoral defence surveillance, smart mines and missiles in such a way as to create 'A2AD', anti-access and area denial.[2] A solution was needed to break down an A2AD 'bubble' and reassert American operational superiority.

The logical extension of 'joint' operations (across air, land, sea and space) and new technological integration (in the communications, informational and electronic environment) was designed for greater interoperability between systems to defeat A2AD. Frank Hoffman and Michael C. Davis wrote an article that drew on a UK joint doctrine publication on the human domain, and they reflected that being able to exploit the human aspects of warfare, which had been the lesson of counterinsurgency operations in the 2000s, and, combining those with the new technologies, led to a new conceptualisation.[3]

The third step therefore came a few years later, in 2017, when the United States' doctrine incorporated a more multi-dimensional approach as 'MDOs'.[4] One iteration of the concept, written by the US Air Force, describes 'Joint All-Domain Operations' reflecting a recognition of the need to bring all assets together under a singular framework for planning and the execution of operations.[5] The essence of the concept is to be able to detect, decide and act faster than the opponent.

MDI: Incorporating Allies and Partners

The assumption of MDOs is the integration of allies and of the civilian instruments of defence. In practice this has meant allied interoperability with the United States, partnerships between the private sector or state-owned industries and government, and rapid innovation, experimentation and implementation with a variety of new technology companies with defence research establishments. These were worthy goals but were harder to achieve in practice, particularly as the US has a faster and larger procurement system and is better at experimentation than other NATO member states. Moreover, the US can afford to experiment and have failures that can be replaced, compared with the smaller, more constrained budgets of some European states.

There are demonstrations of interoperability, such as US aircraft flying from the decks of UK aircraft carriers and vice versa. Indeed, there is also interchangeability, as it is possible not only to fly allied aircraft on these platforms but to repair them. That said, there have been frictions too. President Biden's decision to abandon Afghanistan, with scarce consideration of NATO partners in Europe, indicated that the integration of political decisions was not guaranteed. Moreover, France, which had irritated the United States in its criticisms and policies in the Middle East, reacted badly when its contracts with Australia were replaced by Washington and London in the AUKUS deal. The statements emanating from Paris indicated unfavourable French sentiments about NATO, defence cooperation, and its policy misalignment with the United States. MDI with allies and partners is, as always, still dependent on politics.

The Russian war against Ukraine exposed the challenges of integration across the NATO alliances. While the United States and UK were eager to offer Ukraine armoured vehicles and self-propelled artillery to help Ukraine resume the offensive and conclude the conflict, German allies were reluctant to do so. Swiss partners, outside NATO but critical in the arms industry of Europe, refused to permit certain products to be sent to Kyiv, creating operationally dangerous delays for the armed forces of Ukraine.

NATO takes its lead from the United States on MDI, and, like other close allies, such as Australia, the concept works best when all units that will operate with the US are on the same digitised battlespace grid, with access to the same communications systems. Such integration is easiest to achieve in the maritime space and air space, and, unsurprisingly in low earth orbit and space, given the American dominance there. The complexities occur in the land and informational domains, because of the friction of political preferences and human activity. This is even more pronounced among the European member states, and the question arises about how smaller nations can operate within a US framework. The assumption is that they must be compliant, thoroughly versed in its systems and subordinate to American command and control.

There is a claim that MDI will enable 'information advantage', a reference to being able to acquire, manage and exploit information faster and more efficiently than an enemy. The reality is that, for political reasons, the West refuses to consciously project its influence into the rear of adversarial states, even where this might be possible. As a result, too often it remains reactive. The MDI concept acknowledges there will be windows of opportunity, but most information campaigns take weeks and sometimes months to prepare, since they depend on being able to access the communications and information architecture of a hostile state. It is hard to identify the single organisation among Western governments that gives consideration to a unified national information campaign. The emphasis on winning narratives has not been a successful feature in the West's campaigns.

The evolution of the concept to include cross-domain defence and security led to considerations about how armed forces would be affected even before a conflict was declared. The emergence of 'grey zone' or subthreshold coercion meant that, by the time the United States had started to move its forces, it might find itself already under some form of attack, from sabotage or long-range missiles carrying weapons of mass destruction. There were anxieties about supply chain security, critical national infrastructure and the future of deterrence, which were exacerbated by the announcement by China and Russia that they had developed hypersonic missiles, a weapon far harder to detect than ballistic systems and capable of delivering conventional and nuclear warheads.

Russia's alleged prowess in information manipulation in the 2000s was called into question by its lamentable performance in information operations during the conflict against Ukraine. While able to dominate the television news within Russia, the West's skilful release of intelligence and clear-cut case of Russia's breach of international law, not to mention the immoral conduct of the Russian army, meant that the West's media was aligned with its national governments.

In terms of technological development, much of the multi-domain concept remains 'potential' rather than actual, which gives NATO member states an opportunity to integrate. However, technological innovations have been coming on stream at a rapid rate for some years, and while it is possible to list a few areas where we have not yet seen a full development, such as the deployment of artificial intelligence, the internet of things and swarm-control, we can point to the use of drones and various guided-missile technologies (1960s), the developments of integrated global navigation systems (1990s) and the introduction of military robotics for tasks like ordnance disposal (2000s). These have brought about their own transformation, without the need for adherence to an imagined concept of MDI. The development has been evolutionary, taking place in the space of just a few decades.

Analysis of MDI and MDO

The critical approach to MDO and MDI is to examine their ontology, why they exist, their meaning, and how they are conveyed. A brief survey of MDI tells us much about the architects of the idea. The epistemology of MDI is a combination of a sense of anxiety and opportunity. There is a fear of obsolescence, of the superiority of rivals, and the fear that new technological developments are occurring so quickly that Western defence establishments just cannot keep up. The fear of this disruptive technology is that it could bring to an end the culture and ethos that the armed forces pride. The bond pilots enjoy with their supporting ground crew would be terminated by purely robotic craft. The ship's company and its captain would be transformed beyond recognition by sole reliance on automated ships and missiles. The army would not be organised by the close-knit regiment and division but consist perhaps only of technicians and remote decision-makers. Perhaps these changes are necessary, but the ethos of fighting personnel could potentially survive in special forces or elite fast boat squadrons and ace fast air individuals with the dexterity to manage two or more swarms in close combat.

The MDO-MDI concept is used as a rallying point. There is an emphasis on systematic solutions, technological approaches and the promise of greater odds of success against the adversary as well as ways to impose friction. This is a particularly important theme given the foreign policy failures in Iraq, Libya, Syria and Afghanistan, as well as pusillanimity over Russia's illegal annexation of Crimea (2014) and growing assertiveness of China. There is an assumption that MDO will work in high tempo conventional operations, and MDI will support that, and, moreover, be applicable to these situations of hostile state coercion.

The purpose that MDO claims is the transformation of defence to address the threats that have emerged and to take advantage of the opportunities afforded by new technologies.[6] But it is really a search for a significant 'edge' over any near peer adversary that would give rise to a 'decisive' battle. The problem is that not all enemies will offer themselves up for destruction. Decisiveness is elusive, and conflicts between peer adversaries can degenerate into protracted, stalemated and more costly struggles, such as the Korean War (1950–53). Militias and proxy actors may be less well trained and therefore vulnerable, but that may mean their preferred fighting style is to disperse, use stealth and contest urban areas where fires and manoeuvre advantages enjoyed by regular forces are diminished. States may try to use proxy actors, arming and supplying them to drain the strength of a more effective force and avoid direct confrontation. There may be a complete avoidance of the multi-domain force, with attacks directed instead only at critical infrastructure with a variety of munitions, or a biological attack on the domestic population. There are weaponised energy and financial aspects to consider too. The confrontation between Russia and the West in 2022, while manifest as a war in Ukraine, was also an economic war.

Protracted wars among populations are more common than decisive 'conventional' conflicts, and while battles can individually or collectively turn the fortunes of a particular campaign, wars tend to be far more expansive and encompassing than localised combat. Neither mass nor alleged technological superiority can necessarily determine the outcome of a campaign. The Western-led coalitions in Iraq and Afghanistan, while enjoying supremacy in technology and quality of forces, could not change the political realities that would decide the long-term outcomes. Similarly, Russia's inability to turn its advantage of mass to defeat Ukraine was in part due to the Ukrainians unwillingness to accept Russian political control.

In the early 2020s, given the examples of Ngorno-Karabagh and Ukraine, the dependence on missiles and the tactical-operational value of drones were the most striking features. However, many continuities mattered too. Levels of training, the determination and morale of military personnel, and logistics were all important factors.

The integrated character of Azerbaijan's operations generated enthusiasm amongst the advocates of the multi-domain concept, but in the fighting in the north of Ngorno-Karabagh, drone operations were far less successful. Communications and electronic warfare played an important part too. Although Armenia possessed mobile electronic warfare equipment, Azeri drones sought out these assets and destroyed them early on. This in turn adversely affected Armenian communications and their integrated air defence. It exemplified the Western aspiration to break down A2AD in order to push forward its air operations and deliver precise fires. It is also essential for communications, and Western forces are dependent on their communications security to enable any ground unit to work with its air forces in real time, to deliver fires, intelligence, resources or lift by helicopters. Equally, the dependence on constant communication is a weakness of current operating models.

Despite the claims of futurists, contemporary conflicts show how little has changed even with the deployment of new technologies. Some tasks have become easier and faster, and precision fires have become more common since the 1990s, but lethality remains largely unchanged, and ranges of ground-based weapons are only marginally greater than they were last century. Urban fighting is still attritional, protracted and exhausting, absorbing great volumes of resources, as the fighting at Mariupol (2022) demonstrated. Close-quarter combat is no less brutal and levelling than it was in the past. Naval battles are still over in a matter of minutes; air-to-air combat in seconds.[7]

There will be significant limits on the ability to deliver transformation to MDI. Some are obvious and longstanding. There are the cultures of the separate armed services, and there are budgetary constraints, which may be affected by global recession and inflation in the 2020s. These are set against a backdrop of increasing economic competition (regionally and globally), time limitations and a lack of agreement on how far to go. Transformation is always difficult because of the legacies that exist, and relics of the past are not easily jettisoned. In many cases, they exist for a reason.

This is a reminder that the most important domain remains the human one. The ability of sensors and effectors to 'talk' to each other and the speed and lethality they promise will be in competition with analogue human networks and the various manifestations of the human condition. Sometimes this will be fear and flight, but at other times it will be obdurate resistance, mobilisation and defiance.

In Ukraine, Russian armour proved vulnerable to smart antitank systems, particularly when it was not deployed in a 'joint' setting. Russian ground forces did not enjoy complete air supremacy and were exposed to artillery and missiles directed by lightweight drones.[8] Small numbers of well-armed and determined defenders are capable of neutralising apparently unstoppable and massed forces.

For each of the characteristics of MDO, there are counter measures. Western forces look to synchronise their actions and achieve simultaneity while dislocating their enemies. They seek efficiency while imposing friction. They look to operate deep in the enemy's rear while protecting their own lines of communication. They try to achieve balance in forces and posture to ensure there is always a reserve and a high level of readiness while overloading and off balancing the enemy. They look to sustain a high tempo of activity, while delaying their opponent. They look to shape and then defeat the adversary at the centre of gravity while avoiding dependencies and exposure to enemy pressure, by shifting axis.

There are sometimes trade-offs to be made. Remaining dispersed avoids presenting the enemy with a target but occasionally forces and firepower might need to be concentrated to achieve local superiority. Being on the offensive enables a belligerent to retain the initiative and impose decisions on the adversary. Nevertheless, sometimes a tactical defence can be the means to inflict significant losses on an opponent, as an interlude between pulses of offensive action or to avoid reaching a culmination point (where resources are exhausted and further progress is rendered impossible).

The multi-domain concept aspires to 'create and exploit' synergy, but many have already asked how different this is from 'joint'. If we accept that there is a single operating dimension, it may even be superseded by 'all domain fusion' at some point. Centralisation has to be balanced against a loss of specialisation as well as cohesive and motivating identities. Synergy is rare, so synchronisation of different elements might remain the realistic alternative, but only after a great deal of rehearsal. Synchronisation and speed are the products, too, of devolved entities. Ponderous centralised command structures cannot hope to keep pace with events and would have to limit themselves to intention, timing and parameters, within which subordinate entities can create and effect real change at speed and conduct the sort of instantaneous tactical actions envisaged in the concept of MDO.

Western defence has emphasised the importance of sensing, ensuring surveillance and understanding. The reality is that, in both strategic and tactical situations, one has to fight for understanding. The myth of the panopticon, or the frictionless battlespace, emerged in the 1990s with the US idea of 'full spectrum dominance'. It has never existed, and will never be realised, except as an episodic moment. Like so many aspects of MDO, it will be harder in practice to achieve all that the concept promises in theory.

In the opening days of an armed conflict, given the lethality and accuracy of modern weapon systems, one might expect losses of warships, aircraft and personnel. Regeneration after the first few weeks would be a serious challenge, particularly for advanced technical equipment, weapons and sensors. Other than the United States, it is hard to see European armed forces and their defence ministries really prepared for such an eventuality. One solution would be to develop stockpiles of millions of robotic and automated systems. Another would be to develop ways to dismantle the adversaries' arsenals systemically. Either way, the requirements have serious implications for force development in MDI and suggest a rapid development of non-military requirements, including the mobilisation of financial measures, sanctions, energy restrictions and a comprehensive information campaign.

Conclusions

The risk of all studies of future war is to expect 'more': more speed, more resources and more effort. The reality of war is messier. There is a need to decide on recovery plans, regeneration-of-force schemes and legislation for civil contingencies in the event of a major conflict, and how far these must be integrated.

MDI implies NATO needs different armed forces. There is a threat of physical operations that require armoured units on land, electronic and missile warfare at sea and strategic airstrikes from the air domain against much larger hostile formations. Ultimately, MDO implies forces manifest themselves as largely automated systems with human operators. This envisages a force that is just emerging: low altitude sea skimming robotics or maritime uncrewed air systems that can be launched from submarines; high altitude, loitering gliders that make use of the explosive potential of relatively small nanotechnology; entangled-photon encryption between drones or multiple stealth attacks by individual drones against key installations; and the willingness to conduct operations in the area known as 'strategic deep fires', including grey zone operations. All these systems need to be plugged into an existing architecture if MDO is to be comprehensive and effective over time.

MDI might prepare for some aspects of warfighting and the sub-threshold space, but it leaves much unanswered. The difficulties are considerable, not least because of the reticence of political leaders to commit military forces where that might trigger escalation and conflict. Calibrating the right response or getting ahead of a threat are challenging political questions and may require very different levers of national power than defence, except in a supporting or enabling role. The exception could be in cyber and information operations, economic warfare, special forces missions, and the enablement of proxies, partners and allies.

The integration of allies is the biggest challenge. Ensuring that interpretation of a situation and that political objectives align will remain the most significant hurdles to overcome. The answer perhaps lies in joint training, combined planning and familiarity with systems long before the next major international crisis breaks.

3

THE NATO 2022 STRATEGIC CONCEPT
GUIDING, ALIGNING, BINDING?

Tim Sweijs & Tara de Klerk

Thirty NATO allies adopted NATO's new Strategic Concept at the Madrid Summit in the summer of 2022, only a few months after the beginning of Russia's war of aggression against Ukraine. The war marked the definite end to the post-Cold War holiday from geopolitics that many European NATO members had taken for granted. It led to the wholesale reappreciation of the importance of defence and security, not just for Germany but for the alliance as a whole—a true *Zeitenwende*. The Strategic Concept is the result of an extended process of political and diplomatic negotiations, making it in effect the lowest common denominator agreed upon by allied governments that each have different threat perceptions, strategic cultures and military strengths and weaknesses. The Strategic Concept is nonetheless a vision document that can help the alliance navigate a critical transition period in its existence. Ideally, it can guide the way forward, align transformation efforts, and bind alliance members in order to safeguard the security of the

Euro-Atlantic area. It does so against the backdrop of three important challenges.

First, the Strategic Concept appears at a time when NATO has returned to a state of 'persistent confrontation' that is likely to endure at least for the coming decade.[1] The resurgence of Russia traces a historical pattern of rivalries between opposing power blocs that exhibit 'momentum shifts, unexpected twists, and outright reversals of fortune' and tend to be hard to eradicate.[2] This pattern follows from the Punic Wars between Rome and Carthage, the One Hundred Years War between France and England and the rise of Nazi Germany following the crushing defeat of Wilhelm's Germany and continued contestation with other major powers over the dominance of Europe. Russia's militarism and attempt to re-establish a position of power following a period of decline continues this historical pattern. Its abysmal military performance and the weakening of its conventional military power should not be taken as a source of solace in this regard. Rivalries tend to have second, third and fourth Acts. NATO must act accordingly.

Second, for three consecutive presidential administrations now, the United States has endeavoured to pivot towards Asia, not merely by political proclamation but also through the incremental withdrawal of troops from Europe.[3] The Russian threat, at least for the time being, has forced the Biden administration to redirect its attention to the European theatre, haunted by the real world variant of the Michael Corleone syndrome—'just when I thought I was out, they pull me back in'.[4] This is happening after the credibility of the US commitment towards Europe significantly eroded under President Trump, who threatened to exclude NATO allies from the benefits of US protection.[5] Although Biden has made attempts to restore faith in America's 'unshakeable' commitment to NATO, it is clear that the Beltway's main emphasis is on strategic competition with China.[6] The

White House considers China 'the pacing challenge' against the background of bipartisan support for a military reorientation to the Indo-Pacific.[7] This, in combination with the surge of populist sovereignism in the US heartland, has already incrementally been reshaping US traditional foreign policy priorities. The possibility of a more drastic shift in US commitment to Europe's security in the coming years cannot be entirely discarded. This will leave European states to fend for themselves. Developing stronger military capabilities, commitments and cohesion among NATO members is, therefore, an essential capstone for a renewed robust force posture of the alliance.

Third, while passing a heavier burden onto European shoulders is clearly advantageous from an alliance management perspective, such a strategy does not enjoy universal approval within the alliance. While US retraction from the Euro-Atlantic area would enable it to focus energies on the Indo-Pacific, it requires stronger European defence capabilities, including greater levels of—what Europeans refer to as—'strategic autonomy', which is achieved through the sharing and pooling of European resources and the integration of European defence industries. This requires the US to devolve itself from any involvement that might impede European progress, even if it may result in a reduced position for US defence industries and a diminished US ability to shape European policy. For the Europeans, the conundrum is the other way around; they want more independence but fear American abandonment. Many Europeans are acutely aware that they lack the requisite capabilities to confront Russia alone and therefore remain highly dependent on US troops and resources, and they are therefore still very much inclined to hide under the US aegis. Here, there is a clear line of contention between European actors, with some loyal to American leadership regardless of geography while others are keen to crystallise the division between the Euro-Atlantic and Indo-Pacific theatres. Americans and Europeans will need to find a way to see eye to eye on this in order for alliance cohesion to endure.

Against the backdrop of these challenges, the Strategic Concept can be instrumental in articulating and codifying a vision for the future role and posture of NATO by offering a clear assessment of its external environment, identifying key threats and challenges, formulating clear goals in light of these and outlining lines of effort to achieve these objectives. Such efforts will include working with important stakeholders and taking into account organisational strengths and weaknesses, both hard ones (capabilities and capacities) and softer ones (culture and cohesion). It can thereby help rally individual members around a common goal, coalesce collective action, guide investment and transformation efforts and bind the members—the smaller and middle powers but also the Gulliver, the US. Ideally, the Concept is sufficiently clear to serve as guidance but also sufficiently flexible that it can accommodate geopolitical changes. The fundamental question, therefore, is whether the 2022 Strategic Concept adequately performs this role, not only guiding allied members through a highly volatile and threatening security landscape but granting them the tools to shape it in their own interests. To answer that question, this chapter proceeds as follows: first, it briefly examines the use and utility of Strategic Concepts through a historical survey of their varying purposes and functions in NATO's history and lays out seven requirements that it applies in an assessment of the current Strategic Concept. It concludes with a synthesis of the key findings.

The Use and Utility of Strategic Concepts

Students of war and strategy are fond of critiquing the broad application of the term strategy and the loose meaning attributed to it. Undeniably, the term has travelled a long way, originally descending from the Ancient Greek term στρατηγός ('the art of the general') and its first French translation of Byzantine emperor Leo VI's *Taktika* with *strategique* in the late eighteenth century.[8] Following widespread adoption in the nineteenth and twentieth centuries, strategy has extended beyond the military realm. Yet the reality is that in today's world, organisations in the private and public sector tend to publish strategy documents in order to articulate objectives and identify the road to attaining them, including NATO, the largest political-military alliance in existence.[9]

In NATO speak, a Strategic Concept is defined as a 'statement of what is to be done in broad terms sufficiently flexible to permit its use in framing the military, diplomatic, economic, informational, and other measures which stem from it'.[10] It constitutes a key document that reaffirms NATO's purpose and strategic trajectory in the given geopolitical circumstances. The Concept, therefore, simultaneously codifies past practices and builds on a collective assessment of the security environment to guide future political and military development.[11] The Concept also fulfills an external public diplomacy purpose as it announces intentions and establishes relations with wider audiences.[12] NATO itself conceives of the role of the Strategic Concept by means of the following characteristics: it '(1) sets the alliance's strategy; (2) outlines NATO's enduring purpose and nature; (3) formulates fundamental security tasks; (4) identifies 'challenges and opportunities in the security environment'; and (5) offers 'guidelines for political and military adaptation'.[13] Since its formation in 1949, NATO has released eight iterations of the Strategic Concept: four during the Cold War (1950, 1952, 1957, 1967) and four since then (1991, 1999, 2010, 2022). The summaries of these Strategic Concepts, their key objectives and geopolitical contexts can be found in Table 1.

Whereas previously Strategic Concepts were classified originating under the Military Committee, the most recent four are public documents of a 'political-diplomatic' nature.[14] The Strategic Concepts also evolved along the axis of their key goals, which marked three key periods.[15] First, the Cold War Concepts clearly prioritised the concept of deterrence and defence in the context of tense relations with the Soviet Union. These Concepts remained closely aligned in their military focus, attuning their strategic dial between deterrence by punishment and deterrence by denial in accordance with their respective geopolitical contexts. For instance, the outbreak of war in Korea, fuelling NATO fears of Soviet-sponsored aggression in Europe, called for a strengthened defence by denial posture in the Strategic Concept of 1952.[16] The maturation of the Soviet nuclear arsenal led to the threat in NATO's third Strategic Concept of 1957 that US bomber forces would respond with 'massive retaliation' in the face of Soviet aggression. The Strategic Concept of 1968 further developed these core tasks to accommodate a broader threat spectrum, 'ranging from covert operations to all-out nuclear war'.[17] Second, the Strategic Concepts of 1991 and 1999, published in the immediate post-Cold War period, reflected NATO's renewed hope for great power peace. The alliance sought to capitalise on its non-military toolkit, focusing on crisis management with disarmament, arms control and dialogue. Third, the penultimate Concept of 2010 appeared in the post-9/11 era. It broadened the concept of security to a global level and accommodated new challenges such as terrorism, cyber security and climate change.[18] Overall, Strategic Concepts have evolved in tandem with important geopolitical developments so they could address the security concerns of their time. Only when Strategic Concepts are understood in terms of their respective security environments can we grasp their instrumental value and assess their ability to guide allied members towards a state of security.

Table 1: NATO's Strategic Concepts—A Survey

Name & Date	Main Objective	Geopolitical Context	Key Concepts / Focus
Strategic Concept for the Defense of the North Atlantic Area (1949)	'To coordinate, in time of peace, our military and economic strength with a view to creating a powerful deterrent to any nation or group of nations threatening the peace, independence and stability of the North Atlantic family of nations'.[19]	Use of American atomic weapons, response to Soviet aggression and use of aggression by measures short of war.	Deterrence by punishment (traditional military power); deterrence by denial (arrest enemy advance with the position of adequate forces as far east as possible; defence (use of atomic weapons if deterrence fails).
The Strategic Concept for the Defense of the North Atlantic Treaty Area (MC 3/5) (1952)	'The main principle is common action in defense against armed attack through self-help and mutual aid. The immediate objective is the achievement of adequate collective self-defense among the North Atlantic Treaty nations.[20]	Background of Korean war.	Deterrence by punishment; deterrence by denial (strengthened); cooperative measures

Name & Date	Main Objective	Geopolitical Context	Key Concepts / Focus
The Sword and the Shield: NATO's Third Strategic Concept (1957)	'Chief objective is to prevent war by creating an effective deterrent to aggression'.[21]	Advent of nuclear weapons and first reference by name. Growing threat of Soviet troops and nuclear arsenal, economic considerations.	'Massive retaliation' by the 'nuclear 'sword' (US strategic bomber forcers); defence by denial by NATO's Shield (forward deployed forces)
Overall Strategic Concept for the Defense of the North Atlantic Treaty Organization Area (MC 14/3), January 16, (1968)	'To preserve peace and to provide for the security of the North Atlantic Treaty area primarily by a credible deterrence, effected by confronting any possible, threatened or actual aggression, ranging from covert operations to all-out nuclear war, with adequate NATO forces'.[22]	Growing nuclear parity between USSR and US. Non-nuclear crises (e.g. Berlin (1958) and Cuba (1962)).	Focus on Warsaw Pact capabilities and their possible forms of actions against NATO; policy of 'flexible response' through three levels of 'graduated escalation': direct defence, deliberate escalation, general nuclear response; reinforcement and rapid augmentation of shield forces.

THE NATO 2022 STRATEGIC CONCEPT

Name & Date	Main Objective	Geopolitical Context	Key Concepts / Focus
Alliance's New Strategic Concept, November, (1991)	'To safeguard their security, sovereignty and territorial integrity. The Alliance's security policy is based on dialogue; cooperation; and effective collective defence as mutually reinforcing instruments for preserving the peace'.[23]	Fall of Berlin Wall and breakup of Yugoslavia.	De-emphasis of deterrence; focus on crisis management with disarmament, arms control and dialogue; focus on cooperative security
The alliance's Strategic Concept, April 24, 1999	'NATO's essential and enduring purpose, set out in the Washington Treaty, is to safeguard the freedom and security of all its members by political and military means'.[24]	Balkan wars that required common defence in wider Euro-Atlantic area.	Security, consultation, deterrence and defence, crisis management and partnership
Active Engagement, Modern Defence (2010)	'NATO's fundamental and enduring purpose is to safeguard the freedom and security of all its members by political and military means'.[25]	Terrorist attacks (9/11). Europe enjoying era of relative peace and Russia listed as potential partner.	Collective defence, crisis management, cooperative security.

Like many of its predecessors, the 2022 Strategic Concept was adopted during a major transition in NATO's security environment. Russian revanchism alongside China's rise and concomitant increasingly assertive stance has drastically altered the regional and global security landscape. If anything, they disrupt a thirty-year period of great power peace that featured relatively harmonious great power relations. It compels NATO's Strategic Concept to offer allies a template for cohesive action. The Strategic Concept should, therefore, be able to map the contours of its external environment, sketch out the goals that follow and outline defined pathways to achieving them. In tandem, the Concept should consider NATO's internal capabilities to ensure allies can still meet the demands imposed on them by emerging challenges. To determine whether the Strategic Concept of 2022 performs these required functions, a comprehensive assessment will be informative. Accordingly, inspired by organisational strategies, we have derived a robust set of seven requirements that was previously lacking for assessing NATO Strategic Concepts. Primarily, these seven requirements, further explained in Table 2, trace existing business and organisational frameworks, to which Michael Porter has made tremendous contributions.[26] On top of this, they take inspiration from requirements identified in brief expert assessments within the international security community, both before and after the Concept's release.[27] This framework does not purport to offer a clairvoyant vision for NATO success but can be used as a tool to gauge NATO members' ability to deflect future threats and mould the security landscape in their own interests.

Table 2: Assessment Framework—Requirement and Explanation

Nr	Requirement	Explanation
1.	Clear assessment of the security environment	Does the Strategic Concept clearly and comprehensively portray NATO's security environment?
2.	Defined goals and objectives	Does the Strategic Concept outline a set of goals that have been clearly defined and presented in a prioritised manner?
3.	Clear lines of effort	Does the Strategic Concept offer a clear outline of steps to be taken for achieving its objectives?
4.	Recognition of own capabilities	Does the Strategic Concept accurately and clearly identify its internal strengths and weaknesses?
5.	Analysis of relevant stakeholders	Does the Strategic Concept describe the functions of different actors both within and outside NATO?
6.	Influence on national defence efforts	Is the Strategic Concept used as a template for the development of national defence policies and/or subsequent allied policy implementation?
7.	Durability	Is the Strategic Concept sufficiently flexible to accommodate changes in the security environment?

NATO's Strategic Concept 2022: An Assessment

Does the Strategic Concept conduct a clear assessment of its security environment?

The NATO Strategic Concept offers a fairly comprehensive assessment of NATO's external security environment, characterised by 'strategic competition, pervasive instability and recurrent shocks'.[28] Rich in refreshingly clear terminology, the Concept recognises the Russian Federation and terrorism as the two principal threats to the alliance's collective security. The former is described as the 'most significant and direct threat to Allies' security and stability in the Euro-Atlantic area',[29] which clearly places Russian aggression at the forefront of NATO's military and political thinking. The reference to terrorism, although diluted throughout the remainder of the Concept, accommodates the concerns from countries on NATO's southern flank. The most pivotal innovation of the Concept comes with the description of China posing a 'systemic challenge' to the alliance by using 'its economic leverage to create strategic dependencies' in multiple domains and 'undercutting the rules-based international order'.[30] Receiving ten mentions, China presents an unprecedented departure for NATO, inaugurating the Indo-Pacific's first appearance in a NATO strategic concept'.[31] It constitutes a signal to the Americans that NATO cares about the Indo-Pacific without entering into any commitments that extend beyond the North Atlantic Treaty area. Widening NATO's geographical focus, Iran, Syria and North Korea are further designated as 'hostile states' with reference to their development or use of Chemical, Biological, Radiological and Nuclear materials (CBRN).[32] The Concept identifies three other security concerns: conflict and instability in NATO's southern neighbourhood, emerging and disruptive technologies and climate change. Nevertheless, 'pervasive instability' lends itself to a broad range of interpretations that simultaneously seeks to assuage concerns of southern allies without necessitating NATO action. Alongside terrorism, these threats from the southern flank receive, comparatively to the eastern threat, little strategic attention. Although comparatively lacking in depth for state-centric threats, the Concept's treatment of climate risks and the vulnerabilities of diverse social groups in conflict settings reflect the concerns of different allies. Overall, the Concept offers a largely comprehensive picture of the global security environment, flagging most of the major topics discussed in preceding summits and general annual reports.

Does the Strategic Concept outline a clear set of defined goals?

Performing the second step of clearly articulating a set of goals to be achieved within this security environment, the Strategic Concept effectively lays out and prioritises its goals. Viewed holistically, however, the Concept fails to paint an overarching vision for the contours of a new security order. The deteriorated security environment has revitalised the alliance's *raison d'être*, infusing it with a renewed commitment to deter and defend against a bellicose Russia. To this end, the Concept provides guidance for how the alliance can position itself in a resurging realist world order. Echoing its predecessor, the current Concept stipulates three core tasks which are all in support of collective defence. The first, and explicitly foremost, is deterrence and defence, to which 15 paragraphs are dedicated. This prioritised core task has pushed the partially renamed task of crisis prevention and management to the sidelines, which, although a previous priority in the post-Cold War Concepts of 1991, 1999 and 2010, has this time only been given five paragraphs. The third task of cooperative security has also been sidelined by NATO's deterrence focus and, apart from the complete erasure of NATO–Russia cooperation, echoes the key themes discussed in the 2010 concept, including its open-door policy and active engagement with strategic partnerships. The core tasks directly respond to incoming threats but are not sufficient in proactively shaping the security environment according to NATO's goals and values.[33] Illustratively, although the task of deterrence and defence dominates NATO's strategic vision, pushing forth a more robust deterrence by denial posture, the Concept fails to adequately address the overall scope of these commitments and does not clarify what constitutes Russian defeat. As such, the Strategic Concept responds to what the 'West is fighting against' but has less to say about 'what they are fighting for', leaving allies without a collective vision of a new order.[34]

In addition, the Strategic Concept also does not specify the degree to which military responses will be executed. We find no corollary to the Cold War policies of 'massive retaliation' and 'flexible response' drawn up in the Concepts of 1957 and 1968, respectively. Both provided allied members with a visual road map for countering Russia, which is more useful than only stating the end-goal of 'defending every inch of Allied territory'.[35] Although the current Concept has certainly reinvigorated NATO's shield forces, referring to its forward deployed forces first established in the concept of 1957, it has not reforged its 'sword' (its counterpart of nuclear capabilities). Although commentators have referred to the 2022 Strategic Concept as 'a very nuclear text',[36] NATO's nuclear policy remains impassively stagnant in the face of Russian developments, such as its escalate to de-escalate strategy. Equally, while the Concept promotes nuclear power states, namely the US, the UK and France, to ensure the ultimate security of the alliance, it fails to explain how the growing nuclear dependence falls in line with NATO's continued commitment to the Non-Proliferation Treaty.[37] The clarity of the Strategic Concept could hereby be enhanced by an updated nuclear policy that reflects

NATO's security assessment and how NATO will incorporate arms control into its agenda. The same can be said for hybrid threats, for which the Strategic Concept fails to demarcate clear policy objectives. Both Russia and China's apparent willingness to engage in tactics that fall below the mutual threshold of Article 5 is not yet adequately matched with a commitment to develop a robust counter strategy. The failure to elevate resilience as a core task represents a missed opportunity in this regard because it would increase the concept's ability to address the spectrum of challenges threatening allies' critical societal functions.

Regarding the crisis management and prevention task, the Strategic Concept is short on detail. Ambitious and innovative initiatives to 'develop the capability to train and develop local forces' in crisis zones and form 'civilian crisis management capabilities', found in the Strategic Concept of 2010, have been replaced with policy reaffirmations that struggle 'to convey a clear message regarding NATO's added value within these domains'.[38] It may be reflective of the fact that, as one observer put it, large scale allied out-of-area operations died in Kabul on 31 August 2021 and were subsequently buried in Kiev on 24 February 2022.[39] While the Concept acknowledges vulnerabilities in the Middle East, North Africa and Sahel regions, they are not linked with the exacerbating effects of Russian and Chinese hostilities nor met with a clear mission statement. By abandoning a clear southern strategy for tackling instability, NATO does not address the security threats that converge on its southern borders and expose the alliance to indirect attacks from its main adversaries. The lack of a shared vision on what pervasive instability means further compounds this issue, which must be met with a more comprehensive approach that accounts for the multifaceted nature of the challenges at hand. Finally, for the third core task of cooperative security, the Concept clearly reiterates the alliance's open-door policy and the previous membership decisions taken with respect to Georgia and Ukraine'.[40] The Concept therefore affirms that enlargement remains critical to the attainment of the alliance's Euro-Atlantic aspirations. In short, the Strategic Concept clearly lays out a prioritised set of core tasks, with the most pressing being well-defined. Nonetheless, how they function holistically under the umbrella of collective defence is not adequately elaborated upon.

Does the Strategic Concept specify clear lines of effort to achieving its goals?

To translate aspiration into reality, the Strategic Concept provides NATO allies with a series of strong implementation guidelines, yet this falls short of a full-fledged blueprint. First, the Strategic Concept has provided added impetus to the many initiatives taken since 2014 that were designed to enhance NATO's conventional capabilities. These come under the overarching shift to deterrence and defence, which comprises three pillars: more forward deployed combat formations, more high readiness troops and more pre-positioned equipment.[41] The first seeks to enhance NATO's forward battlegroups, which are now stationed on a rotational basis in eight Baltic states and are assigned specific defence plans. Put numerically, the troops have increased from a battalion size of around 1,500 troops to the larger brigade format of over 4,000 troops. The most radical change, however, takes the form of NATO's New Force Model, which avows to increase the quantity and effectiveness of NATO's high-readiness reinforcement forces on the eastern flank. The model replaces NATO's Response Force, which could deploy 40,000 troops in 15 days and is structured in three tiers: tier 1 represents the 100,000 troops that would be available within 10 days; tier 2 adds an additional 200,000 troops within 10 to 30 days; and tier 3 promises at least 500,000 troops within one to six months.[42] The New Force Model's main body comprises European troops, which signals a departure from US military dominance in favour of a beefed-up European presence. This is reinforced by the endorsement of Sweden and Finland's membership, following Finland's accession, which has recalibrated the alliance's defence in Northern Europe with the expansion of the Supreme Allied Commander Europe's (SACEUR) land area of operations by over 866,000 km^2.[43] This added layer of support around the Baltic states effectively solidifies the 'NATOisation of Europe' and provides reassurance that NATO can carry out its defensive promises.[44]

The increase in the quantity of military troops is matched with a focus on improvement in quality, with NATO starting to follow the US's extensive exploration of MDOs.[45] This is best captured by General Philippe Lavigne's vision for developing the alliance's ability to synchronise military and non-military activities across all five operational domains.[46] This further elevated the question of allied interoperability, which brought about the first NATO Multi-Domain Operations Conference in the UK in March 2022.[47] The regional concentration and assignment of troops to defend specific allies is testament to this approach as it increases their familiarity with joint force operations in local terrain. Combined, these reflect clear attempts by NATO to synthesise its members' varying practices and capabilities into one cohesive defence programme. At the same time, NATO's recognition of this interconnectivity is again betrayed by the minor attention given to the interlinkage between the three core tasks and the overarching mission of collective security. For instance, strengthening deterrence by denial efforts for non-allied nations could be a key line of effort within cooperative security programmes, something that the Concept ignores. The same can be said for resilience, which permeates into all three core tasks to sustain the alliance's collective security. Only by addressing these lineages can NATO optimise its MDOs approach and act as one concerted whole.

Despite NATO's military compass firmly pointing east, the Concept firmly articulates the need to engage in a '360 degree' approach that can also address the systemic challenge of China through 'shared awareness', 'enhanced resilience and preparedness', strengthening Indo-Pacific partnerships and exploring cooperation with China where feasible.[48] These guidelines have sowed the seeds for future policy development, but this has not yet come to full fruition. For now, the Concept lacks concrete countermeasures, exposing the alliance's division and uncertainty on how to deal with the China's growing threat.[49] The same can be said for NATO's mission regarding cooperative security, where states such as Georgia and Ukraine have been pulled closer into NATO's sphere of security but have not been granted a clear temporal pathway towards full NATO membership. Finally, although the Concept devotes significantly more attention to climate change than in the past, it still does not communicate clear lines in how to respond to this threat in a cooperative manner. In sum, the Strategic Concept initiates a clear guide to defending NATO territory, increasing troop strength so that they guard NATO's eastern borders all the way to the Black Sea. Critically, however, these guidelines exhibit a loss in clarity when discussing NATO's secondary core tasks and inadequately account for the interlinkages between tasks.

Does the Strategic Concept acknowledge its internal strengths and weaknesses?

Even with a clear line of effort identified, when a Russian push comes to shove, can NATO feasibly activate its military power? The Strategic Concept responds with little certainty as it downplays the alliances' internal weaknesses while overstating its strengths. It argues that the source of NATO's strength comes from its members, prompting the continuity of its open-door policy and the recent accession of Finland and, soon to follow, of Sweden, which has made 'NATO stronger, and the Euro-Atlantic area more secure'.[50] Not only does NATO enlargement facilitate military burden sharing, but it also allows for a more robust defence posture building on states' respective capabilities. The Concept boasts its nuclear capabilities, explicitly outlining the strength of US strategic forces, the buffer potential of specific Balkan states and it qualifies that British and French nuclear weapons are cornerstones of NATO's nuclear deterrent.[51] This clearly places NATO's centre of gravity in Northern Europe and the Western Balkans but exposes NATO's southern vulnerabilities.[52] In broader terms, the Concept shows little recognition of NATO's capability shortfalls. The ability of European forces to meet the requirements of the Force model is questionable, especially considering the dilapidated state that many European armed forces are in after a quarter century of budget cuts while current inflationary pressures are not being alleviated by higher NATO defence spending.[53] Therefore, the question remains of whether the Concept's ambitious rhetoric can be credibly carried through. With allied forces only obliged to spend 2% of GDP on collective defence, as agreed back in 2014, the proposed action plan may not be feasible.

Moreover, the Concept fails to fully address the NATO divide across Euro-Atlantic and Indo-Pacific spheres. NATO's Strategic Concept gave way to increased military backing from the US, with the Biden administration promising an additional 14,000 troops to reassure European allies, bringing the total number of US troops in Europe to nearly 100,000.[54] Yet, despite this reassurance of the US's commitment to European defence, the Biden administration has not specified the longevity of this engagement and to what extent it can be undercut by competing responsibilities in the Indo-Pacific. Additionally, despite NATO's values lying at the heart of the alliance, how to safeguard these, and how to promote internal cohesion within the alliance, receives relatively short shrift. In particular, the Concept largely overlooks its democratic foundations, which are a source of concern in light of a global trend of democratic deconsolidation.[55] Without a secure democratic foothold, members of the alliance are less equipped to deal with these lowered levels of democratic support and the potential erosion of member states' institutions. Overall, the Strategic Concept's preoccupation with revisionist states has had a harmonising effect on member states and spurred them into action. However, NATO offers little internal reflection on the limits of its total capabilities and those specific to its members.

Does the Strategic Concept specify the role of relevant stakeholders?

In extension to NATO's internal considerations, the Strategic Concept looks outward and can be praised for its resolve to collaborate with a wide range 'of relevant stakeholders in the international community'.[56] With more actors affected by the deterioration of their security environment, NATO addresses the need to lengthen its list of partnerships, with the Concept's specific mention of deeper relations with 'Bosnia and Herzegovina, Georgia and Ukraine',[57] and the Summit Declaration's added promise of support to the Republic of Moldova.[58] New partnerships in the form of Australia, Japan, New Zealand and South Korea have also materialised in the pursuit of strengthened dialogue in the Indo-Pacific.[59] Inviting these states to the Madrid Summit has narrowed the gap between Euro-Atlantic and Indo-Pacific security affairs, binding Europe with America's broader geopolitical interests. The Concept also provides elaborate attention to the EU as a 'unique and essential partner'. This explicit reaffirmation of EU–NATO cooperation signals NATO's growing appreciation of EU security capabilities and paves the path for a clearer division of labour between the two organisations. This rhetoric of rapprochement, however, adds little clarity on how these two institutions will divide their tasks whilst maintaining policy coherence. The delay in the publication of the NATO–EU Joint Declaration, which was only released in January 2023, attests to the difficulties in operationally aligning these two bodies, although it certainly represents a marked improvement on the past.[60] On the contrary, the Concept does not identify partner countries in the Middle East and North Africa, Sub-Sahara and the Sahel, even though a transatlantic taskforce of external experts noted that 'strengthening regional partners[hips with countries] such as Israel, Jordan, Iraq, Morocco and Tunisia' are critical to achieving cooperative security.[61] Therefore, such an omission may undermine existing engagements with these countries that require diplomatic upkeep. These stakeholders are deprioritised at the same time as the concept fails to recognise how they are positioned at the epicentre of competition with Russia and China. It could be argued that a southernly extension of NATO's defensive shield would account for Russia and China's role in cultivating crisis and instability in the south and further counter their authoritarian interests.[62]

Apart from Eastern European states, the Concept does not clarify how their sought-after partnerships will take shape. For example, NATO has clearly sketched out the shape of its partnership with Georgia through the upgraded Substantial NATO–Georgia package.[63] Yet it still does not clearly stipulate paths to membership. For stakeholders in the Indo-Pacific, the nature and focus of the relationships remain unspecified. Without clearly defining the parameters of its bilateral relationships, NATO runs the risk of muddling through and diluting its capacity deliver on them.[64] Therefore, to enhance the cogency of NATO's cooperative strategy, the alliance should state the scope of its partnerships and 'prioritise those that may best advance Alliance interests'.[65] Finally, the Strategic Concept devotes little time to the functions of the private sector. Receiving only one mention in relation to digital innovation, the Concept does little to address the growing importance of private actors in accomplishing key NATO missions. To conclude, the 2022 Strategic Concept clearly draws up NATO's diplomatic map by broadly addressing the actors intertwined with NATO's security interests even though NATO's position towards its southern neighbours and to Indo-Pacific states remains relatively unclear. Although this helps allied members plan for bilateral and multilateral alignments, the way in which partnerships will manifest remains open for now.

Does the Strategic Concept influence national defence efforts?

The Strategic Concept impact is clearly demonstrated by its use as a template for subsequent Allied defence efforts. This rings especially true for the European militaries who are undergoing numerous operational changes. The recent full integration of the Royal Netherlands Army battalions with German divisions illustrates the large-scale restructuring of European armed forces and has set the precedent for achieving effective deterrence and defence through permanent interoperable military formations.[66] Put in writing, the Dutch Ministry of Defence hopes the armed forces will possess 'higher levels of readiness and deployability', 'targeted improvement of combat power' and 'more agility', which will simultaneously enhance Dutch capability and envelope it neatly into NATO.[67] For Germany, the Strategic Concept acts as reaffirmation of its *Zeitenwende*, which underpins the rapid rupture of relations with Russia and its outward Transatlantic Outlook. In line with the Concept's pushback on Russia, Germany promised 3,000 soldiers to be reserved for deployment to Lithuania when necessary as well as to maintain 15,000 soldiers, 60 aircraft and 20 naval units in the Baltic Sea.[68] Emmanuel Macron, a leading advocate for Europe's strategic autonomy, has also geared France to NATO's line of direction, shifting from counterterrorism and intervention missions abroad to the active defence of its territory and that of its neighbours.[69] The French national security orientation underscores a closer alignment with NATO strategy, counting four explicit references to the Concept and promising to translate this into national specificities.[70] Even Turkey, the country most adrift from NATO policy, has shown a degree of support to NATO ambitions. Despite many reservations, opposition parties have expressed their overall appreciation for the NATO alliance during electoral campaigns, and ministers have pointed to the relevance of NATO's collective challenges to Turkish security.[71] Overall, the Strategic Concept is a wholly collaborative doctrine, built upon agreement and compromise, which facilitates its absorption into national security practices. Central European states are collectively transitioning towards a deterrence by defence military posture, whilst Eastern European states are adjusting their security apparatus to accommodate the reinforcements from their Western neighbours. Even southern powers, despite still requesting additional fortifications on their southern flanks, are using the Strategic Concept as a template to design their own strategic planning and are voicing their commitments to increased defence spending.[72]

Is the Strategic Concept sufficiently flexible to accommodate change?

It can be argued that the Strategic Concept is in theory sufficiently flexible to accommodate change over the course of the next few years. This is mostly facilitated by the promise to maintain 'open channels of communication' and 'reciprocal transparency' with its adversaries as it allows the alliance to quickly recognise changing relations and respond to escalating threats.[73] The Concept further acknowledges the impact of rapid advancements of technology and the blurring of lines between war and peace. This makes NATO well-positioned to plan against future contingencies, allowing it to establish itself as a vital force for stability in an evolving security landscape. Still, only time will really tell whether the Strategic Concept will continue to direct NATO policymaking and unite its members.

Conclusion

Overall, the Strategic Concept stands as a useful beacon that helps member states navigate the shifting geopolitical landscape and allows them to coalesce around shared security goals. Table 3 on the next page summarises the key findings of our assessment. Whether the Strategic Concept will continue to inspire the full transformation of NATO operations and steer future development is unclear because its ultimate impact is dependent upon the member states themselves and how seriously security and defence policy makers, their domestic audiences, and their ultimate decisionmakers will commit to their own and NATO's collective defence. Yet, the Concept certainly helps guide and shape national defence efforts while binding a diverse coalition of allies. In that light and bearing on the three principal challenges outlined in the introduction—rivalry with Russia, US commitment and European capabilities—two main takeaways can be considered particularly heartening. First, the alliance has clearly recalibrated its security purpose and fully recognises the extent of the threat posed by a resurgent Russia. Second, from an alliance cohesion perspective, the Concept's recognition of the interrelatedness of the European and Indo-Pacific theatres in combination with Europe's strengthening of its defence capabilities and industries, this time applauded rather than obstructed by the US, may ultimately help cement transatlantic ties and bind the alliance together in a sustainable and balanced way going forward.

Table 3: Assessment of the Strategic Concept

Requirement	Explanation	Assessment
1. Clear assessment of the security environment	Does the Strategic Concept clearly and comprehensively portray NATO's security environment?	**The Strategic Concept offers a fairly comprehensive assessment in refreshingly clear terms.** • Russia and terrorism defined as two key 'threats' for NATO (terrorism receiving comparatively little attention). • China described for first time as a 'strategic challenge'. • Iran, Syria and North Korea designated as 'hostile states'. • Four other secondary security concerns identified as: terrorism, conflict and instability in NATO's southern neighbourhood, emerging and disruptive technologies, and climate change. • Threats on southern flank not sufficiently elaborated.

Requirement	Explanation	Assessment

2. Defined goals and objectives	Does the Strategic Concept outline a set of goals that have been clearly defined and presented in a prioritised manner?	**The Strategic Concept outlines a mostly defined set of goals but offers no overarching vision for the establishment of a new security order.**
		• Identifies three core tasks now in support of collective security:
		  ○ Deterrence and defence (clearly core priority).
		  ○ Crisis prevention and management (limited attention).
		  ○ Cooperative security (little change from previous concept).
		• No elevation of resilience as an important task and no comprehensive NATO strategy against hybrid threats.
		• Minor attention is devoted to interlinkage between three tasks and collective security.
		• The majority of the threats and challenges are covered under the core tasks, although some more explicitly than others.
		• There is no contemporary corollary to 'massive escalation', 'flexible response' or 'deterrence and détente'.
		• The nuclear strategy lacks innovation in the face of Russia's 'escalate to de-escalate strategy'.

Requirement	Explanation	Assessment

3. Clear lines of effort	Does the Strategic Concept offer a clear outline of steps to be taken for achieving its objectives?	The Strategic Concept is bolstered with many initiatives that act in support of NATO's goals, although a clear plan for both political and military action is lacking.
		• Ambitious military initiatives:
		  o Deterrence and Defence programme.
		  o NATO New Force Model.
		  o Multidomain brigades.
		• No clear lines on membership paths to activate open-door policy.
		• Scant attention to internal cohesion.
		• The lines of action towards China and the Indo-Pacific remain ambiguous.
		• Efforts to tackle climate change are swiftly covered.

Requirement	Explanation	Assessment
4. Recognition of own capabilities	Does the Strategic Concept accurately and clearly identify its internal strengths and weaknesses?	**The Strategic Concept offers little recognition of capability and capacity shortfalls.** • There is little consideration of the weakened state of the European armed forces. • No regard is given to how resources will be provided, distributed or sustained. • Values are mentioned but given short shrift, which is especially relevant considering 'democratic deconsolidation' also within the alliance.
5. Analysis of relevant stakeholders	Does the Concept describe the functions of different actors both within and outside NATO?	**The Strategic Concept recognises a wide range of existing and potential stakeholders but neglects the Global South.** • Explicit and elaborate attention to EU as a key partner but other organisations, such as the Organization for Security and Cooperation, are not mentioned. • Not much attention is paid to partner countries in Middle East and North Africa (MENA), Sub-Sahara and the Sahel. • Little consideration of private sector (one explicit mention).

Requirement	Explanation	Assessment
6. Influence on national defence efforts	Is the Strategic Concept used as a template for the development of national defence policies and/or subsequent allied policy implementation?	The Strategic Concept has a substantial influence on national defence efforts, with allies refocusing their efforts towards deterrence and defence. • European militaries are refocusing their efforts following guidance in light with priorities set out in the Strategic Concept.
7. Durability	Is the Strategic Concept sufficiently flexible to accommodate changes in the security environment?	It can be argued that the Strategic Concept is sufficiently flexible to accommodate change over the course of the next few years.

4

MARITIME-STRATEGIC INTEGRATION AND INTEROPERABILITY IN NATO
THE CASE OF STANDING NATO MARITIME GROUP 1 (SNMG1)

Steinar Torset & Amund Lundesgaard

Soon NATO will likely consist of 32 independent states. That is 32 different strategic outlooks and military cultures that have entered into an alliance, yet, fundamentally, there is a requirement for reasonably aligned perceptions of the strategic situation, as well as a general agreement on the ends, ways and means to deal with this environment over time. Strategic integration between the different countries and military interoperability are consequently key issues facing the alliance. The question is: what do the composition and activities of Standing NATO Maritime Group 1 (SNMG1) say about NATO strategic integration and military interoperability in the maritime domain? Before answering this question, it is necessary to state what SNMG1 is, clarify what we mean with strategic integration and military interoperability and explain the methodical choices and sources that form the foundation of this chapter.

SNMG1 started as a quick reaction force for the maritime domain in 1967. It consisted of four to nine frigates and/or destroyers and often a fleet tanker or auxiliary ship.[1] Contributors to this force were NATO members with coastlines facing the Atlantic Ocean. After conducting several maritime security operations in the Mediterranean and off the Horn of Africa during the 1990s and early 2000s, the force has returned to its roots as a quick reaction force.[2] Furthermore, and as the name suggests, it is supposed to be a standing force that is available on a permanent basis, and it is part of the NATO Response Force. When Russia invaded Ukraine for the second time in six years on 24 February 2022, NATO put its Graduated Response Plans into action. As the maritime component of the NATO Response Force, SNMG1 is part of that plan.

Strategic integration and military interoperability are central to this chapter. National perceptions of the strategic situation will naturally vary within NATO and so will national ends, ways and means. In other words, the extent of strategic integration between the individual nations will differ, and since the strategic environment is fluid, the degree of strategic integration will fluctuate.

Consistent SNMG1 activities over time are an indication of what the alliance collectively considers to be the most important maritime-strategic issues. For example, if the force engages in and trains for maritime security operations, it is natural to assume that this is seen as the main strategic challenge by the alliance as a whole. That may not be the case for individual nations, or even most alliance members, however. Some nations may have other strategic reasons for participating, such as maintaining the goodwill of one or several of the other nations. In other words, the nations may have differing perceptions of the ends they are trying to achieve with SNMG1 but still agree to the ways and means. The activities of SNMG1 are nevertheless an

MARITIME-STRATEGIC INTEGRATION

indication of the general maritime-strategic consensus among the NATO members that normally contribute to the force. They are, in other words, a strategic base line. A state's commitment of ships to the force indicates that the activities of the force align sufficiently with a state's strategic goals. The activities and composition of SNMG1 are therefore indications of nuances in maritime-strategic integration within NATO.

Military interoperability is, according to NATO's definition, 'the ability for Allies to act together coherently, effectively and efficiently to achieve tactical, operational and strategic objectives'.[3] Interoperability is therefore at the heart of strategic integration, and the frequency and types of exercises indicate both the ambition for and level of interoperability. Large-scale and complex warfighting exercises suggest both a high level of ambition and a significant degree of interoperability. Passing exercises, defined as 'training occasions between two or more navies consisting of partial exercises in navigation and communication while ships manoeuvre alongside and around each other', are less complex and imply a lower ambition for, and level of, interoperability.[4] On top of such official exercises, SNMG1 also conducts a range of joint and multinational training that aims at improving interoperability. Such training may include allied and partner aircraft and ships and is a frequent occurrence for SNMG1, even though they are not part of the official NATO exercise schedule. Also important to note is the fact that the ships dedicated to the force itself train and exercise regularly together throughout a semester, independently of official exercises and other activities that involve alliance or partner forces that are not part of SNMG1. Being part of SNMG1 is therefore, in and of itself—and as long as there is more than just one ship in the task force—a contribution to interoperability.

This chapter does more than just provide a chronology of SNMG1 over the past few years. It uses the activities of and participation in SNMG1 to draw quite general conclusions about NATO strategic integration and interoperability in the maritime domain. It is important to point out that the chapter is based on major activities such as exercises and deployments. However, other activities, such as training either as a force or together with units from various alliance or partner nations as well as port visits and other representational tasks, make up a significant part of the operational baseline for SNMG1. The major exercises are nevertheless the most significant indications of strategic integration and military interoperability.

The timeframe of this study stretches from the first semester of 2019 (January 2019) until the end of the first semester of 2022 (June 2022), as well as the first semester of 2017. On 15 December 2016, NATO ended its seven-year-long participation in the anti-piracy Operation Ocean Shield, arguably a maritime-strategic paradigm shift establishing a new baseline for strategic integration: in-area, conventional naval operations. Indeed, SNMG1 and 2 had alternated for deployments to Operation Ocean Shield between 2009 and 2014, with each force spending one semester on deployment and one in training for a new deployment during that period.[5] The wholesale return of NATO to home waters in 2017 set the stage for a new normal for SNMG1 and is therefore a natural point of inclusion for this study as it provides a starting point as well as a point of reference for the later semesters. The first semester of 2022 shows the alliance's reaction to the crisis in, and subsequent wholesale invasion of, Ukraine.

SNMG1 Activities: A Chronology

First Semester 2017: Lacking Contributions

The first semester of 2017 (Figure 1) was signified by quite humble contributions, with three frigates sailing at most (the

Figure 1: Overview of the First Semester of 2017

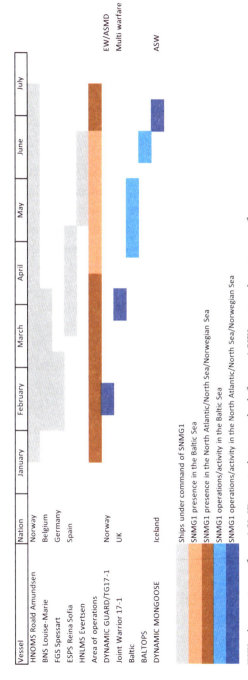

EW: electronic warfare; ASMD: anti-ship missile defence; ASW: anti-submarine warfare.

Spessart is a logistics vessel while the other ships are frigates). As the later semesters also show, spring 2017 indicates the typical pattern of contributions. The semesters usually start off with just the flagship, reach a peak around the major exercises and deployments, and then taper off towards the end of the semester, finishing with just the flagship.

The first major activity this semester was participation in the annual air defence and electronic warfare exercise Dynamic Guard, a NATO Maritime Command led exercise hosted by the Royal Norwegian Navy and aimed at maintaining proficiency in maritime electronic warfare and anti-ship missile defence.[6] Following the conclusion of Dynamic Guard, SNMG1 then participated in the Norwegian fleet's annual Exercise Task Group 17-1, an exercise that 'supports the training and qualification of new submarine commanders, in addition to focusing on improving warfare capabilities'.[7] During Joint Warrior 17-1, an exercise that emphasises warfighting capabilities 'across multiple domains and environments', SNMG1 was given tactical control, but not official command, of three additional ships, making it a six ship task force for the duration of the exercise.[8] Interoperability was a significant aim in this exercise.

SNMG1 usually spends its Baltic Sea deployments exercising and cooperating with both allied and partner nations, often with the express intention of improving cooperation or interoperability.[9] The cooperative nature and multinational aspect was evident under Exercise BALTOPS 17. BALTOPS is an annual exercise that is 'designed to enhance flexibility and interoperability, in order to demonstrate the ability to provide sea control and project power from the sea' in the Baltic Sea region.[10] During the 2017 iteration of the exercise, the two SNMG1 ships were complimented with four additional ships that were under SNMG1 control for the duration of the exercise, although not officially under SNMG1 command: a US destroyer, a Danish

Figure 2: Overview of the First Semester of 2019

Vessel	Nation
USS Gravely	USA
TCG Gokova	Turkey
HMS Westminster	UK
ESPS Almirante Juan de Borbón	Spain
ORP General Pulaski	Poland
FGS Rhön	Germany
FGS Spessart	Germany
Area of operations	
DYNAMIC GUARD/TG 19-1	Norway
Joint Warrior 19-1	UK
Baltic deployment	
BALTOPS	Baltic Sea
DYNAMIC MONGOOSE	Norway

Ships under command of SNMG1
SNMG1 presence in the Baltic Sea
SNMG1 presence in the North Atlantic/North Sea/Norwegian Sea
SNMG1 operations/activity in the Baltic Sea
SNMG1 operations/activity in the North Atlantic/North Sea/Norwegian Sea

EW/ASMD
Multi warfare
Multi warfare
ASW

EW: electronic warfare; ASMD: anti-ship missile defence; ASW: anti-submarine warfare.

command ship, a Swedish corvette and a Finnish minelayer.[11] The final, major, activity of the first semester of 2017 was Exercise Dynamic Mongoose, an annual anti-submarine warfare exercise also aimed at interoperability.[12] This iteration of the exercise was in the waters off Iceland and included eleven surface ships from nine countries, as well as a NATO Research Vessel, all under tactical control of SNMG1.[13]

First Semester 2019: US Flagship and Substantial Contributions v.1.0

The United States was in command of SNMG1 for all of 2019 (Figure 2). These two semesters stand out in terms of contributions to the force, as the size of the SNMG1 force swells when there is a US flagship. During this semester, the group conducted a series of activities, including Dynamic Guard,[14] Joint Warrior, BALTOPS and Dynamic Mongoose as well as having presence in the Baltic region and the North Sea.

This iteration of Joint Warrior was particularly large, including 13 nations, 10,000 personnel, 45 ships and 5 submarines.[15] The Baltic deployment included several activities aimed at reassuring allies and building relationships within NATO, such as escorting a military-chartered merchant vessel, port visits and visits to two NATO headquarters in Poland and the leaders of the Baltic Air Policing mission.[16] A significant aspect of these activities was interoperability across the board in NATO, not just between nations and in the maritime domain. As the commander of SNMG1, Rear Admiral Edward Cashman stated, 'NATO is inherently a Joint service as well as Combined nation Alliance, it is essential that we maintain good links between the various components as we do among the Allied nations'.[17]

Figure 3: Overview of the Second Semester of 2019

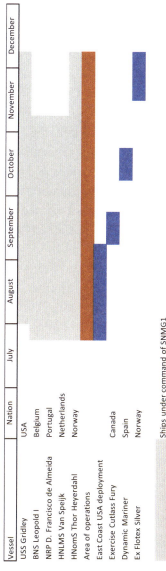

NRF/M: NATO Response Force Maritime.

Second Semester 2019: US Flagship and Deployment to US East Coast

This semester also featured a United States flagship and kicked off with a deployment to the US East Coast, and as with the previous semester, had significant contributions compared with the other semesters. Notably, the semester departs from the established deployment pattern (Figure 3).

The deployment to the US East Coast included participation in exercise Cutlass Fury in Canada. Cutlass Fury is a biennial, medium-scale exercise off the coast of Nova Scotia and Newfoundland, with the purpose of unifying Canada's Atlantic Fleet, allied navies and other joint elements in tactical-level warfare to improve their warfighting skills and interoperability.[18] Also participating were HMS Northumberland and HDMS Peter Willemoes and several ships from US and Canadian navies and coast guards, although these ships appear not to have been under SNMG1 control.[19]

When the group returned to European waters, SNMG1 participated in Exercise Dynamic Mariner in Spain. The exercise was a significant one, consisting of 32 surface ships, 2 submarines and 18 air assets, including Maritime Patrol Aircrafts and helicopters. The stated goal of the exercises was to improve interoperability between allied navies, including between SNMG1 and SNMG2, in a crisis response scenario, testing 'NATO's Response Force Maritime Component (NRF/M) and its interoperability with integrated NATO forces'.[20] SNMG1 concluded the semester by conducting exercise Flotex Silver in Northern Norway in November. However, the group at this time of the semester consisted of only two units.

Figure 4: Overview of the First Semester of 2020

Vessel	Nation	January	February	March	April	May	June	July
HNoMS Otto Sverdrup	Norway							
HDMS Absalon	Denmark							
HMS Sutherland	UK							
FGS Rhön	Germany							
Area of operations								
COVID-19 outbreak								
Cold Response	Norway							
Passex French Navy								
Joint Warrior 20-1	UK							Multi warfare
BALTOPS 20	Baltic Sea							Multi warfare
Dynamic Mongoose								ASW

Ships under command of SNMG1
SNMG1 presence in the Baltic Sea
SNMG1 presence in the North Atlantic/North Sea/Norwegian Sea
SNMG1 operations/activity in the Baltic Sea
SNMG1 operations/activity in the North Atlantic/North Sea/Norwegian Sea
Period affected by initial outbreak of Covid-19

ASW: anti-submarine warfare.

First Semester 2020: COVID-19 Arrives

The first semester of 2020 was marked by the arrival of COVID-19 (Figure 4). Exercise Cold Response was cancelled due to the pandemic, and it is clear that the disease had a significant impact on NATO activities in general, and it is natural to assume that the virus had some influence on whether to participate in SNMG1 activities or not. For most of the semester, SNMG1 consisted of a mere two ships and was expanded with another two ships during the most exercise-intensive phase in March and April.

In terms of the pandemic, there is a significant difference between engaging in exercises and contributing to SNMG1, however. During exercises, ships can choose to exclusively engage at sea, and it is therefore relatively easy to avoid contact between the ships' crews, and in that way reduce the risk of spreading the virus from ship to ship. That is not as easy when sailing as part of SNMG1, since port visits and engagements in person are an integral part of the force's activities, which increased the risk of spreading the virus.

For SNMG1, the activities for this semester mainly focused on traditional activities, such as presence operations in Northern Norway and the Baltic region, with the task group consisting of two units. The semester was also characterised by more cooperation between SNMG1 and its mine-clearing counterpart, the Standing NATO Mine Countermeasures Group 1 (SNMCMG1) than usual.[21] The mutual dependence between the two maritime groups is however important, with SNMCMG1 requiring force protection when conducting mine countermeasures operations and SNMG1's requirement for safe passage in areas with a potential mine threat.

SNMG1 officially consisted of only the flagship during exercise Dynamic Mongoose in July, but as with previous iterations of the exercise was handed tactical control of the other surface ships in the exercise. In total, Dynamic Mongoose brought together seven nations to exercise anti-submarine warfare and to maintain and improve military interoperability.[22]

Although downscaled in spring 2020, Joint Warrior performed much the same function, with SNMG1 as a central part. SNMG1 participated in several exercises and operations this semester that, despite the persistence of the COVID-19 pandemic, aimed at improving interoperability and strategic integration. Indeed, the force exercised with both the Swedish, Finnish and French navies and coast guards, as well as participated in BALTOPS and in exercises with NATO's SNMCMG1. Furthermore, SNMG1 monitored Russian activity in the English Channel as part of a larger allied force.[23] Thus, in spite of the pandemic and the limited contributions to the force, there was a real effort to maintain and improve military interoperability this semester, and the monitoring of Russian activity shows that the force can be used for operations as well.

Second Semester 2020: Baltic Deployment

Much as with the first semester, contributions for the second semester of 2020 were modest, with a maximum of three ships (Figure 5). The impact of the pandemic on contributions is uncertain; however, as some NATO activities suggest, COVID-19's influence on exercise schedules was limited. The semester was carried out in a traditional pattern, with the deployment to the Baltic Sea taking up a sizeable chunk of the semester but also including deployments to Northern Norway and waters around the UK. The Baltic Sea deployment saw the force visiting and conducting training together with Latvian, Lithuanian and German forces, as well as training with units from NATOs Baltic Air Policing mission and cooperation with USS Ross (DDG 71) operating in the Baltic Sea under national command. At the end of the Baltic deployment, SNMG1 trained with the Finnish

Figure 5: Overview of the Second Semester of 2020

Vessel	Nation	July	August	September	October	November	December
NRP Corte Real	Portugal						
HMCS Toronto	Canada						
BNS Leopold I	Belgium						
Area of operations							

Baltic deployment		
Exercise Brilliant Jump 2020	UK	VJTF deployment
Joint Warrior 20-2	UK	Multi warfare
Flotex Silver 20	Norway	Multi warfare

- Ships under command of SNMG1
- SNMG1 presence in the Baltic Sea
- SNMG1 presence in the North Atlantic/North Sea/Norwegian Sea
- SNMG1 operations/activity in the Baltic Sea
- SNMG1 operations/activity in the North Atlantic/North Sea/Norwegian Sea

VJTF: Very-High Readiness Joint.

MARITIME-STRATEGIC INTEGRATION

Navy as well as SNMCMG1 before heading towards Scotland for participation in Joint Warrior 20-2. The deployment towards Scotland was conducted as a part of NATO exercise Brilliant Jump.[24]

Joint Warrior had been scaled up significantly since the spring iteration of the exercise. This time, 'more than 6,000 personnel, 81 aircraft, 28 ships, and two submarines from 13 nations' participated, making it a large exercise.[25] The scope and scale of this exercise suggest that the pandemic was no longer a significant obstacle to partaking in exercises, presenting less of a hurdle for contributing to the SNMG1.

First Semester 2021: Continuing Modest Contributions

Despite a significant exercise and deployment programme, the first semester of 2021 continued where 2020 had left off, with limited contributions to SNMG1 (Figure 6). Several of the exercises during both semesters were major undertakings with several participants, suggesting that the pandemic did not limit the willingness or ability of nations to contribute if there was significant incentive, whether it be strategic, operational or both. Indeed, France, which is generally known to dispatch its ships to SNMG2 in the Mediterranean rather than SNMG1, contributed one of its ships for a three-week period.

There were three major exercises this semester: Joint Warrior, which included the Royal Navy's Queen Elizabeth carrier strike group; BALTOPS, which involved '16 NATO and 2 partner nations [that] will provide approximately 40 maritime units, 60 aircraft, and 4,000 personnel'; and Steadfast Defender.[26] As in previous Joint Warrior and BALTOPS iterations, SNMG1 was bolstered with additional ships under its tactical control; five ships in Joint Warrior and four during BALTOPS.[27] SNMG1 was also bolstered by two additional ships under its tactical control during Dynamic Guard 2021.[28] Although the sources do not address

Figure 6: Overview of the First Semester of 2021

Vessel	Nation
HMCS Halifax	Canada
FGS Spessart	Germany
FS Latouche-Tréville	France
HDMS Absalon	Denmark
FS Bretagne	France
Area of operations	
PASSEX with GER and NL Navy	
TG 21-1	Norway
Ex Dynamic Guard 21	Norway
Baltic deployment	
PASSEX NL Navy	
Joint Warrior 21-1	UK
Steadfast Defender 21	Portugal
BALTOPS 21	Baltic Sea
Dynamic Mongoose 21	Norway

Legend:
- Ships under command of SNMG1
- SNMG1 presence in the Baltic Sea
- SNMG1 presence in the North Atlantic/North Sea/Norwegian Sea
- SNMG1 operations/activity in the Baltic Sea
- SNMG1 operations/activity in the North Atlantic/North Sea/Norwegian Sea

TG 21-1: ASW
Ex Dynamic Guard 21: EW/ASMD
Joint Warrior 21-1: Multi warfare
Steadfast Defender 21: Multi warfare
BALTOPS 21: Multi warfare
Dynamic Mongoose 21: ASW

EW: electronic warfare; ASMD: anti-ship missile defence; ASW: anti-submarine warfare.

Figure 7: Overview of the Second Semester of 2021

Vessel	Nation	July	August	September	October	November	December
HMCS Fredericton	Canada						
NRP Corte Real	Portugal						
HNLMS Van Amstel	Netherlands						
HNOMS Maud	Norway						
ESP Almirante Juan de Borbón	Spain						
FS Normandie	France						
BNS Leopold I	Belgium						
FS Bretagne	France						
Area of operations							
Baltic deployment							
Dynamic Mariner 21/JW 21-2	UK						
FOST	UK						
FLOTEX Silver	Norway						

Ships under command of SNMG1
SNMG1 presence in the Baltic Sea
SNMG1 presence in the North Atlantic/North Sea/Norwegian Sea
SNMG1 operations/activity in the Baltic Sea
SNMG1 operations/activity in the North Atlantic/North Sea/Norwegian Sea

NRF/M
Multi warfare

NRF/M: NATO Response Force Maritime.

the command and control arrangements of Exercise Dynamic Mongoose, previous practice makes it natural to assume that the surface vessels were under tactical control of SNMG1 in 2021 as well.

Second Semester 2021

The second semester of 2021 was notably different from the previous three semesters (Figure 7). For most of the semester, SNMG1 was an unusually robust force, with a maximum of seven ships at one time and at least our ships for a total of 12 weeks, although the activities themselves do not stand out as very different. One difference, although not a great one, was that for the first time, Dynamic Mariner and Joint Warrior were combined into one exercise. Although the sources for this semester do not address command and control, it is plausible that SNMG1 had tactical control over ships not under its command.[29] In a rerun of the previous semester, France once again added a ship to SNMG1 command for three weeks, and another French vessel was put under SNMG1 tactical control for the duration of Dynamic Mariner/Joint Warrior exercise.[30]

First Semester 2022

With the second Russian invasion of Ukraine as a sinister backdrop, the first semester of 2022 stands out from previous ones (Figure 8). The high turnover of ships is a key break with what the above has shown to be the operational baseline for SNMG1.[31] However, during this semester SNMG1 experienced an unusually high turnover of flagships. When the Netherlands assumed command of SNMG1 on 7 January 2022, the 'group' consisted of 1 ship: HNLMS Rotterdam. In early February, the German tanker FGS Berlin joined the force and soon became the new flagship of SNMG1. In mid-March, the Commander of SNMG1 and his staff embarked the Dutch ship Zeven de

Figure 8: Overview of the First Semester of 2022

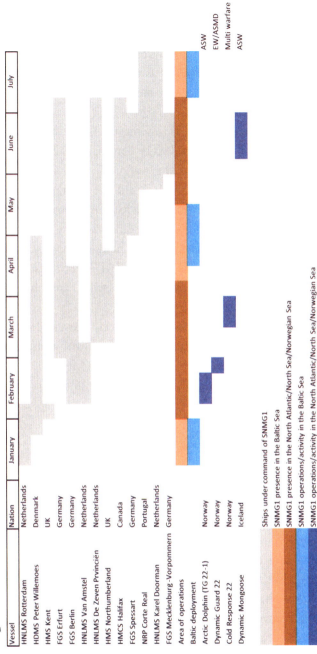

EW: electronic warfare; ASMD: anti-ship missile defence; ASW: anti-submarine warfare.

Provinciën, which stayed on as the flagship throughout the semester. In other words, during the period of 7 January to 15 March, SNMG1 had three different flagships. This is not necessarily a significant challenge as the Commander of SNMG1 with his staff can embark any ship suited to carry a maritime task group staff.

What is also notable for this semester is the high number of ships under continuous SNMG1 command throughout the period from the outbreak of the war until early July. Also of importance is the fact that SNMG1 did not engage in Exercise BALTOPS, which was a regular activity throughout the period covered in this chapter and, indeed, since 2016.[32] Rather than join the exercise, SNMG1 deployed to the Baltic Sea a few weeks after the end of BALTOPS. Besides BALTOPS, the exercise schedule adhered to the operational baseline that had been established since 2017.

As with some of the previous semesters, the sources do not disclose the nature of the command-and-control arrangements for the exercises, but again it is likely that the SNMG1 commander was given tactical control over ships not officially under their command.

Military Interoperability: The Backbone of Maritime-Strategic Integration

As was mentioned above, the period from the first semester of 2017 until the end of the first semester of 2022 shows that a baseline of operations had been established for SNMG1. In terms of activities, the baseline is a busy exercise schedule with slightly more activities during the first semester of a year and a somewhat lower tempo in the second. The exercises are generally recurring ones, usually annual or biannual, and they emphasise either certain aspects of conventional warfare at sea or combinations of such aspects. Geographically, the exercises are mainly concentrated in the Baltic Sea and the northern-most parts of the North Atlantic.

Baseline contributions are between one and three ships under SNMG1 command. The question is what the baseline, and the inevitable deviations from it, suggest about military interoperability, strategic integration and the relationship between them in NATO's maritime domain.

First, despite the challenge of maintaining a common strategic perception in an alliance of 30 nations, the mere existence of SNMG1 as an active force and as a part of the NATO Response Force implies a reasonably similar awareness of the maritime-strategic environment within the alliance. Furthermore, it is proof that NATO also has reasonably similar views on the ends, ways and means necessary to deal with that environment, which pertains in particular to the contributors to the force. The exercise programme's strong emphasis on conventional operations is evidence of a general agreement on the nature of the threats and challenges in the North Atlantic region. The major exercises, such as Dynamic Mongoose, Joint Warrior, BALTOPS, Dynamic Guard and Dynamic Warrior are all exercises that, in large part, are aimed at maintaining and improving proficiency in conventional maritime operations. To reiterate, the fact that these kinds of exercises dominate the SNMG1 schedule is evidence that there is a significant maritime-strategic integration within NATO.

Nevertheless, the pattern of participation in the force is an example of the limitations of this integration. The force's baseline composition, between one and three surface ships, is far from the intended four to nine ships. The natural implication of this is that there are other maritime-strategic considerations more important than keeping SNMG1 at full strength during peacetime. The pattern also suggest that the force is more strategically important to some nations than others. Certain nations, such as Belgium, the Netherlands, Germany and Norway are frequent contributors, while the United Kingdom, the United States, France, Spain and Denmark are less frequent. It is worthy of note that several of the frequent contributors are small countries in the north-west of Europe, while the large maritime nations seem to have different priorities. This suggests that, at least in terms of SNMG1, there's a small but noteworthy difference in the maritime-strategic integration between the two blocks of nations, although certainly not a fracture.

The above shows the limits of what is a relatively high level of maritime-strategic integration, but every 'rule' has exceptions and SNMG1 has three major such exceptions. The first of these is when the United States is in command of the force. Compared with the other semesters, the two semesters of 2019 saw significant contributions with between five and seven ships at times, although the holiday seasons in winter and summer attracted fewer participants. Strictly speaking, the deployment to the East Coast of the US is far away from the maritime challenges that Northern Europe faces, but the allure of US command clearly overrode any such concern. Sailing under US command is therefore clearly an attractive proposal, which seems to increase strategic integration for the duration of the command. Whether regular US participation, without commanding the force, would have a similar effect is difficult to ascertain, as the US generally does not contribute except when it is in command of the force.[33]

The second exception is crisis, as both the last semester of 2021 and first of 2022 show. The lead up and eventual invasion of Ukraine on 24 February 2022 showed an alliance that coalesced and galvanised politically, economically and militarily in the face of Russian aggression. The SNMG1 adds a maritime aspect to this overall picture, confirming the impression of an alliance that aligned strategically in Europe. Indeed, both semesters saw SNMG1 contributions comparable to when the US had command in 2019. One could say that the Ukraine war's effect on the willingness to contribute to SNMG1 was equal to that of US command of the force.

The third significant exception to the baseline are major exercises, where SNMG1's numbers are regularly and routinely boosted by additional surface ships put under its tactical control. Exercising with SNMG1 seems to be strategically attractive to NATO members on the Atlantic coast, which suggests that there is significant agreement over their conventional nature. In short, the practice of putting ships under tactical SNMG1 control confirms the relatively high level of maritime-strategic integration in NATO, and especially among the nations on the North Atlantic seaboards.

Although strategic integration is showcased through exercises, they are about more than just that. Indeed, they are central in developing what is arguably the backbone of strategic integration in NATO: interoperability. If the purpose of NATO is to defend its members, aligning strategic interests is only part of the solution since an effective fighting force operates jointly and as seamlessly as possible. In other words, it is necessary to cultivate interoperability, and the only way to do this is to train and operate together as interoperability is a natural consequence of these activities. This chapter has shown that SNMG1 is a hub for maritime training and exercises and therefore a central piece in achieving interoperability between maritime forces in NATO. There are several large, official exercises every semester, and although not addressed in much detail in this chapter, it is also important to note all the tactical training both within the force and between the force and other units.

Interoperability is not just treated as a side-effect of training and exercises. Indeed, as this chapter shows, interoperability is put front and centre, either implicitly or explicitly, in nearly all major exercises. The sheer number of larger exercises, about seven per year, and the scale and complexity of these, suggest a high degree of maritime interoperability within NATO in general. SNMG1's role as a hub for allied exercises and training, as well as the tactical training and exercising that does not feature on the exercise schedule, shows that the force is at the core of NATO's maritime interoperability. Indeed, the contributors to SNMG1 arguably prioritise interoperability over strategic integration, evidenced in the habitual surge of contributions in periods with large exercises, as well as the transfer of tactical control of ships to SNMG1 during exercises. Even though the surges and the transfer of control also are indications of strategic integration, the integration would have been greater with a larger number of contributions throughout the semesters.

The force's role in interoperability is central to strategic integration in two ways. First, it acts as a symbol of such integration. The existence of SNMG1, the contributions to it and its activities signal that the alliance's perception of the strategic environment, as well as the ends, ways and means to deal with this environment, sufficiently align to attract contributions to the force. Second, it is also likely that SNMG1 acts as a driver of strategic integration within the alliance. It has been argued that the intertwined nature of NATO's political bodies, bureaucracy, agencies, exercises and training act as a gravitational force to draw the alliance's nations together.[34] The existence of SNMG1 and its activities fit neatly into this argument.

Conclusions and the Way Ahead

Although this chapter is an initial foray into SNMG1's role in NATO's strategic integration and interoperability, it has shown that the force is a hub for, and contributor to, both. It has also shown the practical interplay between the two terms in the

MARITIME-STRATEGIC INTEGRATION

maritime domain through mainly two avenues. First, without sufficient maritime-strategic integration, SNMG1 would not exist, or its activities would be markedly different. Second, the backbone of maritime-strategic integration in NATO is interoperability. As SNMG1 acts as a hub for both in the northernmost Atlantic Ocean, it arguably has two main roles: it is crucial in showing alliance solidarity and unity; and it is central in preparing the alliance as a collective—as opposed to individual nations or bilateral arrangements—for conventional maritime warfare. Although training with partner nations has not figured prominently in this chapter, the Baltic Sea deployments show that SNMG1 also plays this role vis-a-vis partners such as Finland and Sweden. Indeed, it is a distinct possibility that SNMG1's joint activities with Swedish and Finnish naval forces have contributed to easing their way into alliance operations once they officially enter NATO. This, however, is a topic for future research.

Questions about SNMG1's relevance as a quick reaction force are legitimate because its baseline of between one and three ships is hardly 'an overwhelming force presence'.[35] On the other hand, the track record from the events leading up to and including the Ukraine war shows that, when strategic integration is sufficiently aligned, NATO can muster quite significant naval power. SNMG1's emphasis on interoperability likely enables these forces to assemble rather quickly. This approach nevertheless has a weakness, as it depends on the availability of allied ships and on a sufficiently high level of maritime integration.

This chapter has identified a baseline for SNMG1 activities in the northernmost region of the Atlantic. This pattern of activities affords NATO significant leeway for assisting allies in need while at the same time avoiding misunderstandings related to escalation of crises or conflicts. As with the relationship with its partners, the role of SNMG1 in NATO deterrence and reassurance is another aspect that is ripe for study. Finally, the motives and strategic calculations behind individual nations' participation—or lack thereof—in SNMG1 is another topic that requires more in-depth study, as this chapter has only scratched the surface.

PART TWO

THE WAR IN UKRAINE
STRATEGIC SHOCK, STRATEGIC CHANGE?

5

RETURN TO A BLEAK PAST?
THE RUSSIAN INVASION OF UKRAINE AND THE INTERNATIONAL SYSTEM

Beatrice Heuser

The switch made in February 2022 by the Russian government from unattributable military support for a feeble independence movement in the Donbas (Eastern Ukraine) to a full-scale classic military invasion caught the EU in a period of stagnation or even disintegration. European integration that had started with great élan after the Second World War was stunted militarily in the mid-1950s when the project to form a European Defence Community foundered on a French parliamentary veto. Subsequent steps towards integration always came under counter-pressure from sovereigntists—the extreme defenders of sovereignty, i.e. the freedom from any influence by and concern for other parties in one's own decision-making—especially where defence was concerned. Meanwhile, NATO, to which the defence of Europe was and still is largely delegated, has remained an inter-governmental, not a supra-governmental, organisation. Even the small steps towards more European cooperation in matters of common security and defence made since the end of the Cold War have not in fact produced a full European defence capacity outside NATO or even within NATO. Attempts to make progress in this direction during the Yugoslav Wars of the 1990s (i.e. to pacify this crisis without the help of the USA) foundered, despite the benevolent attitude of the US administration that was more than happy to leave this can of worms to the Europeans. Except they could not deal with it on their own and the US had to step in. The construction of a European Pillar of NATO, capable of standing alone if need be, was obstructed at the time by Turkey in a bid to prevent Cypriot and promote Turkish membership of the EU. Since then, little had been achieved.

Defence is the last bastion of sovereignty. While the majority of EU members were ultimately willing to surrender part of their fiscal sovereignty to the European Central Bank by making the Euro their currency, they have baulked at a common defence. As multiple analyses of the foundering European Defence Community project of the early 1950s agreed, the problem with taking steps towards including defence in the supra-national part of the EU is that it makes no sense without integrated, supra-national policymaking in this domain. In other words, it makes no sense without a transfer of sovereignty in this domain to a European government, and that does not exist.

What could be and has been agreed upon in a number of cases is joint procurement, such as with the Eurofighter, as this could be done in times of peace via inter-governmental negotiations. Also, military units of various sizes from different states have been merged or put under common command or at least have worked to standard procedures in military exercises. The Netherlands has been most serious about this: at the end of March 2023, it put its last remaining brigade under German command by merging its *13th Light Brigade* of 3,000 soldiers with the German Army's 10th Panzer Division. They have been true to their own decision, reflected in their 2020 white paper,[1] to focus their defence efforts 'on a stronger, more self-reliant Europe'. By contrast, in 2017 when France under President Macron tried to prod its neighbours into discussing further European cooperation and perhaps even integration in matters beyond joint procurement, he got little or no response, especially when it came to discussing nuclear weapons.[2] France's Presidency of the EU in the first half of 2022 coincided with the all-out Russian attack on Ukraine, and let some of France's planned initiatives for European integration— some already delayed by COVID—pale against the need to take a stance on Russian aggression. Arguably, time was lost by Macron's attempts—in line with his course of a third option rather than alignment in emergent US–Russian and US–Chinese bipolarities—to show himself as the great mediator who would keep diplomatic talks open and believed he had Putin's ear.

The states that have joined NATO and the EU since the end of the Cold War seem to be interested only in the alliance with America when it comes to defence: in the 1990s, concerted attempts by European diplomats to get them to apply for membership of the Western European Union (which was later dissolved with its mutual guarantee clause alone retained in the Lisbon Treaty) misfired as they insisted that only NATO as the framework for US backing would satisfy their security needs. The Southern tier European countries have been preoccupied with a distinct problem affecting them disproportionately, mass immigration across the Mediterranean, an issue that has little or nothing to do with Russia's neo-imperialist expansionism. Meanwhile, Britain has taken the paradoxical position of strongest possible military-political commitment in opposing Russia (admittedly with the luxury of a greater physical distance from Russia than most continental Europeans: Russian tanks are unlikely to roll into the home counties even in a Third World War), while withdrawing from far less risky mutual commitments in the domain of economic and fiscal cooperation in the EU. As Hungary and Poland were deviating from key EU constitutional and political values, the European integration process seemed to have peaked. It was and still is suffering from overstretch and a resurgence of narrow nationalist selfishness in the wake of the 2008 financial crisis that forced governments to take measures of austerity that in turn alienated voters and drove them into the arms of populists all across Europe. The EU members had barely recovered from this when COVID-19 hit in 2020 and again forced emergency government spending resulting in new government debts. In parallel, possibly augmented by the greater sensitivity to the forces of nature which the pandemic generated, younger people in particular woke up to the long existing calls by scientists for serious and very expensive measures to be taken throughout Europe to mitigate what is already inescapable climate change. This was and is classically a domain in which EU members can achieve more jointly than they can by going it alone, but also one where interests diverge widely: Poland and Hungary deem it impossible to abandon coal quite yet as they would be fiscally unable to afford the switch. Meanwhile, Germany, the stomach of the EU (to use the imagery of John of Salisbury's *Policraticus*), drew its energy to keep the whole body going from cheap Russian oil and gas imports, without a fall-back.

No war comes at a good time, but the Ukraine war definitely did not from the point of view of the European project. One might have hoped that it could have rekindled interest in and commitment to it, especially as signs had been clear for over quarter of a century that American interests had slowly but steadily been shifting away from Europe and the Middle East and towards the Western Pacific.[3] The war should indeed have reinvigorated the European project, because so very much is at stake, even if other states are not combatants. What is at stake is the current world order, which despite gravest structural flaws is still the most pacific the world has known and thus much in the interest of the Europeans to defend. Let us have a look at how it has emerged and what the alternatives would be.

Patterns of Behaviour in Relations Between Polities

We can distinguish different patterns of behaviour in recorded history in relations between organised larger human societies.[4] Such patterns—often referred to as 'systems'—changed over time, sometimes abruptly, sometimes incrementally. I use the term 'systems' reluctantly to describe these because definitions of 'systems' tend to include the notion of order. We shall use it here with the strong caveat that it should not be understood to resemble a system of planets invariably obeying the same laws of physics, but as a *pattern* of behaviour, even if this is not always adhered to. Focusing only on the Euro-Mediterranean world, successive or sometimes parallel systems can be identified. Rather than analysing the successive systems of interactions between European polities chronologically, let us identify the recurrent themes.

The two most popularly famous are that of the universal empire and that of competing or rivalling powers. The idea of the universal empire or monarchy can be traced back to the third millennium BC.[5] It evolved, of course, as the knowledge about geography and reach of those aspiring to such universal rule increased. As their horizons widened, people discovered ever more distant civilisations, sometimes other empires with a universalist claims. Sometimes this led to long-standing competitions as between Persia and the Roman Empire.

Universalist claims tended to be based on religions that claimed to pertain to all of mankind rather than just to one people or tribe or on ideas of manifest destiny or historical inevitability.

The notion of being God-willed, being the earthly version of His heavenly rule gave the idea a self-righteousness that would survive until the Reformation, and that can be compared only to the missionary zeal with which the Muslims embarked on their wars of conquest and (still ongoing) proselytism, the Mongol notion of 'Heaven's Will', or the historical inevitability of the spread of communism, aided by all tools of strategy, hard and soft. Of these, Islam and communism were directly inspired by the Romano-Christian model, of which Russia saw itself as a new incarnation, with Moscow as the 'Third Rome', with an imperial mission burning brightly again today.

Empires, in establishing an internal monopoly on the use of force, could implicitly or explicitly promise peace within their boundaries—think of the Pax Augusta or the Pax Britannica. While this has given rise to some enthusiasm for them,[6] even among historians,[7] such peace tended to be bought at some cost of internal *Gleichschaltung*, homogenisation, intolerance of (religious or other) deviation, a loss of self-determination and a reduction of self-rule. In general, this was pretty disagreeable for a large part of the population who could be massacred, enslaved, expelled and often starved to death in the process. Many empires in world history have thus been brutally repressive or beneficial only to a ruling elite. On the whole, being colonised by force is not a welcome experience.

There are exceptions: even before the Reformation kicked the religious underpinnings away from under the feet of the emperor, the Holy Roman Empire, which had long ceased to expand, had evolved into an internal power-sharing system with several layers of sovereignty that was constrained by the need for consultation. Minus the figure of the emperor/empress, it was the structure that has most in common with today's European Union. Several of the European colonial empires were marked in part by the humane desire to share the fruits of the enlightenment, of medicine and sanitation and good governance with colonised peoples, with the aim of helping them towards a better life, and ultimately, independence. While the Russians certainly had a similar sense of mission, both in tsarist and in communist times, they had no intention of eventually letting go of any part of their vast empire. The Russian elite's track record of behaviour towards its own lower classes—serfdom was not abolished until the end of the nineteenth century—is similar to its attitude towards conquered nations, captured in Vassiliy Vereshchagin's famous painting *The Apotheosis of War* (c. 1870), in the context of Russia's wars in Central Asia. It shows a pile of skulls in a barren desert, and he dedicated it 'To all tyrants, past, present, and future'. Communist China's treatment of its Uyghur population today suggests that Chinese imperialism also has miserable victims. The universal monarchy of one nation that is self-appointed to dominate all others is not the ideal state system.

The aim of establishing a universal monarchy was never realistic, and emperors or US, Soviet and Chinese presidents never quite went so far as to espouse it. But some of their court ideologues did, provoking denunciation by rival entities that set out to counterbalance such ambitions. This leads us to the second principle of rivalry among two or more polities, in which entities ganged up to keep others in check, touted as (re)creating or maintaining a 'balance of powers'. Some entities did aspire to dominate a (regional) system as hegemons, others merely to prevent their rivals from achieving hegemony. As the Renaissance freed European minds from the inherited belief that Christendom should really present a monolithic entity, it clearly was not (as Christian entities—monarchies, city-states, republics—competed with each other) driven by the desire for aggrandisement at the expense of others. The Reformation, with its confessional wars, was merely an interlude. The French diplomat Philippe de Commynes described (around 1500) these rivalries in binary terms. He was perhaps also the first to describe these rivalries as positive, designed by God to keep all parties 'in fear and humility'.[8] Over the following centuries, this notion was developed further into a theory of (positive) balances of power by which different polities kept one another in check, preventing universalist ambitions.[9]

Others, however, identified in such rivalries—whether or not couched in terms of 'balance of powers'—drivers for war. And indeed, in modern times, and until the Second World War, Europe was perhaps both the most bellicose and the most war-torn continent of the world. Clearly, looking back, such a system, dominated by aggressive rivalries in the name of counterbalancing other powers, was not in the interest of a pacific and prosperous life for Europeans.

Battered from the Napoleonic Wars, five great powers who shared the aim of stabilising Europe by co-operating among themselves to settle outstanding issues emerged in Europe.[10] Ruling one of them, Russian Tsar Alexander I, coming from a country that had known neither Renaissance nor Reformation, was driven by medieval ideas of Christian unity and called for a Holy Alliance among the great powers to assure peace for Europe. But then, as in the Middle Ages, rivalry among them prevailed over Christian brotherhood. These big five, who had set out to rule Europe, if not the world, peacefully from the mid-nineteenth century, fell out in a series of bi- or tri-lateral wars of great power competition, culminating in the cataclysmic world wars of the twentieth century. Even those great power wars of the nineteenth century left deep scars as collective memories of their bloody battles with conscripted mass armies show: think of Solferino (1859) that pitted French and Italians against Austrians, the Battle of Dybbøl (1864) in the German alliance war against Denmark, the Battle of Königgrätz/Sadowa (1866) in the Austro–Prussian War or the Battles of Gravelotte or Sedan (1870). Thus, the voluntary great power cooperation or collusion of the first half of the nineteenth century turned into great power competition and wars (1853–1945), an international system that could hardly have been worse for the Europeans.

One should have known better after the First and Second World Wars than to once again entrust the fate of the world to the voluntary cooperation of a pentarchy of great powers. Yet this is what was done both in founding the League of Nations in 1920, and the United Nations (UN) in 1945. Not just great power rivalry but also ideological rifts paralysed both global organisations. Ideological clashes and colonial rivalries between the great powers in the League's Council facilitated the rise of Mussolini's Fascist Italy, imperialist Japan and Nazi Germany and their long-unchecked expansion. Ideological rivalries soon led to the paralysis of the UN's Security Council for most of the Cold War.

And yet, the Cold War was a period of unparalleled peace for Western Europe, and of great prosperity. Under the threat of nuclear war, the two alliance systems, NATO and the Warsaw Treaty Organisation, kept each other in a situation of stand-off. Under America's nuclear umbrella, European integration, previously impossible while the Europeans had lived by the law of balance-of-power rivalry, was made possible by singularly auspicious alignment of the stars: all countries involved happened to be liberal democracies with free-market economies balanced by social welfare schemes. Its ideational roots, however, were much older and revolved around having the heads or representatives of the European states resolve any problems jointly, as equals, around a council table.[11] It took the fratricidal wars of the nineteenth and early twentieth centuries to turn theory into practice, by shaking up the Europeans to the point where they were willing to dampen their own nationalistsovereigntist selfishness in the interest of cooperation. But the positive effect was tremendous: Western Europe prospered and has enjoyed a period of peace exceeding any in recorded history. It got better still when communism collapsed in Europe and Central Asia without bringing down the world in a Third World War. Eastern Europe now could benefit from the trade and economic freedom which had made the West so prosperous. A short period ensued in the 1990s in which the UN's Security Council functioned with the harmony that its creators in 1945 had hoped for.

But communism—even if with Chinese peculiarities, as China's leaders never cease to note—has not disappeared in the Far East. And nationalism-cum-sovereigntism is back, including in its extreme imperialist, expansionist form that dominated the world in the nineteenth century, especially in Russia, but also in other parts of the world—think of Turkey and India.

The League and the UN were not, however, mere extensions of the nineteenth-century pentarchy. Both also built on older ideas of a *universal, all-inclusive* state system, now extended to the whole world. Both include a novelty: the principle, introduced by US President Wilson in 1917 that every people, every nation, have a right to self-determination (i.e. to be independent from foreign domination, again an idea with much older roots).[12] But it was elevated to a principle governing international relations only with the creation of the League of Nations, which was designed to overview the gradual emancipation of all colonies that eventually were to become independent sovereign states and members, and the UN. It is the negation of empire, of the formal domination of some peoples or even states by others. Contrary to previous centuries, international law had now developed in principle to declare all states equal and sovereign.

Thus, both the League and the UN contained a fundamental contradiction in fusing the earlier pattern of the rule of five great powers—the pentarchy—with that of equality of the over 150 members to which the UN would grow. This contradiction persists to this day, as well as the problem that all three successive pentarchies had in common, namely, that the great powers were also rivals and could block each other, a system formally enshrined in the UN Security Council with the veto right of the big five.

This deficiency of the UN was recognised early on and resulted the creation of the two military alliances to complement it, NATO in the West and the Warsaw Treaty Organisation in the East. The latter was dissolved at the end of the Cold War as East European countries escaped Russian hegemony, instead seeking protection in the American-led defence pact from a post-communist Russia they did not trust. While some former Soviet republics—the Baltic States—also managed to gain admission to NATO, other Soviet republics were left to fend for themselves. Georgia was such a one, attacked by Russia in 2008 as the West stood by; subsequent promises of admission to NATO never got beyond initial announcements of intent. From 2014, Ukraine was infiltrated by Russian soldiers in uniforms without markings, Crimea was annexed to Russia, and again, the West promised a NATO membership which has not yet materialised and will probably not as long as the war is ongoing. Security is demonstrably divisible as the UN is incapable of acting: those who are in NATO seem to be protected, those who are outside it clearly are not. While it would be in the interest of all weaker powers the world over if the renunciation of war as an instrument of statecraft were upheld throughout the world, *Realpolitik* suggests that it is in the interest of the Europeans at least to keep out of the fray and protect the security they have in the short term in this two-tier world.

What is at Stake in the Russo-Ukrainian War?

All this needs to be kept in mind when analysing what the Russo-Ukrainian War is about and what is at stake in this war. For the Ukrainians, it is their independence, founded on the right to self-determination on which our world order—this is what we can now call this system as it is underpinned by international law—has rested since 1928. For Russia, it is the claim to have a manifest imperial destiny to rule over others, the very negation of the right of others to self-determination. Therefore, what is at stake in this war is whether its outcome will throw us back to the system of the nineteenth century in which might was right and in which even international law conceded that any sovereign state had the right to go to war in pursuit of its interests (a principle that was explicitly relinquished with the Briand–Kellogg Pact of 1928, an abjuration confirmed by the UN Charter). Alternatively, if Ukraine can expel the Russian forces, it will be a victory for the order established in 1928/1945 that banished war as a tool of state interest and confirmed the right to self-determination.

In their own defence, the Russians say that other infringements on the rules of the order based on the UN Charter have occurred, indeed made by one or more members of the pentarchy. They point to the Western air campaign against Serbia in support of Kosovo in 1999 or to the US and British involvement in the Iraq War of 2003–11. Neither, however, was aimed at the conquest of territory, and indeed the former ultimately defended the principle of self-determination, the latter ostensibly aimed to ensure Iraq's adherence to its own renunciation of producing weapons of mass destruction. While the latter was based on scandalously misconstrued intelligence information, both in principle upheld the rules-based international order (RBIO), which we shall use as a shorthand for the rules enshrined in the Briand-Kellogg

Pact, the UN Charter and the order that was founded on related international norms and covenants.

The RBIO is not without its contradictions, as we have seen: the fundamental paradox in the UN's constitution that declares all states to be equal but pronounces the pentarchy of great powers 'more equal than others' by giving the latter permanent seats and veto rights in the Security Council is not resolved. The system itself is constructed so that any member of the pentarchy can block reforms going against its interests, and each has the interest to preserve its special powers. Much thinking has been put into how to reform a system that can only be explained by which states held power when it was created, not in terms of, say, proportional representation of humans on this planet. Even then, the problem would remain: what can justify giving India, Brazil and Nigeria a place among the great powers, if this leaves further billions of people without such representation, merely because they happen not to be citizens of one of the population-richest states?

Be that as it may, the outcome of the war will determine whether one of the big five powers can go against the rules and get away with it, whether might is right, as it was before the establishment of this order, which would not only undermine the order but encourage other revisionist powers to follow Russia's example of returning to the use of force to pursue state interests.

What Possible Outcomes are there to the War?

So let us pass review on possible outcomes of this war and what they would mean for the rest of the world. One would be the achievement of Russian war aims. These have taken several guises. All of them, however, imply a return to features of the nineteenth century pattern of interstate relations, by which great powers, which were simultaneously imperial powers, had the right to dispose of other states and peoples, in rejection of any right to self-determination. The achievement of Russian war aims in any of its three forms is thus diametrically opposed to any interest in upholding today's RBIO.

The first of Russia's war aims is, or perhaps was, simply to bring Ukraine 'heim ins Reich', back into the 'Russian World' empire, *Russkij Mir*. The analogy with the Austrian 'Anschluss' to Hitler's Third Reich in 1938 imposes itself: in Putin's self-delusion springing from his articulated conviction that Russia and Ukraine do not constitute distinct nations,[13] he clearly hoped that Ukrainians would welcome or passively condone such an 'Anschluss'. It would, however, have needed a coup in Kyiv to accomplish this back in February/March 2022, and this coup did not materialise. Instead, Ukrainian national identity was strengthened if anything along with the determination to resist.

As of the time of writing, the impression is that a fall-back definition of aims is to keep the already annexed Crimea and secure 'New Russia', Novaya Rossiya, in Eastern Ukraine, both areas settled with Russians under Catherine the Great in the late eighteenth century. Both options—full annexation or partial annexation—would signify a return to pre-UN practices, the very practices adopted by the rogue states Germany, Italy and Japan in the 1930s that ushered in the Second World War. Both options are incompatible with upholding the current RBIO. Interestingly, once the Second World War was over, Stalin was cautious about changing frontiers by force, and indeed the Soviet Union under his successors foreswore the change of frontiers by force in the Helsinki Final Act of 1975. Putin's Russia is thus visibly going back, not even to Soviet practices of the Cold War, but to the great power practices of the nineteenth century and of the 1930s prelude to the Second World War.

A third option was put forward by Russia in December 2021 as an alternative to a full-scale invasion and was then ignored by the West that remained and remains wedded to the principle of self-determination: to force Ukraine to abjure any application to join the EU or NATO and to guarantee its neutrality by a great-power congress, involving Russia itself and America, of course, and NATO collectively (Bismarck must be laughing and weeping in his grave). Such a proposal not only flies in the face of the principle of self-determination but has also been deprived of any credibility by the behaviour of Russia itself as it had entered into just such a great-power agreement with the Budapest Memorandum of 1994. In this, the US and Britain stepped in as guarantors of an agreement between Russia on the one hand and Belarus, Kazakhstan and Ukraine on the other that if the latter surrendered to Russia the nuclear weapons stationed on their territory at the time the USSR was dissolved, Russia in turn would promise not to touch their frontiers. Which Russia, in the case of Ukraine, has blatantly ignored since 2014.

All three options are thus unacceptable to any country whose own security depends on the upholding of the RBIO, which is the case for all EU and European NATO members. Only a full reversal of Russian aggression would be acceptable by the standards of the EU. The distribution of military power in Europe is such, however, that this is not only the less likely outcome than the at least part-realisation of Russia's aims, but also an outcome which one would realistically have to expect Russia under Putin or a similar successor regime would seek to reverse, returning to the initial charge as soon as possible.

European Reactions

Have the Europeans understood what is at stake and the dilemmas this poses? One might turn, initially, to what is modestly called the EU's 'Strategic Compass', a sort of update and supplement to the EU's Global Strategy of 2016.

We must keep in mind that the process of drawing up a national or alliance security strategy is one that is more important than its product. Such a strategic concept—under whatever name, Integrated Review, Compass or Strategic Review—is a bureaucratic exercise, and its main intended or unintended aim is to forge consensus through arduous discussions at least within government or within an alliance, on what must be done and how, and how to finance it. Such an exercise is outdated as soon as it is published, a fate that befell the British, French and NATO strategic concepts which were published before the Russian invasion of Ukraine on 24 February 2022. The invasion also almost derailed the EU's strategic compass, which, in a Herculean effort, was adapted to this new situation in the weeks before its publication on 21 March 2022 (Britain had already had to come up with an 'Integrated Review Refresh' on 13 March 2023[14]). If published, such a document by definition tends not to articulate some important concerns. Thus, among the European products (counting these here to include the British Integrated Review), only the Dutch review of 2020 was bold enough to address the European nightmare of American disengagement and draw out the consequences.[15]

Being, again by definition, compromise documents that needed to please all sides sufficiently for them to sign up to them, one must expect a certain amount of ambiguity in language, of passages that paper over the cracks that mark divergences of interest and values among parties signing up to them. In the EU's Strategic Compass of 2022, a commitment is unsurprisingly spelled out 'to uphold the principles of the UN Charter and restore peace in Europe together with our partners'. Given what we have said above, however, it is unclear how the second part of this commitment can be realised, either soon or durably, without abandoning the former.

New measures to this effect include the 'establish[ment of] a strong EU Rapid Deployment Capacity of up to 5000 troops for different types of crises', which is of course tiny in the face of a Russian mobilisation of somewhere in the ballpark of 200,000 men for the war against Ukraine. A series of other measures aim to give Europe a better space and maritime defence capability, to augment its capacities in matters of intelligence analysis, cyber security, instruments to combat information manipulation by adversaries, other 'hybrid' tools of strategy and so on. The Compass also articulated the resolve more boldly to 'combine our diplomatic and economic instruments, including our sanctions regimes, with civil and military assets to prevent conflict, respond to crises, contribute to peacebuilding and support partners'.[16]

Indeed, aligning actions with pronouncements, the EU has collectively imposed package after package of sanctions on Russia (ten by the time of writing), and individual member states have added to these. The grand strategy, if one may call it that, of the EU has thus been to fight back Russia's deft use of its own non-military tools of its grand strategy—the export of cheap gas, oil and grain—with equally non-military tools.[17] Effects on Russia's economy, let alone on the civilian population of which up to 75% seem to give their full support to Putin's 'special military operation' against Ukraine, seem to be if not negligible, too small to cause enough pain to raise protests among the great majority of Russians.[18] By contrast, soaring inflation and energy prices are affecting most EU citizens, especially those on lower incomes. The sanctions themselves contribute to this pain on the side of the EU: sanctions generally hurt both sides.

The enforcement of sanctions largely remains under the competence of EU members. They, plus the UK, have also individually furnished arms to Ukraine and several are training Ukrainian soldiers to use them. But of the roughly 200 tanks that Ukraine's government says it needs to fend off the invader, only penny-packages of 14 or 15, and moreover of different makes (Challengers, Leopards, Abrams), have been promised or are being delivered.

The fear of doing more can of course be linked to the terrible threat of a nuclear escalation of the conflict which cannot be excluded. This is the most important way in which the present differs from the 19th century or even the 1930s. Polls suggest overall support among European populations for Ukraine, yet the former seem far from fully aware that the international order is at risk, an order that emerged so late from centuries, nay millennia, of bloody wars, particularly in Europe.

Europeans have got used to a comfortable life. Reductions in state spending or salary augmentations below inflation rates resulting from fiscal deficits have in 2023 caused strikes in Britain, France and Germany. In the winter of 2022/23, European willingness to 'put up with the cold and turn down the heating' in support of Ukraine was limited. And political leaders of parties at both extremes of the political spectrum act as mouthpieces of Russia by constantly reiterating the trope that the Russian war on Ukraine was in some form merited by NATO for having accepted the refugee states from the Warsaw Pact into its fold. Ensuing 'peace demonstrations' work for the Kremlin as much as they did in the early 1980s, when Western demonstrators focused their anger exclusively on Western nuclear weapons, not on those deployed by the Soviet Union. The EU, in short, is at risk of being turned from a paradisical Continent of Peace into a paradise of fools who do not know what precious acquis they have, and that they must make efforts to protect it as it is at risk an being fought over—In Ukraine.

6

THE UNITED STATES AND EUROPE
REFORGING THE NATO ALLIANCE

Andrew A. Michta[1]

Three Decades of Strategic Slumber

The Russian invasion of Ukraine and the brave response of Ukrainians who stood up and fought in defense of their country's right to remain sovereign has become a system-transforming war at multiple levels. So far, it has had three principal consequences. First, it has resulted in a level of transatlantic political unity unseen since the end of the Cold War, strengthening the US position of leadership on the continent and muting differences that surfaced within NATO during the two decades of America's Global War on Terror, especially in the wake of the second Iraq War. Second, Ukraine's staunch resistance has begun eliminating the two-frontier crisis the Sino-Russian alliance has tried to put in place at a time when the US military is formatted to fight in only one major theater of war and one limited engagement in a secondary theater. Today, the Ukrainian armed forces—a non-NATO military—is grinding down the Russian land forces on non-NATO territory, buying America and its allies badly needed time to rebuild their forces for state-on-state conflict, in the process sequencing the threats the United States faces in both the Atlantic and the Pacific theaters. Third, and arguably most significantly, it has awakened NATO's political leadership to the reality that over the past three decades, the European allies have effectively disarmed to a point that, notwithstanding their population resources and wealth, they would be unable to defend themselves without America coming yet again to the rescue. It has returned NATO to its original role, placing collective defense once again front and center.

The war in Ukraine has laid bare flawed assumptions about the nature of the international system, the alleged benefits of 'globalization' and 'complex interdependence,' refocusing the minds of American elites on the irreducible national security function of the state. Gone is the era of 'it's the economy, stupid,' whereby the fundamentally flawed 'end of history' assertion led us to prize economic efficiency of 'just-in-time' supply systems above all else. According to this thinking, not only would Western companies be able to leverage labor arbitrage in China, but in the process Western foreign direct investment and 'export-driven modernization'—it was believed—would bring about greater pluralism in the People's Republic of China, just as *Wandel durch Handel* and Germany's *Energiewende* would foster Russia's interdependence with Europe and ensure a more stable and peaceful world.[2] On 24 February 2022, Russia reminded us in no uncertain terms that history had not in fact ended; rather, it had come full circle, bringing us back to a future where hard power is once again key, where real exercised military capabilities are central to the survival of democracy, and where it is less about efficiency and more about redundancy when it comes to manufacturing capabilities and, by extension, stockpiles of weapons and munitions 'just in case.'

THE UNITED STATES AND EUROPE

After three decades of globalist fallacy, the United States and its NATO allies have finally awakened to the hard realities of state-on-state competition and war. Not only has communist China failed to become a 'responsible stakeholder in the international system'—to quote but one notorious phrase from that bygone era—but it now stands enriched with money, knowledge and technology the West so glibly provided when it moved entire production lines there, brought the China into the World Trade Organization and opened its universities and research laboratories to Chinese students and researchers. For three decades, we fed Western technology, Western expertise and research and development to a 1.4-billion-strong communist state on a flimsy and unsupported assumption that growing prosperity and interdependence would lead to a more open and pluralistic China—that 'they' would become more like 'us.' China has used these 30 years to accomplish the most impressive economic and military modernization in history. The end result is not a more democratic but rather a more nationalistic and geostrategically assertive China, intent on not only competing toe-to-toe with the United States but also intent on replacing America and the global normative system and security architecture it has put in place. Augmented by extortion of intellectual property—reportedly, one in five American companies doing business in China had to supply their intellectual property in exchange for market access—and its theft of technology, China has been rapidly closing the gap between its research and development base and that of the United States and its democratic allies. To recall President Richard Nixon's words shortly before his death, we have created a Frankenstein.

China has not been the only beneficiary of three decades of post-Cold War policies in Washington and other major capitals. Ten years after the disintegration of the Soviet Union, Russia under Vladimir Putin was firmly back on its revisionist path, seething with resentment over its loss of power and status. Twenty years of Putinism witnessed a narrative of Russia's betrayal by the country's politicians—cowardly Gorbachev, drunken Yeltsin, you name it—to produce a Russian equivalent of the Weimar Republic era *Dolchstoßlegende*, which gave interwar Germany Hitler and its final drive to empire that lit Europe and the world on fire yet again. Putin used the last twenty years of access to the West to increase Europe's dependence on Russian energy. For instance, Germany's dependence on Russian gas went up from 35% in 2014 to close to 60% on the eve of Russia's invasion of Ukraine in 2022, to say nothing of the two Nord Stream pipelines bypassing the flank countries, effectively isolating Ukraine and other frontier states. Putin used this revenue to centralize power, build a patronage system and increase his information operations across the West. Twenty years of largely unfettered access to Western technology has allowed Russia to selectively modernize its military, with significant advances in attack submarine technology, hypersonic propulsion and cyber technology. Russia used military power repeatedly and directly, first subduing Chechnya in a series of campaigns that lasted from 1999 to 2009, then invading Georgia in 2008 to seize Abkhazia and South Ossetia, Ukraine in 2014 to seize Crimea, and Syria in 2015 to prop up Assad's regime and return Russia to its former status as a player in the Middle East. Each time Putin used military power, he scored a significant geopolitical win, with little to no consequences when it came to his relations with the West. A case in point, after he invaded Georgia he still got Nord Stream 1, and after he invaded Ukraine in 2014, the Nord Stream 2 contract was finalized and the pipe built. Clearly, in 2022 Putin expected not only a quick win, much like in 2014, but also virtually zero reaction from the West.

THE UNITED STATES AND EUROPE

Sweden and Finland in NATO: A Geostrategic Gamechanger for the 'Intermarium'

Arguably, no other event in the wake of the Russian invasion of Ukraine in 2022 would prove as transformative for the geopolitical map of Europe and the future of NATO as the decision of Stockholm and Helsinki to abandon their neutrality and apply for membership in the alliance. Although as of this writing it is unclear whether Turkey and Hungary will ultimately relent and allow for Sweden to join, Finland has now joined the alliance. The entry of Finland in particular changes the geostrategic picture in the Baltic, Scandinavia and the European High North in that it forces Russia to deal directly with an additional 830 miles of NATO's border in the northeast. Furthermore, this round of NATO enlargement will in effect transform the Baltic Sea into a space surrounded by NATO countries—a 'NATO lake' of sorts. Next, it will provide the strategic depth needed for the defense of the three Baltic States, dramatically improving their security and the ability of the other allies to come to their assistance if attacked. Moreover, both Sweden and Finland will bring with them considerable military capabilities, especially when it comes to air power (Finland has placed an order for 64 F-35 aircraft[3]) and overall system integration across the region. In a key development, on 16 March 2023, Finland, Sweden, Denmark and Norway signed an agreement to pool their air forces together. The four states will be able to use their 250 fighter aircraft as a single fleet based on NATO interoperability standards.[4] The Danish air force noted that they want to develop a 'Scandinavian concept of joint air operations.' It is likely that the agreement will serve as a basis for creating a joint Nordic center for air operations that could also house the United States and Canada under a single command structure. The deal marks a seminal shift when it comes to the security of NATO's Nordic/

Baltic/Central European area, strengthening NATO's capabilities and further complicating Russian military planning.

In order to fully appreciate the shock delivered by the Russian invasion of Ukraine to how Sweden and Finland historically thought of their neutrality and approach to defense, one needs to acknowledge that the decision to apply for NATO membership was made within three months of the attack.[5] Simply put, it became clear both to Stockholm and Helsinki that being merely a NATO partner did not offer any meaningful guarantees, and nothing short of Article 5 would suffice going forward. Their decision to join NATO, once finalized and in combination with Poland's massive expansion of its land forces, air force and air defense capabilities, will significantly shift the center of gravity when it comes to the military capabilities to the continent's northeast, all the more so as the 100 billion euros reinvestment in the Bundeswehr, promised by Chancellor Scholz in this so-called *Zeitenwende* speech to the Bundestag on 27 February 2022, has yet to yield significant results in terms of real military capabilities.

This geostrategic reconfiguration of NATO's Northeastern flank will have a long-term impact on how NATO will be reforged going forward and how the United States will posture its forces in Europe. First and foremost, from Washington's vantage point it is becoming increasingly clear that the north–south 'intermarium' from the Baltic to the Black Sea represents the most committed group of European allies when it comes to investing in real exercised military capabilities. Today, while NATO remains politically unified regarding its response to the Russian invasion of Ukraine, nonetheless member countries have shown different appetites for risk taking, depending on their geographic proximity to the conflict, with countries along the eastern flank all in on supporting Ukraine, and those farther west, including Germany and France, less eager to provide weapons and support and more desirous of a political settlement that would freeze the conflict. Poland in particular has become indispensable to providing assistance to Ukraine, with its transportation hub and airport at Rzeszów-Jasionka being a key shipping point for Western military and humanitarian assistance to Kyiv. Since the Biden administration has declared its commitment to support Ukraine 'for as long as it takes,'[6] Warsaw's influence in the alliance has continued to grow, with Washington having announced that it would establish a permanent US army headquarters in Poland.[7] In short, the entry of Sweden and Finland into NATO, taken together with the growing US military footprint in the region, especially in Poland, suggests that a reforged NATO will rely more heavily on the contributions of the northeastern flank allies, while the US legacy military installations in Germany will shift more to training and reinforcement roles, with Germany remaining a principal entry point for US forces into Europe.

Ukraine in NATO?

The largest unanswered question looming over the horizon is what happens to Ukraine once the war is over, assuming that the country will be able to defend its sovereignty and independence. Today Ukraine commands the most powerful military in Europe after the United States. Any talk of rebuilding Ukraine postwar must begin with the question of how to ensure the country's security going forward, for no private investment will go there if Ukraine finds itself under constant threat of attack and further destruction. And so while most of the conversation in Western capitals has focused thus far on bringing Ukraine into the European Union, this discussion will have to increasingly shift to addressing how the country's security would be provided. Simply put, one of the key issues that NATO leaders will have to address is whether, and if so when, Ukraine would be brought into the alliance as a full member. This question will remain one of the key decision points that will shape a reforged NATO after the war in Ukraine has ended.

The future of Ukraine, and whether the United States and its European allies are ready to talk NATO membership for Ukraine, remains key to how the alliance will be reforged going forward. Ukraine is a large European state, with over 52 million citizens in 1991 when it declared its independence; in 2022, following the Russian annexation of Crimea and the invasion of Donetsk and Luhansk, it had some 42 million people. It is a country with vast natural resources, arguably the best land in Europe when it comes to agricultural production, a highly educated population and—until the Russians began to attack the country's industrial base and its critical infrastructure—a robust defense manufacturing base. In geopolitical terms, Ukraine is a lynchpin state for Russian neo-imperial ambitions and thereby for European security: a Russia that does not control Ukraine cannot pose a direct threat to Europe and return to European great power politics. Moreover, a successful, democratic Ukraine anchored in the West will all but ensure that Lukashenka's dictatorship in Belarus will implode, yielding the conditions for a region-wide solution to the security equation in Europe's 'crush zone' in the east.

Simply put, bringing Ukraine into NATO would be transformative for the region and for European security. It would effectively block Russia's pathway to Europe, returning Russia to its status as a Eurasian medium power for the first time in some 300 years. Furthermore, it would redefine the entire Nordic/Baltic/Central European 'intermarium' region, bringing together the military resources of Ukraine, Poland, the Baltics, the Nordics and NATO allies around the Black Sea—a belt of countries with a combined population of close to 140 million that share, on account of their histories, the same threat perception when it comes to Russia and determination to work closely with the United States in NATO.

THE UNITED STATES AND EUROPE

Admittedly, governments across the alliance are today nowhere near the requisite consensus when it comes to inviting Ukraine into NATO, for while the northeastern flank countries would welcome the idea, Germany, France and others in Western Europe remain opposed to it. Most importantly, the debate in Washington has not yet reached a point where the US government and Congress would be ready and willing to take up the question. Still, especially if Ukraine is successful in its planned 2023 spring offensive, the question of NATO membership for Ukraine is likely to percolate ever-closer to the surface of allied debate.

The Interlocking Challenges of NATO Planning

NATO's challenge today, as it grapples with the long-term consequences of the second Russian invasion of Ukraine, is fundamentally two-fold: first, revamping its strategic, operational and tactical planning to meet the challenge of a possible large-scale war in Europe and second, addressing the urgent need to rebuild Europe's defense industries and to rearm its militaries. In June, NATO formally adopted a new Strategic Concept to guide the alliance's approach to modernization and readiness through to 2030.[8] The core component of this framework is the new Concept for Deterrence and Defense of the Euro-Atlantic Area (DDA), or more simply, the Deter and Defend strategy that is currently being put in space. While top level plans cover the entire Euro-Atlantic area, others cover specific geographic regions or domains, such as maritime and space domains.[9] It also covers the cyber domain and logistics. The DDA is a hierarchy of integrated plans that cover peacetime, crisis and war. All the plans are integrated, with DDA aiming to triple forces available to support NATO's military objectives, with enhanced command and control.

The DDA concept represents a significant breakthrough, especially at the level of integration and planning of allied military capabilities. It was progress on the DDA framework that has allowed NATO to strengthen its posture, shielding the allies before and after the war that the Russian invasion of Ukraine started, in the process reducing the risk of the conflict widening and even jumping across the NATO fence. Since it exponentially increases NATO force integration, the concept also reinforces the alliance's unity. As part of this process, in 2022 NATO enhanced its forward presence along the eastern flank by establishing four new multinational battlegroups in Bulgaria, Hungary, Romania and Slovakia in addition to the existing battlegroups in Estonia, Latvia, Lithuania and Poland, which have been in place since 2017. It has increased training in these new battlegroups, to improve readiness and enhance force integration.

The cross-domain aspect of DDA is key to its transformative impact on NATO's readiness as it also aligns with the United States' 'Army 2035' Modernization Strategy that is intent on transforming the Total Army—Regular Army, National Guard, Army Reserve and Army Civilians—into a multi-domain force by 2035 to meet the requirements of the Joint Force, provide for the defense of the United States and retain its position as the globally dominant land power.[10] Since in the Euro-Atlantic space the US Army's role will be pivotal to NATO's deterrence and defense planning, the alignment of NATO's DDA concept with the Army Modernization Strategy is an important step towards strengthening force integration and effectiveness in the Euro-Atlantic theater. Similar to the Army Modernization Strategy, Supreme Headquarters Allied Powers Europe (SHAPE) plans for alliance members to view air, land, sea, space and cyberspace as warfighting domains.[11]

There is one especially germane aspect that links NATO's adaptation under DDA with further modernization plans for the US Joint Force. A critical element of military modernization pursued by NATO is to ensure interoperability through modernization and technology-based cooperation between the allied nations as the US begins to carry out its vision for next-generation Joint All-Domain Command and Control (JADC2). Already in 2022 the Pentagon indicated that with respect to JADC2 it will pursue earlier integration with the allies.[12] This will be critical to planning for deterrence and defense of the Euro-Atlantic area at every level, ensuring better integration between US and European systems. There has been a growing awareness that NATO needs to have not only interoperability when it comes to doctrine and exercising together, but also to be able to communicate with each other and have compatible systems.

The Urgent Challenge of Europe's Rearmament

The most daunting problem facing European NATO members today is a lack of readily available weapon systems and munitions. The three decades of the so-called 'peace dividend' left some of the formerly vaunted armed forces in Europe, especially Germany's Bundeswehr but also the militaries of France and the United Kingdom, as pale shadows of their former selves. Those 30 years, including 20 years of out-of-area operations, have reformatted the armed forces across Europe in a way that left them woefully unprepared for the kind of state-on-state conflict unfolding in Ukraine. It is now widely acknowledged that the rates at which weapons, especially munitions, have been consumed in that conflict have shown NATO's stocks to be simply inadequate to the task. This situation also made supplying Ukraine a daunting problem, with shortages of basic explosives putting in question Europe's defense industries' ability to produce the requisite number of shells that Ukraine would need.[13]

The situation of the German defense industry is a good illustration of the results of three decades of neglect. The CEO of Rheinmetall stated that Leopard 2 tanks could not be refurbished and supplied to Ukraine before 2024,[14] provided that contracts for such work were issued by the German government.[15] A similarly dismal situation prevails when it comes to munitions production, with Rheinmetall again unable to deliver the first batch of 155 mm howitzer ammunition to Ukraine before July 2023, with government orders key to ramping up production.[16]

In general, compared with where the Bundeswehr was at the end of the Cold War, today's German military has undergone a two-thirds reduction in personnel and shed about 90% of equipment units from that time. For example, as the Cold War ended what was then West Germany had more than 3,500 tanks; today Germany has just 225, with only a portion of them drivable and in usable condition.[17] In effect, successive German governments, especially during the tenure of defense minister Karl-Theodor zu Guttenberg, have treated the defense budget as a source of spending for other programs, leaving the military starved for both modernization and maintenance of existing stocks. But this sorry situation is not limited to Germany. The United Kingdom has neglected its army to the extent that—by its own admission—it would take the British army 5 to 10 years to be able to field a war-fighting division of some 25,000 to 30,000 troops backed by tanks, artillery and helicopters. About 30% of the UK's forces on high readiness are in fact reservists who would be unable to mobilize within NATO timelines. And the deficiencies in weapons, equipment and munitions are not that different from Germany's, with the majority of the British army's fleet of tanks and armored vehicles built between 30 to 60 years ago, with no replacements planned.[18] The situation of the French army is not much better. Six years ago, a RAND study estimated that Germany, France and the United Kingdom could muster and sustain one heavy brigade each for the defense of the Baltics, albeit at different rates; sustaining these forces would require significant strain.[19] Today even those targets would be difficult to attain.

There are some bright spots, however, when it comes to investment in defense, but they are mainly happening in countries along the eastern frontier of NATO. Here, Poland is a clear leader, having committed to spending 3% of GDP on defense and building a 300,000-strong armed forces, with projected investment reaching 4% next year. Poland has placed an order for 250 of the M1A2 sepV3 tanks, the most advanced version of the Abrams, plus 32 F-35 aircraft.[20] Recently, the US State Department approved the sale of 18 HIMARS rocket launchers and almost 500 launcher loader module kits along with ammunition to Poland.[21] In order to offset the equipment losses due to sending all of its modernized T-72 tanks, the PT-91 'Twardy' tanks, a number of its Leopard 2s and its Krab self-propelled howitzers to Ukraine, in July 2022 Poland signed a number of contracts with the Republic of Korea worth $5.8 billion to buy 189 K2 tanks and 212 K9 self-propelled howitzers, in what is the Asian country's largest-ever arms deal. Poland is also buying 48 FA-50 light combat aircraft and 288 K239 Chunmoo rocket artillery launchers.[22]

Others along the eastern flank have followed Poland's lead. Last fall, Romania announced that it would increase its defense budget to 2.5% of GDP, with contracts for attack helicopters and drones included in the package.[23] Other smaller states, such as Slovakia and the Baltic states, have also increased their spending to meet and exceed the 2% NATO target. But the picture remains uneven across the alliance, which raises an important political consideration, (i.e. the extent to which the United States Congress will allow for continued free-riding across the alliance).

'*Burden-Transferring*': *Whither NATO?*

There is not a quick and easy fix to decades of European disarmament. In fact, analysts agree that the United States will need to bridge capabilities in Europe for as long as another decade, provided European NATO demonstrates that it is serious about rectifying its deficiencies. As pressures in the Indo-Pacific increase and pull in more of US military resources, the European allies will need to assume an ever-greater role when it comes to conventional deterrence and defense of the Euro-Atlantic area. During the two decades of Global War on Terror, the United States' military was reformatted to fight only one major theater campaign and one secondary. Although not so much a resource decision as a political one, the reduction in size of US forces bears direct impact on the role that America's European allies will need to play to ensure deterrence in Europe holds, and should it fail, to decisively defeat a Russian invasion. In effect, NATO's talk of 'burden-sharing' needs to be replaced with a more direct commitment to what I would call 'burden-transferring,' whereby Europe provides the bulk of conventional forces in NATO, with the United States continuing to provide the nuclear umbrella and high-end enablers.

This means that a reforged NATO needs to move away from arguments over percentages of GDP on defense and focus instead on what specific capabilities this money will buy. The DDA concept and the attendant plans will rely on specific capabilities that each nation will need to provide, which the Supreme Allied Commander Europe (SACEUR) can then bracket within regional plans. In short, NATO needs to return full circle to working specific scenarios and exercises that are devoid of hypotheticals.

Much of NATO's evolution going forward will depend on the final outcome of the war in Ukraine and the decisions the alliance takes when it comes to ensuring Ukraine's security for years to come. Since the Euro-Atlantic and the Pacific theaters are interconnected, what happens in Europe, and specifically in Ukraine, will shape Beijing's perceptions as to the allies' unity and staying power in a conflict and will impact how the competition in the Indo-Pacific unfolds. Nonetheless, the imperative of NATO rearmament remains vital for the alliance's future, for without it it will fail to fulfill its collective deterrence and defense mission in the dangerous period of systemic instability that is upon us.

Europe's rearmament will remain the key variable in shaping a viable path to a reforged NATO. The question of European rearmament is directly linked to the future of the DDA concept and NATO regional plans, for without real exercised capabilities, planning will remain just that—planning that does not move to the implementation phase. It will take a serious political commitment from Europe's leaders to step up in this time of need. It is understandable that after three decades of the 'peace dividend' many in Europe—especially those further away from the eastern flank—are still somewhat reluctant to acknowledge how radically the world has changed. Nonetheless, the sooner they realize it, the better. If NATO fails to rearm it will become a hollowed-out structure, irrelevant in the current security environment regardless of how many meetings and strategic concepts it produces in years to come. If the European allies fail to rearm, there will be less and less support in Congress for the United States to remain committed to European defense, and—should the United States depart from Europe—the costs and the risks to the continent would be orders of magnitude greater than what is needed to restore NATO to its requisite military strength. There is no time to waste.

7

THE THREAT POSED BY RUSSIA AND CHINA AFTER THE UKRAINE WAR

Kori Schake

Every good strategist is a desperate paranoiac, seeing spectres of complication and failure at every turn. Russia has proved a poor strategist in the choice and prosecution of its invasion of Ukraine. We in the West have proven timid but creative; our staying power, always considered the Achilles heel of free societies, is now being tested. And China is not likely taking the lessons we hope they would from Russia's failing prospects.

Lessons Russia Should Be Learning

From what is detectible outside Russian councils, the invasion of Ukraine should go down in history as one of the great examples of hubris. An authoritarian leader, isolated by 20 years of increasingly repressive rule and fears of pandemic contagion, having successfully prosecuted barbaric military campaigns in Chechnya, Syria and Ukraine, flush from concluding a 'friendship without limits' with the most powerful fellow challenger to the liberal international order, convinced of the decadence and decline of the West and reveling in the degrading abandonment of Afghanistan by the US that even managed to aggravate the allies that had let affection for America draw them into 20 years of war there, seized the moment, ignoring military concerns, and catapulted its army into a neighbouring country to prevent Ukraine from choosing independence and association with the Western world.[1]

Russia had a 12:1 force ratio in the north, yet failed to take Ukraine's capital.[2] It threw 80% of its army into the fight, has had to denude positions in Kaliningrad and elsewhere, mobilized 300,000 additional troops and thrown them into battle untrained. It cannot adapt its approach at anywhere near the speed its opponent is able to. It has likely suffered at least 100,000 casualties and is experiencing desertion rates between 20 and 40%.[3] Its equipment has been felled by corruption and lack of maintenance, while Western sanctions are forcing it to humiliatingly import North Korean artillery and Iranian drones. These reverses have decimated the reputation of Russia's military as an effective fighting force. Before the invasion, Russia was widely considered to have the second-best military in the world; now it is derided as not even having the best military in the former Soviet Union. The United States could defeat it, Britain or France could defeat it, and Poland could very likely defeat it. The combined power of NATO militaries has never been so predominant in the history of the alliance as it is now.

Russia's threat to use nuclear weapons has had no effect on overt and direct Western supply of weapons, intelligence and economic support to Ukraine. President Biden voices concern about avoiding 'World War Three,' and he must bear the moral weight that his incrementalist caution is being paid for in Ukrainian lives, but his policies undertaken have not buckled despite Russian threats. Nor has the commitment of NATO allies, even those exposed to risk of attack. Europeans have borne up impressively under skyrocketing gas prices, sabotage and threats. The European Union has proven stalwart and even creative in sanctioning Russia. Germany is being shamed into overcoming its sanctimonious aversion to participation (including by its own pacifist Green Party, 97% of whom support arming Ukraine).[4] Sweden and Finland set aside centuries of non-alignment and applied for NATO membership.

Russia's invasion of Ukraine has produced a staggering set of power-diminishing consequences diametrically opposed to what Vladimir Putin and those who keep him in power say they want. NATO is stronger and united behind American leadership. Germany has embarked on a *Zeitenwende* of greater responsibility. American allies in Asia now participate in sanctions, join NATO meetings and contribute to Ukraine's war effort. Ukraine is undeniably a nation and undeniably Western, likely to retake all of its internationally recognized territory. Russia will remain under debilitating sanctions as long as Vladimir Putin remains in power. Confiscated Russian money will be used to reconstruct Ukraine, giving it the most modern infrastructure of any country. China is vocally supporting but economically and militarily withholding assistance, and it is now denouncing Russia's nuclear threats. Both the G-7 and G-20 condemn Russia's war. It is a struggle to think of a historical example of an outcome so disastrously at variance with intention, or one so costly. What lessons should Russia take from this shattering of national prowess?

Extravagant war aims require overwhelming battlefield victory. Russia will keep only what it wins on the battlefield. Its conduct—both in military performance and its war crimes—has collapsed the space for negotiated settlement. Lawrence Freedman highlights the 'gap between Russia's assertion of its war aims and its ability to prosecute the war to achieve them…

After nine months of fighting Russia has yet to achieve a single war aim through force of arms ... embarrassment in battle has not led to a corresponding scaling down of war aims.'[5] Russia is not the only country to have underestimated or refused to bring its ambitions and resources into alignment; the same is certainly true of the 2003–10 US war in Iraq, and the 2001–21 US war in Afghanistan, but the US had, and has, a much wider margin for error than Russian policy and military choices produced. The strategic consequences are crippling for Russia with regard to both the initial incongruity of ambition and resources and its inability to acknowledge and constrain its objectives to something its forces can achieve.

Targeting civilians backfires. Russia's battlefield failures caused a shift to targeting civilian infrastructure in an effort to break Ukraine's will to fight. At least so far, it does not appear to be working. Ukraine remains colossally courageous and united. Nor does the history of civilian targeting give much encouragement of eventual success.[6] The strategy is also reputationally and practically detrimental. It has destroyed the credibility of Russia's argument that the invasion was for the benefit of Ukrainians, marks Russia as villainous and makes any negotiated settlement more difficult. Fighting militaries rather than burning villages is not just a nicety of international law, it's a practical measure that preserves resources for the main effort and keeps open diplomatic possibilities to attain the war's political objectives.

Liberal societies are resilient. Russia's only remaining hope of success in this war is breaking Ukrainian will or Western assistance to Ukraine. Putin's theory of the case is evidently that we in the West are so solipsistic that our own cosseted well-being is all we care about, so dragging out the conflict will result in fracturing of the West. But Western countries show no signs of crumpling, changes in government in Sweden and Italy and change of leaders in Britain have not changed policy, and in the cases of both Germany and the United States, reluctant governments are being pushed to do more by their publics.

Political science data demonstrates pretty conclusively that while democracies are slow to coalesce domestically or undertake international obligations and alliances, they are the regime type that is most enduring in carrying out commitments.[7] In order to undertake commitments, governments have to win the domestic political argument and that provides a solid foundation for sticking to agreed policy when costs mount. Ukraine's incredible resistance and Western solidarity with Ukraine both refute the autocrat's assumption that just because free societies are loudly disputatious they must be incapable of sustained unity of effort.

Nor are governments the only source of strength: civic activism is the true superpower of free societies. And that has been on remarkable display throughout the West. Businesses have donated extravagant assistance both financially and operationally to Ukraine: Microsoft is helping police its networks while Starlink has kept its internet functioning. Charities like World Central Kitchen are feeding hundreds of thousands of civilians. Civil-society organizations have formed to donate money, clothing, weapons and even foreign soldiers to Ukraine, are ridiculing Russian diplomats and merrily building support for Ukraine in the West—even the hackers collective Anonymous has joined the fight on Ukraine's side. It's all such a gratifying reminder that free societies can be motivated to exceptional sacrifice because they are participants in deciding what to do.

For less than 4% of the US defense budget given in military aid to Ukraine (and considerably more proportionally from the Baltic states, Poland, Luxembourg, the Czech Republic, Slovakia, Slovenia, Britain, Norway, Sweden, Canada and Denmark), Ukraine has dramatically reduced the Russian threat to allied countries.[8] Russia cannot now reasonably expect to win a war against the West, or coerce it into meaningful political concessions.

But it does not necessarily follow that Russia no longer poses a threat to the allied states, those fifty countries who gather monthly under US leadership with Ukraine to determine its military requirements and provide them. Firstly, because Russia's theory of victory has not yet been disproven. Much hard fighting remains for Ukraine to recover its territory, other crises may divert attention, supplies may exhaust on the Western side before they do for Russia, Western publics may balk at the inconveniences and cost of sustained support, Ukrainians may understandably reach a breaking point and capitulate (John McCain used to demur when commended for heroism while a prisoner of war, saying that all of us have a breaking point), Western governments may prove stingy in reconstruction or in extension of membership in Western organizations thus leaving Ukraine still vulnerable, Russia could be forced off Ukrainian territory but remain capable of attacks that forestall investment and reconstruction, Putin may be overthrown by an even more repressive regime, Russia may circumvent sanctions and reparations, China and other authoritarian governments may assist rebuilding of Russia's military: there are always so many ways things can still go wrong.

Allies on NATO's central front (Poland, the Baltic States, Finland, Slovakia and Romania) worry that allies in more secure geography, principally the United States, will consider Russia's diminished threat manageable by NATO's European militaries, whereas their conclusion is that Europe would not have come together to act without American involvement. They worry that too few US forces will remain in Europe to deter a Russia that even if weakened may prove more dangerous: Russia may prefer to lose a war to NATO than to Ukraine. They also fear Russia's heartland will emerge unscathed economically once sanctions are lifted. Worse, they are concerned that upholding global financial practice will mean that Russia does not face justice: Russian central bank holdings currently held in Western accounts may not be used to finance Ukraine's reconstruction.

From an American perspective, Russia looks weak in Europe but still aggressively successful with mercenary forces elsewhere. Russia's military may not be the peer of a Western force, but its brutality is proving adequate to preserve governments in Syria and the Central African Republic. In addition, we may not be seeing the best Russia's military can offer; there may be other wars where they could prevail.

Lessons the West Should Be Learning

Don't drink the water! The temptation is already evident in Western states to congratulate ourselves on efforts in Ukraine, a phenomenon known in the Pentagon as drinking your own bath water. We're incredibly impressed with our assistance to Ukraine, the superiority of our armies and equipment, the effects of our training of the Ukrainian military since 2014, the rapid creation and magnitude of logistics lines of supply, declassification and release of intelligence information, successful neutering of Russian cyber-attacks, creation of new sanctions measures and unity in enacting them. Those things are all true, but not only are such celebrations premature, they also avert what should be a penetrating evaluation of our failings. Because our future adversaries are certainly looking for our vulnerabilities to capitalize on.

Failures of deterrence. Most importantly, our efforts did not deter the Russian invasion of Ukraine. Russia rightly calculated that we would not fight to uphold the foundational principle of the post-1945 order that boundaries change by negotiation and mutual consent not invasion. Russian power prevented President Biden taking as stalwart a stand as President Bush did in 1991 when Iraq invaded Kuwait. We were deterred, Russia was not.

Steering away from direct confrontation with another nuclear power is reasonable, and the President's defenders will say it is even the only responsible position. And our concern for Ukraine is systemic (preserving peace in Europe and the principle of sovereignty, expanding the democratic world) and humanitarian rather than an existential security threat or an alliance commitment. But our decision left a much weaker state to bear the burden of Russian aggression as has our cautious parsing of weapons to forestall escalation. This is evidenced by a discouraging progression of statements: in September 2021 that we could not provide weapons to Ukraine because they would quickly be in Russian hands, in December saying we could only provide defensive weapons, shifting in February to providing offensive weapons but none that could range into Russian territory, then in May providing weapons that could reach Russian targets but making Ukraine promise not to use them that way, then in August when Ukrainians used them to strike Russian bases in Crimea we affirmed that as Ukrainian territory and therefore fair game, and now, with Russia targeting power grids, we are likely to relax restrictions on attacking Russian military targets inside Russia.

Nor have we deterred Russia from committing war crimes on an industrial scale—torture, kidnapping, forced resettlement, purposely targeting civilians—or demonstrated any facility at isolating Putin and his war chiefs from the Russian population.

President Biden and his senior officials have repeatedly expressed their concern about World War Three and been cautious and slow in giving Ukraine the assistance it needs to protect itself. Our evident anxiety about escalation, either horizontal in regard to attacking a NATO ally or vertical in regard to employing nuclear weapons, is rewarding Russian threats and reinforcing the value of possessing nuclear weapons to proliferators.

Deterring Russian escalation is likely to require assuming more risk ourselves, for example threatening to reveal any Russian preparations for nuclear use, providing targeting information and weapons to Ukraine to pre-empt such use, prepositioning NATO Chemical, Biological, Radiological and Nuclear materials teams in Ukraine to attenuate any effects from nuclear use, threatening to hunt down any Russian participating in the policy decision or execution of order for nuclear use—and actually doing it.

All of us who work on strategy in free countries need to revisit Michael Howard, Tom Schelling, Therese Delpeche and make good use of Lawrence Freedman and Geoffrey Blainey while we have them. As Mick Ryan has argued, we need to be identifying 'future challenges for which there no current solutions.'[9]

We are bad at assessing military capability. Virtually no Western military analyst believed Russia was this incompetent. The Biden administration eschewed providing weapons to Ukraine even when it assessed Russia would invade because of the presumption that Ukraine would lose so quickly and completely that the US equipment would end up in Russian hands.[10] The US senior military advisor, General Mark Miley, even believed Ukraine would be quickly overrun.[11] Russia's military instead showed itself bad at virtually every element of warfare.

Russia is not just bad at the higher math of warfare—joint operations, fusing information and establishing kill chains. They have proven both deficient at the fundamentals of organization and operation, such as deconfliction to prevent fratricide. And they seem incapable of adapting to fix their problems. A report by the Royal United Services Institute concluded 'there is a culture of reinforcing failure unless orders are changed at higher levels.'[12] As Rob Lee and Michael Kofman characterized Russian faltering, 'the Kremlin's thinking was increasingly characterized by strategic procrastination and wishful thinking.'[13] Yet we could not see that before the war in Ukraine.

Nor are we particularly good at understanding the dynamic of war termination. General Milley recently scandalized many defense experts and the Biden administration by insisting there was no military solution to the war.[14] It is objectively difficult to determine how proficient a military is and how committed a society will be to its war aims. As Lawrence Freedman cautions, 'Even those with a good knowledge of the competing forces and the terrain over which they are fighting can be caught out by chance developments such as a change in the weather or an effective tactical innovation. During a war's course expectations shift.'[15] The unsatisfying truth is that you cannot tell how good a military is until you fight it. Specifically. Generic assessments must give way to the unique circumstances. But we still ought to be carefully assessing what we got wrong and why we got it wrong in order to improve our tradecraft.

We have not been serious about the prospect of war. Inadequate munitions stockpiles are the clearest proof that Western governments, especially the United States, did not believe themselves likely to have to fight.[16] Russia and Ukraine are burning through weapons and ammunition at rates far exceeding what their or our countries had planned for in our own wars. British forces would expend their stockpiles of critical ammunition in 8 days of high-intensity fighting; at Russia's rate of use, British stockpiles would be exhausted in just 2 days.[17] The US is no better. It ought not to take this war for the Pentagon's procurement head to conclude that 'production really matters.'[18]

The nature of the problem is less 'the return of industrial warfare' than the return of great power war.[19] Warfare at industrial scale did not fall out of fashion, we in the West simply were not fighting countries that had the economic capacity to fight at scale against us with advanced weaponry. Yet our national security strategies have been declaring the requirement for fighting a near-peer to be our policy since the 'pivot to Asia' in 2012. The US and other Western countries have the industrial capacity to produce weapons and ammunition at scale; we simply have not. We could produce more, we simply have chosen not to. This led to constriction of the defense industrial base: in 1991, the US had fifty-one major defense contractors, now it has just five. And we have focused on exquisite systems instead of simpler systems in larger numbers—capability rather than capacity, to use Pentagon jargon.

These are fixable problems, and what we are learning from the war in Ukraine may give us time to remedy the situation before we have to fight such a war ourselves. But we need to get serious, throw money at the problem, commit to longer term contracts so that industry expands production, and relax protectionism in procurement to permit allied countries to restock concurrently.[20]

Grant and Nelson Smile

Much we are seeing on the battlefields of Ukraine we have not seen before in quite the same ways.

The importance of dispersal, firepower and stockpiles is not new, but operations in this war have revealed new dimensions.[21] Drones are new, permitting low-cost persistent surveillance and targeting, but the advancing accuracy in locating enemy forces has been trending for some time. Concealment is more difficult due to layered sensor data, but spoofing is not far behind.[22] Cyber is new, but the anticipated tornado of computer-generated malice did not occur, even though Britain's chief of GCHQ considers Russia's 'use of offensive cyber tools has been irresponsible and indiscriminate.'[23] We were told to expect 'flying sharks with lasers,' and what we got was voluntary assistance from Western businesses, allied trust in sharing information and diligence in protecting networks preventing show-stopping effects.[24] It turns out that good old-fashioned destruction by ordinance is how Russia creates havoc in civilian infrastructure. Reliance on internet connectivity is new, but the quest for reliable and immediate communications is timeless. Tanks have not been proven obsolete, despite the breathless assessments from those distant from the need for protected mobile firepower.[25] Technologies are just giving us new ways to attain enduring objectives on the battlefield.

A volunteer force is expensive—in money, certainly, but for it to be a fighting force more than mercenary, also in commitment to the mission and professionalism about the undertaking. Mission command is hard to teach and requires creativity, initiative, tolerance for subordinate error and the ability to synchronize activity without having control of it. Yet it accelerates the speed of operations, creates and takes advantage of opportunities and produces emboldened commanders of experienced judgment. All that shows incredible advantage on the battlefield. Ulysses Grant and Horatio Nelson's precepts never really went out of fashion, even in the age of industrial warfare or nuclear weapons, but there is little about Ukraine's success and Russia's failure that they would not recognize and take satisfaction from. Pushing past the PowerPoint self-congratulation and actually creating those forces in Western militaries remains challenging.

Lessons to Hope China is Learning

Western military dominance. A strong case can be made that Russia's failing special military operation in Ukraine should be a cautionary tale for China's ambitions to expand its sphere of influence and destabilize the liberal international order. Success in warfare is inherently difficult to predict, and lunging to control Taiwan could fail militarily with devastating effects on the legitimacy of Xi Jin Ping's leadership and Communist Party control in China. The American military remains proficient and motivated, its alliance relations tightening rather than loosening in response to China's efforts to intimidate its neighbours. Western weaponry has shown to advantage Ukraine, and even if China's weapons systems are built on stolen blueprints of American models, as with computer chips, they are iterations behind our upgrades.[26] China remains so fearful of individual initiative that it is designing artificial intelligence to serve the functions non-commissioned officers perform in Western militaries rather than unleash the risks of training and relying on the judgment of its rank and file. Moreover, the Chinese military has not been tested in combat since the 1970s, so any claims of proficiency have not been proven, which ought to inspire caution about prospects for success against the US and its allies.

Financial esprit de corps.[27] Economically, in response to Russia's invasion the West has shown that our central banks dominate the global financial order and are willing to run systemic risks (like sequestering Russian central bank reserves in their possession) to penalize aggression. Our treasuries are remarkably capable of tracking and targeting assets for seizure across the world and developing innovative sanctions to achieve policy objectives. Our societies voluntarily accepted economic costs and rapidly reduced reliance on Russian oil and gas, diminishing Russia's economy not only in the present but in the future.

Values drive Western policy. Western publics support their governments' aid to Ukraine because they have formed views on Russia's actions as wrong, even evil, and see Ukrainians as both innocent victims and co-religionists in the secular sense of sharing the common values of the West. The exalting achievement of a comedian becoming the most towering wartime leader since Winston Churchill is a thrill for free societies, a validation of the core beliefs of individual potential. The toughness of average Ukrainians' endurance draws widespread admiration, and our instantaneous access to visual evidence of Russian war crimes have prevented governments' pressuring Ukraine for concessions to end the war. China's preferred narrative of Western decadence and decline have not been borne out: Western governments have united, Western publics have supported Ukraine and condemned Russia, and the tolerance for individualism at the core of the West is producing success. The ballet dancers and transvestites of the Ukrainian military are defeating the vaunted Russian war machine ostensibly motivated by preserving traditional values.

Lessons China is More Likely Learning

But Western choices may look very different in Beijing. A plausible case can be made that China sees a much more advantageous landscape for its interests in ways that encourage aggression.

Authoritarian regimes are not brittle. Vladimir Putin is unquestionably the architect of Russia's war in Ukraine: he chose it, he sold it, he makes every significant decision (to include whether surrenders and retreats can occur). He has been losing almost since the invasion occurred, yet there are no signs that his hold on power has been shaken. There have been no high-level defections among the cabinet or leading oligarchs, and he has evinced strident support from Lavrov, Medvedev and other prominent political voices. He successfully crushed opposition to the war by Russians, arresting thousands of citizens to tamp down protests. He's cashiered military leaders without protest by those remaining or signs of mutiny from within the ranks and successfully blamed the military for strategic failures of design and execution of the invasion. State media are virulently nationalistic; so much so that he can permit criticism of the war effort. While mobilization produced the exodus of perhaps 300,000 young Russians, it also served as a steam valve further reducing domestic opposition to the war. Sanctions are being accepted without riots. All in all, authoritarianism has held up pretty well in Russia. China may conclude its leadership could likewise remain in power through a failed military adventure.

Nuclear deterrence works. China has dramatically expanded its nuclear arsenal in recent years, and is on form to triple it to 1,500 warheads by 2035.[28] That would make China a third nuclear superpower, unconstrained by any treaty restrictions that bind the US, and partner in a 'friendship without limits' with Russia whose arsenals combined dwarf that of the US, despite President Biden's repeated hand-wringing about needing to avoid World War Three, caution in providing weapons to Ukraine and his rush to get and keep all American defense department personnel out of Ukraine, which all signal American unwillingness to risk involvement in a conflict with a nuclear-armed adversary. China could well conclude that the US would balk at actually defending Taiwan when the costs of fighting China become clear—and the Biden administration has done nothing to prepare the American public for the prospects of a major war. President Biden's breezy commitment to defend Taiwan, repeatedly walked back by his senior administration officials, suggest confusion about policy and could add the humiliation of the US to Chinese satisfaction of using the nuclear umbrella to create the space for conventional forces to attack Taiwan or other US interests in Asia.

Western cupboards are bare. A senior Australian defense official was recently informed by the US that it would take 7 years to replace the weapons Australia has given to Ukraine. That is a very long window of vulnerability. Pentagon officials began to hedge their commitment to arming Ukraine, fearing their ability to carry out US war plans.[29] Even if this does not collapse the flow of arms to Ukraine, it will impede allies' ability to fight China. Our unpreparedness for a long war—or even a short, intense one—signals societal aversion to fighting such a war, a very encouraging sign from the Chinese perspective and one that reinforces their storyline about Western decline.

Sanctions are not debilitating. Russia's economic policymakers have done an astonishingly good job of minimizing the consequences of coordinated Western economic action against Russia since the invasion. What was perceived to be the economic equivalent of 'shock and awe' has proven damaging but not decisive: the IMF estimates Russia's economy will contract by only 3.4 per cent in 2023, and the central bank has succeeded in holding interest rates to 7.5%.[30] The war skyrocketed prices for energy, and Europeans especially had little near-term alternatives. Where hard constraints exist, Russia has found fellow anti-Western governments like Iran and North Korea to provide supplies. Much of the developing world blames the West for the economic impact of the war rather than blaming Russia; China, as the world's largest lender with its Belt and Road Initiative, can expect even more assistance and failure to enforce any Western sanctions.[31]

Even if the West could impose economic penalties on China as it has on Russia, China may doubt whether it would. Russia's GDP is $1.8 trillion, and concentrated in oil and gas export to countries that are also likely victims of its aggression; China's GDP is $17.7 trillion and tightly woven into supply chains for essential Western products like pharmaceuticals and electronics in countries that run no risk of Chinese aggression. Political solidarity among America's allies in Asia is—with the laudable exceptions of Australia and Japan—nowhere near as broad or deep as that in Europe. The British government is warning businesses that the effects of war in Taiwan would be of similar magnitude in effect as Covid, and that is even without any punitive action taken against China, just the supply chain disruptions.[32]

Emerson was right. The American philosopher Ralph Waldo Emerson wrote 'when skating over thin ice, our safety lies in our speed.' Russia signaling its intent with large-scale military deployments in the spring of 2021 and again with the invasion force gathering in August and September 2021 gave the US and its allies time to declassify and share intelligence, prepare domestic publics for the approach of war, coordinate policy among themselves and with Ukraine, develop economic sanctions for quick execution and prepare their own economies for the consequences. China could move with greater alacrity and potentially achieve its objectives before the West could organize itself. That would not obviate the significant structural advantages militarily and economically that the West could bring to bear, but a fait accompli would be more difficult to reverse than to prevent or sustain resistance.

Taiwan is not Ukraine. Ukraine's profound unity in the face of Russia's onslaught and occupation has been a marvel. It is assisted in its resistance by a territorial expanse that permitted strategic depth. Taiwan has no such hinterland from which to continue resistance if a Chinese invasion were to be successful. Ukraine also has the terrifying history of Holodomor within living memory, in which Moscow's actions starved more than 3 million Ukrainians to death as well as current evidence of Russian war crimes. China has no such history with Taiwan, even counting civil war that created a separate Taiwan. While many expected Ukraine's military and security services to be rife with Russian collaborators, the defection of so many to Russia during the 2014 invasion and careful screening by Ukraine since have hardened their defenses to a degree unlikely to be replicated in Taiwan, whose security services are widely believed to be compromised.[33] And then there is the question of the will of the Taiwanese to resist, which is open to question, especially if an onslaught is overwhelming.

A roaring debate is going on in the US about whether China poses a greater near- or long-term threat.[34] If China's leaders believe even a subset of these more emboldening lessons, the risks of Chinese aggression in the near term loom large. Western attention, weapons and economic support flowing to Ukraine reduce their availability for defense of allies and interests in Asia, giving China an excellent window of opportunity, and that window may well be closing as China's economy becomes marooned in the middle-income trap.[35]

PART THREE

THE IMPACT OF THE WAR
ENHANCED MILITARY INTEGRATION?

8

ZEITENWENDE OR BUSINESS AS USUAL?
GERMAN DEFENCE POLICY FOLLOWING RUSSIA'S INVASION OF UKRAINE

Robin Allers & Håkon Lunde Saxi

On 27 February 2022, 3 days after the Russian invasion of Ukraine, Chancellor Olaf Scholz held a landmark speech in the German Bundestag. He declared that Russia's 'war of aggression' marked 'a watershed' (*eine Zeitenwende*) in 'the history of our continent' and committed Germany to respond by undertaking several dramatic changes in foreign, security and defence policy.[1] In addition to stepping up sanctions against the Russian aggressor, these measures included the support of Ukraine with weapons and a massive increase in defence spending which would allow Germany to fulfil and extend its contributions to NATO's collective defence.

Among both Germany's political elite and in the wider public, the speech was generally well received and since the German term '*Zeitenwende*' was used repeatedly throughout, it quickly became the defining reference for the government's intention to adapt German foreign and security policy to a new reality.[2]

Over the following months, Scholz himself would use the term repeatedly in speeches and interviews to describe how the war was changing Germany's approach. Towards the end of the year, an article in the journal *Foreign Affairs* summed up the main elements of this new course and pointed out what Scholz saw as his main achievements for an international public.[3]

Abroad, the speech was widely acknowledged as an important signal. Germany has long been regarded as a country that 'punches below its weight' in European defence, and its allies and partners have for years called on Germany to do more and become a more active contributor to European and international security.[4] Partly in response to this criticism, Berlin formulated its own ambition to function as a 'framework nation' in European defence—a 'backbone'—leading from the centre by contributing more and being an integrative force in European security and defence.[5]

As Russia's preparations for a full-scale invasion became more and more clear, allies became increasingly frustrated with Germany's insistence on finding a peaceful solution to the conflict instead of boosting Western deterrence and arming Ukraine. Following the February 2022 speech, even Germany's harshest critics, many of them in Eastern Europe, were impressed by the willingness to radically shift course towards Russia (especially regarding energy dependence), to hear Ukraine's pleas for weapons assistance and to accept the necessity of substantial investment in the armed forces.

However, as the Scholz government initially remained hesitant to deliver weapons that would make a difference on the battlefield and proved slow to use the new funds for new defence material, allies turned impatient, and many observers asked themselves if the *Zeitenwende* was the radical shift they had hoped for. As one observer noted at the end of 2022: 'The trust deficit between Germany and many of its European partners remains huge'.[6]

ZEITENWENDE OR BUSINESS AS USUAL?

This chapter offers a first of assessment of the policy changes announced on 27 February, judging by how and to what extent they have been implemented one year later. Does the speech really qualify as a genuine turning point in German defence policy? And have decision-makers in Berlin delivered on the promised changes so far?

We propose to answer these questions by examining four key fields: first, we start by asking whether the proposed increase in defence spending is likely to provide Germany with the capabilities that are necessary to become one of the alliance's leading military powers. Second, we look at the speed and extent with which Germany has supplied Ukraine with weapons. Third, we address the question of whether the Scholz government's renewed commitment to NATO's collective defence can remove doubts about Germany's status and reliability as an ally, before we ask, fourth, to what extent the changes in Germany's security and defence policy since February 2022 also include the long-awaited development of a new strategic mindset. Finally, drawing together our findings from these different fields, we discuss if the *Zeitenwende*-speech together with the subsequent measures has the potential to qualify as a real turning point in German defence policy.

Change or Continuity in Defence Spending?

One of the most remarked upon changes announced in Chancellor Scholz's *Zeitenwende* speech was to do with German defence spending. About halfway into his statement to the German Bundestag, the Chancellor announced that Germany would establish a €100 billion 'special fund for the Bundeswehr' to finance 'necessary investments and armaments projects'. Germany would also 'now—year after year—invest more than two percent of our gross domestic product in our defence'.[7]

On the face of it, this was no more than what Germany had already committed to. At the 2014 NATO summit in Wales, Berlin had signed up to a commitment to 'move towards' NATOs guideline to spend a minimum of 2% of gross domestic product (GDP) on defence 'within a decade'.[8] In reality, very few expected Germany to meet this target by 2024. In 2019, the German government had informed NATO that Germany aimed to increase defence spending to only 1.5 per cent of GDP by 2024, considerably below the level agreed in Wales. At the time, Germany was spending about 1.35% of GDP on defence. One key reason for this backpedalling was that there was no consensus on the 2% figure within the 'grand coalition' government in Berlin, with the Social Democratic Party (SPD) opposing it and only the Conservative Party (CDU/CSU) supporting it in principle. The goal of reaching 1.5% of GDP by 2024 was a weak compromise, with at best lukewarm support from the SPD.[9] When the new SPD, Green Party and Free Democratic Party (FDP) coalition government replaced the 'grand coalition' in December 2021, their government platform did contain a pledge for Germany to 'fulfilling its commitments made in NATO', but not a firm commitment to reach 2% of GDP on defence by any given date.[10]

That a Chancellor from the SPD would announce that Germany would henceforth 'invest more than two percent of our gross domestic product in our defence'[11] was therefore groundbreaking. If implemented, it would indeed be, as Chancellor Scholz argued, 'a watershed in the history of our continent'.[12] As one analyst put it:

> If Scholz's proposal is realized, it would represent the largest absolute jump in German military expenditure since at least World War II. Annual spending would increase by 50 per cent in 2022 alone [...] All else being equal, Germany would rank third—up from seventh in 2020—behind the United States and China and ahead of India and Russia.[13]

ZEITENWENDE OR BUSINESS AS USUAL?

Within NATO, the commitment promised to transform Germany into NATOs second largest spender on defence—still well behind the United States but also ahead of the United Kingdom and France.[14] But the announcement would only be a true watershed if implemented. The proof of the pudding would be in the eating.

In the months following the Russian invasion of Ukraine, it gradually became clear that Germany's government—at least initially—did not intend to reach 2% of GDP by way of increasing the regular federal defence budget.[15] Instead, it intended to increase defence spending by drawing on the €100 billion 'special fund for the Bundeswehr' which Scholz had also announced in his *Zeitenwende* speech. The fund would be financed by one-off borrowing.[16] While many observers had initially understood the special fund as coming on top of the commitment to spend 2% of GDP on defence, it became apparent that the fund would instead serve as the primary vehicle for attaining the Chancellor's ambitious spending pledge.

The establishment of such a special fund (*Sondervermögen*) was a common way of financing major multi-year programmes run by the federal government. It would also allow the government to circumvent the constitutional debt brake (*Schuldenbremse*), which limited the federal government's annual structural net borrowing to 0.35% of GDP.[17] In order to establish the special fund, an amendment to Germany's constitutional Basic Law would be necessary, requiring an absolute two-thirds majority in both chambers of the German legislature—the German Bundestag and the German Bundesrat.

After several months of parliamentary negotiations, the constitutional basis for the €100 billion special fund for the Bundeswehr was finally created in June 2022.[18] As such, the SPD, Green Party and FDP governing coalition obtained the two-third majority required. This was principally accomplished by the support of the main opposition party, the Conservative CDU/CSU. However, uncertainty remained over the timeframe and how the €100 billion would be used.

Those expecting massive and immediate increases in German defence spending were soon disappointed. Spending increases in fact proved excruciatingly slow. As the Parliamentary Commissioner for the Armed Forces put it in her February 2023 report: 'in 2022 our servicewomen and men have not yet received a cent from the special fund'.[19] Some critics branded it 'a lost year for the Bundeswehr' and the bureaucratic slowness of Germany's military procurement system was widely criticised—even by members of the governing coalition.[20] But spending not only proved too slow, it also proved insufficient to meet the high benchmark laid down by the Chancellor.

The regular German defence budget in 2023 in fact decreased slightly compared with the year before, remaining relatively fixed at about €50 billion.[21] The government also proposed to maintain a relatively flat base defence budget for the period 2023–26.[22] Meanwhile, the German Ministry of Defence (BMVg) only planned to spend €8.5 billion from the 'special fund' in 2023.[23] About €30 billion had so far been committed (but not spent) on orders for new armed drones, F-35A combat aircraft and CH-47F Chinook heavy transport helicopters. Meanwhile, while it stood unused, inflation and interest rate payments were eating away at the purchasing power of the special fund.[24]

In total, €58.5 billion in 2023 was a far cry from the approximately €75 billion needed to reach the 2% goal.[25] Researchers at the Stockholm International Peace Research Institute had already concluded in April 2022 that the 'special fund' would in any case be insufficient to attain the 2% benchmark—only a sustained increase in Germany's base defence budget would suffice.[26] By February 2023, Germany's popular new minister of defence Boris Pistorius was advocating increasing the base defence budget to €60 billion but was facing stiff resistance from the SPD's left wing and the Federal Ministry of Finance.[27] In short, over a year after the *Zeitenwende* speech, it was still highly uncertain if, how and when Germany would realise the Chancellor's spending pledge.

Against this backdrop, the most severe critics are claiming that the spending pledge made in Scholz's *Zeitenwende* speech 'is a mirage' and contrasting Germany unfavourably with Poland, which aims to reach 3% of GDP in defence spending in 2023.[28] While the creation of the 'special fund' will undoubtedly increase German defence spending in the coming years, it also seems uncertain, and even unlikely, that this boost will be sufficient to reach the ambitious goal laid out on 27 February 2022. Since then, the 2% pledge has been written into a new national security strategy published in June 2023 and was reconfirmed at the NATO summit in Vilnius in July the same year. Yet carefully worded caveats and reluctance towards making the commitment legal, support those who doubt that this goal will be attained anytime soon.[29] As a result, the well-documented deficiencies in the Bundeswehr's equipment, readiness, and stocks of ammunition are likely to persist for the foreseeable future.

Delivering Weapons to Ukraine: Glass Half Full or Glass Half Empty?

On Saturday 26 February, the day before his landmark speech to the German Bundestag, Chancellor Scholz wrote a short entry on Twitter, stating:

> The Russian invasion marks a turning point. It is our duty to support Ukraine to the best of our ability in defending against Putin's invading army. That is why we are delivering 1000 anti-tank weapons and 500 Stinger [air-defence] missiles to our friends in Ukraine.[30]

On the face of it, the short English-language tweet, consisting of only 222 characters, seemed to represent an about-face reversal of existing German policy. The decision went against the spirit of a long-standing German policy commitment to show 'restraint' by not sending arms to 'areas of tension' or 'crisis regions' outside NATO.[31] More importantly, it also represented a *volte-face* on recent German government policy on Ukraine. A mere two weeks before the Russian attack, Chancellor Scholz and his Minister of Foreign Affairs, Annalena Baerbock, were publicly stating that Germany would on principle not deliver 'lethal weapons' to Ukraine.[32] Invoking memories of World War II, the foreign minister argued that Germany had a 'historical responsibility' not to send weapons to conflict zones.[33] This stance drew criticism from some of Germany's NATO allies, who were actively arming and training Ukrainian forces in order to deter a Russian attack. A commitment by Berlin in late January 2022 to provide 'non-lethal' military equipment to Ukraine—most noticeably 5,000 Kevlar helmets—was widely ridiculed.[34]

In his *Zeitenwende* speech, Chancellor Scholz repeated his newfound commitment to provide weapons for Ukraine, reiterating that Germany would henceforth 'supply Ukraine with weapons for the country's defence'.[35] However, while a seemingly clean break with the past, it soon emerged that important restrictions were still in place on Germany's willingness to transfer weapons to Ukraine.

The following two months saw Berlin attempting to restrict arms transfers to 'light' and 'defensive' equipment, holding the line against providing 'offensive' and 'heavy' weapons, such as tanks, infantry fighting vehicles and artillery. The Chancellor suggested publicly that this hesitation was grounded in a fear that such deliveries could escalate the conflict to a direct war with Russia, stating that 'we must do everything possible to avoid a direct military confrontation between NATO and a highly armed superpower like Russia, a nuclear power'.[36] Outside observers pointed also to domestic German politics, including SPD party politics, as the reason for Germany's continued reluctance.[37] However, as international and domestic political pressure mounted, this line became increasingly untenable.

By late April 2022, the line buckled as the German government agreed to provide Ukraine with Gepard self-propelled anti-aircraft guns. Berlin also pledged to begin compensating Eastern European countries ready to send Soviet-made weapon systems to Ukraine with equipment from Germany's stocks (the so-called *Ringtausch*, or 'swap').[38] This arrangement again proved short-lived, as in May Germany agreed to send more heavy weapons directly to Ukraine, including German-made Panzerhaubitze 2000 self-propelled artillery and, shortly thereafter, US-manufactured M270 MLRS self-propelled rocket artillery. While some categories of Western-made heavy weapons—such as main battle tanks, infantry fighting vehicles and combat aircraft—remained off-the-table, the restrictive policy of March and April had given way to a much broader delivery of arms to Ukraine.

By early January 2023, pressure was building on Germany to also enable the delivery of German-made armoured fighting vehicles to Ukraine. Ukrainian authorities argued that they needed 300 modern Western-made main battle tanks to succeed in liberating occupied Ukrainian territories. The largest fleet of such tanks in Europe was the German-manufactured Leopard 2, of which more than 2,000 were in service in NATO and EU countries.[39] Shipment of some of these armoured vehicles to Ukraine would require Berlin's approval, but the German government remained reluctant. Publicly, Chancellor Scholz invoked the Federal Republic's policy of military restraint and multilateralism. At the World Economic Forum in Davos, he stated: 'We are never doing something just by ourselves, but together with others, especially the US'.[40]

In the end, it took US engagement to break the deadlock. Early in January 2023, the US and Germany announced US-manufactured Bradley and German-manufactured Marder infantry fighting vehicles would be sent to Ukraine.[41] Later the same month, the US and Germany announced that they would deliver, respectively, the M1 Abrams and Leopard 2 main battle tanks to Ukraine—and Berlin would enable other European states to provide their German-built tanks to Ukraine. The Abrams would at best take many months to reach Ukraine, since these were to be built by US defence contractors, whereas the Leopard 2s were to be drawn from existing European stocks and therefore would arrive much more quickly.[42]

By the summer of 2023, the German government was regularly updating a long and increasingly impressive list of weapons and military equipment that had been provided to Ukraine so far.[43] International comparisons of military aid to Ukraine also showed that Germany now ranked third—behind the United States and the United Kingdom—as Kyiv's largest weapon donor.[44] In relative economic terms (measured by donor country GDP), the total military and civilian aid provided by Berlin appeared less impressive, with many smaller European states providing more generous support to Kyiv. However, among the major NATO countries, Germany was providing about the same as the US and the UK relatively, and more than France and Italy.[45]

After the initial elation that immediately followed Scholz's *Zeitenwende* speech, Western international opinion quickly soured on Germany. The feeling outside Germany in March and April 2022 had been that Berlin's military aid to Ukraine was always 'too little, too late'.[46] In April 2022, Kyiv had even informed Berlin that the German president was not welcome to visit Ukraine—a strong expression of displeasure. The decision was in part also due to President Frank-Walter Steinmeier being regarded as one of the architects of Germany's failed Russia policy over the past decades.[47] A year later, this external criticism had largely abated. When, in April 2023, German authorities approved a Polish request to transfer ex-German Mig-29 combat aircraft to Ukraine, it caused only a small stir in the international media.[48] This was but the latest in a long and remarkable series of turnarounds, in which virtually all of Germany's former restrictions on arms transfers to Ukraine had fallen like dominoes.

In short, over the course of a year since the Russian invasion of Ukraine, Germany's policy on delivering weapons to Ukraine had evolved from its poor starting point as a criticised and ridiculed laggard, into one of Kyiv's most important military (and financial) backers. While some restrictions still applied, such as the continued insistence on coordinating every step with the US and a continued refusal to transfer Western-made combat aircraft, Germany's record on delivering weapons to Ukraine—both in terms of quality and quantity—was now at the very least one of 'glass half full'. While off to a poor start, Germany had, a year later, largely delivered on Chancellor Scholz's promise on 27 February 2022 to 'supply Ukraine with weapons for the country's defence'.[49]

'Every Square Metre'?—Germany's Commitment to NATO's Collective Defence

With public attention focused on Germany's defence investments and weapons deliveries to Ukraine, it is widely overlooked that the *Zeitenwende* speech included a strong commitment to strengthening collective defence. According to Scholz, Germany was 'absolutely serious' about defending 'every square meter of NATO territory together with our allies'.[50] Germany had already boosted its contributions to the defence of NATO's eastern, northern and southern flank and would continue to do so. Similar assurances came from foreign Minister Annalena Baerbock, from the Green Party, who not only emphasized 'that we will defend every square centimetre of our Allied territory when necessary' but promised 'to step up our engagement even more to enhance the security of our partners'.[51]

In the following months, the Chancellor and other members of his government reiterated these reassurances in numerous speeches, statements and interviews and followed up with concrete measures. At the centre of these efforts was a strengthening of NATO's eastern flank from the Baltic Sea to south-eastern Europe. In Lithuania, Germany reinforced its role as the framework nation for a multinational battalion as part of NATO's Enhanced Forward Presence (eFP), first with additional troops and later with a brigade headquarters that would be joined by combat units on rotation for exercises. Responding to the Lithuanian argument that credible defence and deterrence only works with 'trustworthy in-place capabilities', Germany eventually agreed to further expand its commitment with the permanent stationing of a 4,000-strong brigade in the Baltic state.[52]

The German Air Force had since 2004 contributed to NATO's Baltic Air Policing mission.[53] Now, German Eurofighter combat aircraft joined allies to strengthen the enhanced Air Policing (eAP) mission in Romania. In Slovakia, where NATO established one of four new multinational battle groups, Germany contributed with infantry and air defence forces.[54] At the NATO summit in Madrid in July 2022, the chancellor promised to support the alliance's new force structure by 'keeping an armoured division of 15,000 troops, along with up to 20 ships and 60 aircraft in heightened readiness for Northern Europe'. He also highlighted a 'major contribution to the alliance's defence capabilities through Germany's role as a logistics hub'.[55]

Even before Russia's full-scale invasion, the German Navy had reinforced its presence in the Baltic Sea, and in the following months, the number of German ships exercising and operating along NATO's northern flank (i.e. in the Baltic Sea, the North Sea and the North Atlantic) increased further. Meanwhile, political and military representatives underlined Germany's ambition to assume more responsibility for coordinating maritime operations in the Baltic Sea. The German Navy's objectives for 2035 and beyond include the ambition to 'exhibit high combat readiness and to demonstrate its presence in the North Atlantic Ocean, the North and Baltic Seas, already in peacetime'.[56]

When in September 2022 a series of explosions caused damage and leakages to the Nord Stream pipelines, maritime security on NATO's northern flank gained renewed urgency. While it remained unclear who had caused the damage—though Russia was the main suspect—the incident exposed the vulnerability of critical infrastructure and a lack of capabilities to protect the thousands of kilometres of pipelines and undersea cables on which Western communication and energy security rely. At the same time, increased drone activity around Norwegian oil and gas platforms in the North Sea showed that Europe's—and especially Germany's—main provider of natural gas faced similar threats. At the request of the Norwegian government and coordinated by NATO's Allied Maritime Command (MARCOM), the German Navy joined allies in patrolling the waters around oil and gas installations off the coast of Norway.[57] In November 2022, chancellor Scholz, together with his Norwegian counterpart, jointly presented NATO Secretary General Jens Stoltenberg with an initiative to strengthen cooperation on the surveillance of subsea infrastructure.[58]

In late August 2022, Scholz used his speech on European integration at the University of Prague to launch a new initiative for which Germany would take the lead—closer cooperation on air defence.[59] Already in his *Zeitenwende* speech in February, Scholz had vowed 'to contribute to the defence of our allies' air space in Eastern Europe using anti-aircraft missiles'.[60] In

October, 14 allies signed a declaration of intent to develop an 'integrated air and missile defence system', dubbed the European Sky Shield Initiative, in the framework of NATO. In February 2023, Sweden and Denmark joined as well.[61] New initiatives, like the intention to establish a European sky shield or a centre for the protection of subsea infrastructure, signal a willingness to assume more responsibility for European security. According to chancellor Scholz, Germany's 'crucial role' is 'to step up as one of the main providers of security in Europe'.[62] Increased investments in the Bundeswehr meant that Germany would be able to take on large scale tasks for which it was capable due to its size, 'namely organizing territorial defence'.[63] According to the Chancellor, only the US and Germany would have the necessary forces to organise territorial defence for the entire alliance. Allies could rely on Germany, and the point was to send a signal to Putin saying loud and clear 'don't dare to attack us!'.[64]

As much as they were a necessity in view of Russia's aggression, these signals were also a response to the continued pressure for a stronger backing of NATO's deterrence posture and more leadership in the alliance. Although Germany under Chancellor Angela Merkel had joined NATO's adaptation to a changed security environment, re-focusing on national and collective defence, it was not, according to Bastian Giegerich and Maximilian Terhelle, seen as 'a reliable partner for its allies in the security realm'.[65] In the months and weeks preceding Russia's full-scale invasion of Ukraine, allies and partners had become increasingly frustrated over Germany's unwillingness to cut all ties with Russia—especially the controversial Nord Stream 2 pipeline project—and its hesitance towards arming Ukraine in the face of Russia's military build-up. But they also despaired over armed forces that were 'underfunded, ill-equipped and [enjoyed] poor value for money with its procurements'.[66] On the day of Russia's invasion, Germany's army chief turned to social media and posted a damning judgement on his troops' ability to fulfil their duties.[67]

Scholz's promises that Germany would stand 'unconditionally by our collective defence obligation within NATO' and would invest in a 'a powerful, cutting-edge, progressive Bundeswehr that can be relied upon to protect us' raised high expectations that soon turned into disappointment both inside Germany and among allies and partners.[68] Shortly before the Bundeswehr took the command for NATO's Very High Readiness Joint Task Force (VJTF) in January 2023, several of its Puma infantry vehicles experienced technical problems.[69] The Pumas were quickly repaired, but this and other embarrassing incidents led to questions of whether Germany was able to fulfil its many obligations. Especially in Eastern Europe, but also in the United States, trust in Germany's reliability as an ally suffered significantly.[70]

This criticism is only partially justified. Despite apparent difficulties to overcome a deeply ingrained fear for escalation, and notwithstanding an often-hapless communication strategy, Scholz and his government could argue rather convincingly that they had coordinated each step closely with key allies, first among them the Biden administration.[71] Indeed, the overall strategy to avoid NATO's direct involvement in the war with Russia was backed by all major Western powers from the beginning of the war. Most decisions to provide Ukraine with new types of capabilities were taken in connection with meetings of the so called Ramstein-contact group, chaired by the United States. Few other NATO member states have made as far-reaching commitments to NATO's new Force Model as Germany.

There are no indications that Germany does not intend to live up to its NATO obligations. However, doubts about Germany's ability to fulfil its NATO obligations persist. One year after he infamously remarked on social media that 'German land forces were "more or less bare" in view of the new threats', a leaked memo quoted the chief of the German army considering plans for a sufficiently equipped second division in 2027 as 'unrealistic'.[72]

Towards a New Strategic Mindset? The German Debate on Security and Military Power

If anything, the Chancellor's *Zeitenwende* speech has initiated perhaps the most comprehensive debate about German defence and security policy in decades. Abroad, allies and partners welcomed Germany's newfound apparent willingness to radically change its traditional approach towards Russia and particularly welcomed the commitment to more defence spending. At home, the Chancellor could rely on broad-based political support for his announced policy changes. Criticism comes mainly from those who think that Germany has acted too slowly. Protests against the support for Ukraine remained limited to the far left and far right fringes of the political spectre and to an assemblage of so-called intellectuals.[73]

Looking beyond the first procurements financed through the special fund and the next delivery of weapons to Ukraine, analysts and observers wonder how deep the transformation of Germany's security debate truly is.[74] Is Russia's aggression against its neighbours perceived as a genuine threat against European, and thus German, security? Is the sense of urgency in the political elite and wider society strong enough to push for necessary reforms of Germany's defence sector? Will the commitment to invest more in security and defence survive a future settlement of the war in Ukraine? Is Germany ready to take on a leading role in pushing for a stronger and more coordinated European defence effort? In short, will the current changes in Germany's security and defence policy lead to the long-awaited development of a new strategic mindset?

ZEITENWENDE OR BUSINESS AS USUAL?

To be sure, this is not the first time Germany faces a debate about its strategic culture. The end of the Cold War, the Balkan wars and the terrorist attacks of 11 September 2001 all led to debates about Germany's role and responsibility for European and international security.[75] The latest major debate came in 2014, when federal president Joachim Gauck used the Munich Security Conference as a platform to call for a more active foreign policy, and the ministers of foreign affairs and defence promised that Germany would take more responsibility. Shortly after, Russia's illegal annexation of Crimea and the advances of the terror group IS in Syria and Iraq forced Germany to take action that some saw as a paradigm shift.[76] The following years saw a rise in defence spending and a marked return in NATO to collective defence. These changes were reflected in the white paper of 2016 and found expression in concrete contributions to NATO's new deterrence and defence posture. However, critics bemoaned that these changes in the international security environment never led to a real adaptation of Germany's strategic culture.[77]

This time, the willingness for transformation seems to be more profound. One difference is that the Chancellor himself has set the tone with the *Zeitenwende* speech and continued to drive the debate. Contrary to his predecessor, Olaf Scholz has, from the start of his term, engaged in foreign and security policy decisions as the war in Ukraine has placed the matter firmly at the top of his agenda. Additionally, he has been under pressure from his coalition partners to do more.[78] At the same time, coalition partners have managed to keep their differences within certain boundaries. Despite a significant loss in popularity and fundamental disagreements over energy policy, the governing SPD–Green Party and FDP coalition has proven relatively stable. The government's stability has in turn given increased prominence to members of the German parliament in the security debate. A strong Conservative CDU/CSU opposition has called publicly for the government to stay on course, and individual parliamentarians from the smaller coalition parties have not been afraid to criticise their own government over a lack of boldness in supporting Ukraine and reforming the Bundeswehr.[79]

While the debate engages all political parties, the social democrats are under particular scrutiny. Already when the coalition government was formed in December 2021, many were surprised that the party's left wing, represented by influential figures such as party whip Rolf Mützenich and former youth leader, now secretary general, Kenvin Kuehnert, did not prevent a firm commitment to NATO and continued German participation in alliance nuclear sharing in the coalition agreement. Both were among key party figures that Scholz apparently did not consult before giving his seminal statement of 27 February 2022. This raised the question of whether the Chancellor would have the political backing to see such radical changes through. Many social democrats in the Bundestag and beyond were indeed shocked about the Chancellor's commitment to increased defence spending and his commitment to deliver weapons to Ukraine. In the following months, Mützenich and other social democrats did not hide that they found parts of the new course extremely difficult to support.[80] Nevertheless, they contributed to keeping the party on the course of unity that had brought them victory in the federal elections of 2021. Few, if any, leading party figures joined those on the left who challenged the government's policy of supporting Ukraine and increasing defence spending. Instead, party leader Lars Klingbeil and others tried to get ahead of the discussion by formulating a new foreign policy narrative, even addressing the difficult issue of German leadership.[81]

While they acknowledge the boldness and ambition in the Scholz-government's new approach, sceptics in and outside Germany wonder whether the change is real and sustainable.[82] As Giegerich and Schreer point out 'it can be difficult to change the strategic culture of a nation [like Germany, where the] reluctance to use military force is deeply ingrained in the national psyche'.[83] The debate on foreign and security policy is first and foremost one for the political elites. However, under the impression of Russian war crimes and attacks against the Ukrainian civilian population and infrastructure, the broader German public was also confronted with questions of war, security and defence in an unprecedented way. Opinion polls during the first year since Russia's full-scale attack on Ukraine and Scholz's speech seem to suggest that Germans still lack a real sense of urgency regarding Russia's aggressive behaviour. Many are afraid that military engagement might escalate the conflict further. However, polls also show that the war has transformed the electorate's positions on questions of security and defence.

According to the Bundeswehr's annual study of the public's attitudes towards the military, published in October 2022, a majority see Russia as a threat. Support for defending NATO's eastern flank has also risen considerably. Never have so many Germans (60%) been positive to increased defence spending.[84] A nationwide poll in February 2023 also showed that most Germans support weapons deliveries to Ukraine. The new defence minister, who argued much more forcefully than his predecessor for increased defence spending, quickly became Germany's most popular politician. Meanwhile, calls by so-called intellectuals to stop weapons deliveries as well as efforts to mobilise a new 'peace movement' have failed to gain widespread public support.[85]

The cautious course for which the Scholz-led government earned criticism, results in part from the need to make sure that his coalition, his party base and the wider society (the electorate) supports the proposed transformation. In the longer term, Germany's political elite, the public, but also Germany's allies and partners, expect an explanation as to what the changes entail. The National Security Strategy that Germany published in June 2023 is supposed to be an important steppingstone in this reflection process. The first ever document of this kind published by a German government not only reflects on the *Zeitenwende* but wants to address the complex challenges of an 'age of increasing multipolarity' where 'some countries are attempting to reshape the current international order, driven by their perception of systemic rivalry'.[86]

The ambition to draft a 'comprehensive national security' was already part of the so-called traffic-light-coalition's governing platform of December 2021. In his 2023 *Foreign Affairs* article, Scholz noted that 'Germany's new role will require a new strategic culture' and he promised that 'the national security strategy that my government will adopt a few months from now will reflect this fact'.[87] Significant delays in completing the strategy and compromises in the wording on controversial points, such as relations with China, suggest that reaching a consensus within a coalition government has proven challenging. The proposal to establish a national security council that could clarify responsibilities and streamline decision-making is not even mentioned. Observers acknowledge the strategy's integrated security approach as timely but note a lack of 'concreteness' and 'specifics about defence'.[88] Whether the document helps to shape the debates on security and defence policy since February 2022 in a way that will lead to changes in Germany's strategic culture remains to be seen.

There can be no doubt, however, that the new national security strategy, together with the Chancellor's speech of 24 February 2022, will become a document of reference for the policy changes provoked by Russia's invasion of Ukraine. The identification of Russia as 'the most significant threat to peace and security in the Euro-Atlantic area', commitments to NATO's defence and deterrence posture and to the alliance's spending targets as well as to Ukraine's place in the Euro-

Atlantic security architecture will be difficult to ignore by the current and future governments.

Conclusion

Undertaking a first assessment of Germany's *Zeitenwende* is a challenging task for several reasons. Firstly, this is very much a moving target. In the first few months after the speech, the envisaged €100 billion 'special fund for the Bundeswehr' made it appear as if Germany was about to finally deliver on hiking its defence spending. Meanwhile, Berlin's initial reluctance to move beyond delivering 'light' and 'defensive' weapons (narrowly defined) to Ukraine, made this policy area seem like the biggest let-down.

However, within barely a year, matters had been reversed. Setting up the 'special fund' turned out to be so slow-moving that '[not a] cent from the special fund' was spent in 2022.[89] By contrast, by early 2023, Germany was delivering most categories of weapon systems to Ukraine in significant quantities, with a few exceptions, such as Western-built combat aircraft. At present, Germany appears to have underperformed massively on increasing defence spending, but it has managed far better when it comes to delivering on its promise to provide Ukraine with weapons for the country's defence.

When it comes to collective defence, the impression is mixed. On the one hand, the German government has repeatedly confirmed its strong commitment to the defence of NATO's eastern flank. Chancellor Scholz has promised a bigger role for the Bundeswehr and has launched new initiatives for German leadership on air defence and security for underwater infrastructure. There remain serious doubts, however, if Germany will be able to live up to these promises. Even with more funding and a more active defence minister it will be a huge task to reverse decades of spending cuts and to reform the bureaucratized procurement system.

To achieve this, Germany's political elites must develop a strategic mindset that accepts a higher level of military readiness on a permanent basis. There can be no doubt that the Russian full-scale attack on Ukraine represented a watershed in European security and that Scholz's *Zeitenwende* speech will stand as the key moment in Germany's process of waking up to a new reality. Whether this moment will be regarded as the defining turning point in Germany's security and defence policy and as the starting point for the development of a new strategic mindset is still too early to say.

9

FINLAND'S APPROACH TO MILITARY COOPERATION AND INTEGRATION

FROM ALIGNMENT TO ALLIANCE

Tuomas Iso-Markku & Matti Pesu

Introduction

Finland's decision to seek membership of NATO represents one of the more surprising consequences of Russia's war of aggression against Ukraine in February 2022. Although the so-called 'NATO option' had long been an integral part of Finnish foreign and security policy vocabulary, no one foresaw the rapid and fundamental shift in Finnish public opinion that took place in the immediate aftermath of the Russian invasion of Ukraine—and very few could have predicted just how swiftly Finnish policymakers would exercise the option of applying for membership.

Finland's entry into NATO in April 2023 marked the beginning of a new era in Finnish foreign, security and defence policy. For the first time in its history, Finland is part of a formalised military alliance and can plan its own defence as part of NATO's collective defence. However, while NATO accession is clearly a turning point for Finland, this chapter argues that it is also a logical continuation of—not a radical shift in—Finland's approach towards military cooperation and integration.

Indeed, Finland has practiced threat-based, strategically informed military cooperation since 2014, when Russia's annexation of Crimea and the war in eastern Ukraine highlighted the Russian regime's readiness to use force against its neighbours. Subsequently, Finland developed a network of defence partnerships, encompassing bilateral and trilateral relations with Sweden, the United States and Norway, membership in diverse subregional and minilateral defence frameworks, close ties to NATO and a highly supportive stance towards deepening the defence dimension of the European Union. After Russia's first invasion of Ukraine, Finland duly adopted a strategy of 'alignment', tying itself *de facto* to the NATO-centred European security and defence system without formally joining the alliance.

In the context of Russia's full-scale invasion of Ukraine in February 2022, Finland's model of credible national defence paired with extensive international cooperation was no longer perceived as a sufficient deterrent in view of Russia's increased threat potential, causing Finland to apply for NATO membership. However, NATO accession will not diminish the significance of the military partnerships that Finland has built and enhanced over the years. On the contrary, as a NATO ally, Finland will engage in even deeper cooperation with like-minded allies, both within and beyond NATO structures. Such cooperation can, and should, play a crucial role in executing NATO's defence and deterrence tasks in Northern Europe. This can take the form of joint planning, new multinational command and control arrangements and potentially even basing.

This chapter analyses Finland's approach to military cooperation and integration both prior to and after its accession to NATO. The chapter is divided into four sections. The first one portrays Finland's security conundrum, that is, being a small state located next to a great power, Russia, and explains how Finland has sought to manage this conundrum for most of its history, relying on a combination of nationally generated deterrence on the one hand and diverse reassurance measures on the other. The section also highlights how Finland's strategy changed after 2014, with the balance of its Russia policy gradually shifting towards deterrence—and international military cooperation becoming a key avenue for Finland to strengthen deterrence. The second section looks more closely at the bilateral, trilateral and minilateral military partnerships, involving countries such as Sweden, the US, Norway and the UK, which formed the core of Finland's new deterrence strategy in the post-Crimea years. The third section then analyses the changes brought about by Russia's 2022 invasion of Ukraine, which led Finland to discard the non-treaty-based 'alignment' strategy in favour of formal membership in NATO. Finally, the fourth section discusses the opportunities that Finland's entry into NATO opens up in terms of military cooperation and integration. The chapter ends with a short concluding section.

Managing Finland's Security Conundrum

Throughout its independence, Finland's main security conundrum has been straightforward: how to preserve independence, sovereignty and territorial integrity in the face of a potential threat from Russia or, before it, the Soviet Union. Importantly, the Finnish–Russian relationship has always been marked by a glaring power asymmetry, as well as fundamentally different views of the ideal European security order. As a small state, Finland has advocated a rules-based anti-hegemonic system, whereas Russia traditionally prefers an order based on great-power dominance and legitimate spheres of influence.[1] Consequently, René Nyberg, the former Finnish ambassador to Moscow and Berlin, has aptly called Russia Finland's permanent dilemma—one that Helsinki can never solve but can, and must, try to manage.[2]

Finland has utilised two broad tools for dealing with the Russian conundrum. First, it has relied on deterrence with the aim of preventing a Russian military attack or, more broadly, thwarting any Russian action that could potentially destabilise Finnish society.[3] Second, Finland has simultaneously pursued a policy of reassurance and engagement vis-à-vis Russia. In practice, this has meant that Finnish high-level decision-makers have been both ready and willing to engage in political dialogue with their Russian counterparts. Moreover, Finland has also limited the scope of its defence policy to convince the Russian side about its defensive aims and to emphasise Finland's reluctance to serve as a springboard for any external aggression against Russia.[4] On balance, Finland's two-pronged strategy towards Russia is hardly unique. The elements of deterrence and reassurance have featured prominently in the security policies of the Nordic states, particularly in the cases of Norway and Sweden.[5] Even NATO as a whole has arguably followed a similar path.[6]

Overall, the Finnish approach towards Russia has traditionally been heavy on reassurance. The primacy of reassurance prevailed throughout the Cold War period and continued, to a somewhat lesser degree, during the first three decades of the post-Cold War era as well.[7] This meant that Finnish decision-makers accommodated Finland's defence policy to the security interests of the neighbouring great power. Indeed, during the Cold War, defence policy was almost completely subservient to the objective of maintaining a cordial relationship with the Soviet Union.[8] After the collapse of the Soviet Union, Finland's freedom of action increased considerably. The role of deterrence began to grow almost inconspicuously, as Finland bolstered its defence capabilities with major weapons procurements, such as the American F-18 aircraft acquired in 1992.[9] At the same time, Finland continued to invest in diverse reassurance measures and, most of all, pursued a policy of military non-alignment.

As far as deterrence is concerned, Finland's strategy was for a long time markedly national. From the end of the Second World War to the mid-2010s, Finnish defence policy was underpinned by a deterrence-by-denial model that was built and sustained by national efforts only.[10] During the Cold War years, Finland's international military cooperation was almost non-existent,[11] reflecting the country's limited room for manoeuvre and the primacy of reassurance. In the 1990s and the 2000s, Finnish defence policy began to internationalise gradually with Finland's entry into NATO's Partnership for Peace (PfP) in 1994, the country's accession to the EU in 1995, as well as the establishment of different forms of Nordic military cooperation. However, cooperation in these frameworks focused almost exclusively on crisis management, not on territorial defence, which remained a national prerogative.[12]

Indeed, international military cooperation did not form part of Finland's deterrence efforts until after Russia's first invasion of Ukraine in 2014. The Russian aggression in Crimea and eastern Ukraine marked an underappreciated watershed in Finland's defence policy as well as its approach towards Russia. In the years that followed it, Finland's view of Russia grew increasingly pessimistic. The Finnish government's 2016 report on foreign and security policy noted that '[…] the return of Russia to thinking in terms of power politics, including its internal development, the growth of its military potential and increasing military activity challenge the very foundations of the European security regime and create instability in Finland's operating environment'.[13] The 2020 government report on foreign and security policy, for its part, concluded that 'Russian operations in areas like Georgia,

Ukraine and Syria show that the country has lowered its threshold to use military force'.[14] Accordingly, the balance of Finland's Russia policy started to tilt in favour of deterrence.

At the same time, Finland started to recognise, and appreciate, the potential of international military cooperation for bolstering deterrence. Already in 2015, Finnish President Sauli Niinistö argued that Finland's security rested on four different but mutually complementary pillars: strong national defence; integration into Western political and military structures, including closer defence cooperation with Sweden and enhanced partnership with NATO; engagement with Russia where possible and useful; and continued defence of international law and a multilateral order.[15] Niinistö emphasised that Finland should try to reinforce those pillars it can while trying to uphold all of them to the extent that it was possible. The government's 2016 foreign and security policy report explicitly linked Finland's deepening military partnerships to deterrence, stating that '[b]ilateral and multilateral defence cooperation is an important part of maintaining, developing and using Finland's defence capacity, and [of] deterrence'.[16]

This does not mean that Finland discarded reassurance entirely. Finland continued to emphasise the need for dialogue with Russia on bilateral issues and international security, as well as the possibilities for cooperation on economy, energy, the Arctic and climate issues.[17] Finland also invested in broader great power dialogue between Russia and the US, hosting the 2018 Russia–United States summit in Helsinki as well as meetings between high-level Russian and US military officials. Most significantly, Finland still refrained from formally applying for NATO membership, being concerned about the potential implications of such a move for Finnish–Russian relations and the stability in the Baltic Sea region and mindful of Finnish public opinion, which remained strongly opposed to joining NATO.[18]

FINLAND'S APPROACH TO MILITARY COOPERATION

The beginning of Russia's war of aggression against Ukraine in February 2022 pushed Finland's Russia policy decisively towards a deterrence-based approach as Helsinki's bid to formally enter NATO exemplifies. Political dialogue with Russia will be in a deep freeze indefinitely, and the policy of reassurance is currently reduced to escalation management and keeping the bilateral channels of communication open in case they are needed.[19]

Military Cooperation as a Key Part of Finland's Post-Crimea Deterrence Policy

Finland already engaged in international defence cooperation before 2014, participating in the EU's Common Security and Defence Policy (CSDP), forging a close partnership with NATO and engaging in different forms of Nordic defence cooperation, which gained fresh impetus with the establishment of the Nordic Defence Cooperation (NORDEFCO) framework in 2009.[20] However, while cooperation in these frameworks arguably contributed to strengthening Finland's national defence capability, its role in Finland's deterrence vis-à-vis Russia was very limited, especially in military terms. It was not until Russia's first invasion of Ukraine in 2014 that both Finland's approach towards Russia and the significance of international military cooperation therein started to change. These changes happened rapidly but partly out of the public eye, which is why their significance continues to be overlooked both within and outside Finland.

Finland's changed view of the role of defence cooperation was formulated in a very explicit manner in the Finnish government's 2017 white paper on defence, which emphasised that defence cooperation '[...] strengthens defence in normal and emergency conditions. It also enhances deterrence and improves the chances of receiving political and military assistance when needed'.[21] International military cooperation was duly seen not only as a means to deter any military aggression from Russia's part but also to create the conditions for acting jointly with partners if deterrence were to fail. Despite its non-membership of NATO and prevalent culture of military self-reliance, Finland thus prepared to defend itself in close cooperation with others and as a natural part of the NATO-centred European security and defence system. Relatedly, Finland consistently highlighted the importance of the EU's mutual assistance clause (Article 42(7), TEU), the only formal mutual assistance obligation the country was bound to.[22] Any legal hurdles to mutual assistance were removed in 2017 with the enactment of a law that allows Finland to provide and receive military assistance by combat forces.

While NATO membership continued to be seen merely as an option by most Finnish policymakers, Finland's approach increasingly relied on the idea that in a military crisis or conflict, shared interests would lead to the formation of ad hoc coalitions between key states. This view was most clearly expressed by President Niinistö. During his re-election campaign in 2017, Niinistö argued that '[i]f Finland is attacked, that means that there is a massive war going on. In such a situation, coalitions emerge. Finland is seen as a central actor—thanks to us having kept our defence in order. I think we would even be sought after'.[23]

In line with its assessment of the value of defence cooperation, Finland began to actively deepen its existing defence relationships and forge new ones, primarily concentrating on actors with security interests and the capacity to play a role in the Baltic Sea region and in Northern Europe at large.[24] This resulted in a multi-layered web of partly overlapping bilateral, trilateral and minilateral defence partnerships with close but varying links to NATO. At the same time, Finland also enhanced its cooperation with NATO itself and supported efforts to deepen the EU's defence dimension.

FINLAND'S APPROACH TO MILITARY COOPERATION

Finland's relationship with NATO rose to a new level already in 2014, as the alliance's Wales summit granted Finland the status of an enhanced opportunities partner. Finland also signed a memorandum of understanding on the provision of host nation support for the execution of NATO. Moreover, political dialogue with NATO was enhanced, as Finland and Sweden were invited to participate in NATO's deliberations concerning the security situation around the Baltic Sea in what was then a '28+2' format.[25]

At the same time, Finland's bilateral defence cooperation with Sweden started to take off. The Finnish and Swedish defence ministers signed an action plan for deepened defence cooperation in May 2014, aiming at 'increasing effect and efficiency through combined use of resources, through increased interoperability and through a closer dialogue on common challenges'.[26] While initially developed primarily for the purposes of international crisis management and confined to activities in peacetime, it was clear from early on that the joint activities of the two countries could 'easily bleed into cooperation that is useful during crisis/wartime'.[27]

The Finnish–Swedish action plan was quickly followed by further documents. Especially after 2015, Finnish–Swedish cooperation deepened rapidly—and was increasingly driven by their shared view of the regional security situation, with Russia's assertive posture being the main challenge.[28] In 2018, a new memorandum of understanding between Finland and Sweden was signed, stating that their cooperation aimed at 'strengthening the defence capabilities of the Participants, creating prerequisites for combined joint military action and operations in all situations, and to further common interests in the defence domain, including strengthening the security of the Baltic Sea region'. To underline the depth of the relationship, the memorandum also explicitly stated that the countries' defence cooperation covered 'peace, crisis and war' and emphasised that there were 'no predetermined limits' to deepening the bilateral defence relationship.

The value of Finnish–Swedish defence cooperation partly derives from the complementary structures of their armed forces, with Sweden having a comparably strong navy and Finland fielding a large and capable army. In practice, the military cooperation between Finland and Sweden has covered the three branches of their armed forces. On the naval side, it has included sea surveillance cooperation as well as the establishment of the Swedish–Finnish Naval Task Group and the Swedish–Finnish Amphibious Task Unit.[29] The Finnish and Swedish air forces have concentrated on the interoperability of air operations, base operations and command and control systems.[30] The two countries' land forces have also been building their ability to conduct high-end operations together.[31] Significantly, the two countries engage in joint operational planning covering all situations.[32]

In many ways, Sweden was a natural partner for Finland to work with due to the close historical ties between the two countries but also due to their status as non-NATO countries, which set them apart from their Nordic and Baltic neighbours—and made cooperation easier politically.[33] However, Finland's military cooperation in the post-Crimea years was by no means confined to the relationship with Sweden, instead extending to several NATO allies as well.

Another crucial partner for Finland was the United States, with which Finland signed a bilateral statement of intent on deepening and increasing practical defence cooperation in 2016. The document outlined an agenda that covered dialogue, exchange of information, enhancing defence capability, readiness and interoperability in the context of multilateral operations, increased training and exercises, armaments cooperation, as well as exploring opportunities to enhance Finland's cooperation with

NATO.[34] Importantly, very soon after, Finland, Sweden and the US started to advance trilateral defence cooperation as well. A memorandum of understanding between the three countries was signed in 2018, stating the parties' aim to intensify their trilateral dialogue on defence, develop their political and military interoperability, expand their situational awareness, develop their capabilities and posture, improve their ability to conduct combined multilateral operations, coordinate their strategic communications and promote constructive links between NATO and the EU.[35]

A third close partnership developed with Norway. Finland and Norway first signed a bilateral framework agreement in 2018 and then updated it in 2021. The Finnish–Norwegian agenda, as outlined in the documents, extends from dialogue to interoperability, military security of supply to joint combined situational awareness, and from cyber and hybrid-related cooperation to training and exercises. As with the US, Finland and Sweden also furthered trilateral cooperation with Norway with a particular focus on the northern parts of the three countries. In 2020, a trilateral memorandum of understanding was signed between Finland, Sweden and Norway. It covered, among other things, setting up a trilateral strategic planning group and, significantly, the coordination of national operations plans between the three countries in areas of common concern as well as the possibility for common operations planning in certain areas.[36]

In addition to the bilateral and trilateral frameworks, Finland's defence partnerships also included different minilateral groups. Reflecting the Nordic states' shared concerns about Russia's assertiveness as well as the increasingly close bilateral and trilateral links between them, cooperation within the framework of NORDEFCO advanced with the adoption of a NORDEFCO vision for 2025, which stated that the five countries would improve their 'defence capability in peace, crisis and conflict'.[37] However, in practice, most of the work was done in different bilateral and trilateral constellations.

In 2017, both Finland and Sweden also joined the United Kingdom-led Joint Expeditionary Force (JEF). Originally devised as an expeditionary force able to deploy wherever needed, Russia's first invasion of Ukraine in 2014 led to the JEF reorienting itself increasingly towards Northern Europe, encompassing the Northern Atlantic, the Arctic region and the Baltic Sea region. This made it a highly relevant and interesting format from the Finnish perspective.[38] Alongside the JEF, Finland also joined the German-led Framework Nations Concept (FNC) as well as the French-initiated European Intervention Initiative (EI2). Finland's participation in these frameworks was primarily motivated by its willingness to strengthen its ties with the respective lead nations, Germany and France, as well as to instil Northern European views into the ensuing cooperation.[39] However, to date, neither the FNC nor the EI2 have developed as dynamically as the JEF nor have they been as relevant from the point of view of Northern European security, which is why their importance for Finland has remained more limited.[40]

Finally, Finland also continued to highlight the importance of developing the EU's CSDP as well as the broader defence dimension of the EU. Consequently, Finland expressed strong support for the steps that the EU took, especially after the publication of the EU Global Strategy in 2016, including the introduction of the Coordinated Annual Review on Defence, Permanent Structured Cooperation and the European Commission–initiated European Defence Fund. However, Finland's political commitment to these initiatives did not translate into substantial practical engagement. From Helsinki's point of view, most of these initiatives were welcome in political terms, but of limited value militarily, which is why Finland's participation in Permanent Structured

Cooperation projects, for example, has been at a low level compared with many of its partners.

While Finland's extensive partnerships in many ways—and oftentimes deliberately—blurred the line between alliance and non-alliance, there were limits to the cooperation that neither Finland nor its partners were prepared to cross. These were related, among others things, to issues such as exchange of information and command and control.[41] Finland's and Sweden's trilateral agreement with NATO member Norway also very clearly stated that even if the three countries shared the ambition to be able and ready to conduct operations in crisis and conflict, Norway planned 'to transfer command to NATO in crisis and war'.[42] This qualification made it very clear that there was a difference between the nature of this cooperation and full membership in NATO. Even the very close cooperation between Finland and Sweden as two non-NATO members did not advance to the point where the countries would have introduced mutual security guarantees. Finnish–Swedish cooperation in crisis and war was thus an option rather than an obligation[43]—and the same applied to Finland's other military partnerships as well.

Collapse of the 'Alignment' Strategy and Finland's NATO Membership Bid

Russia's full-scale invasion of Ukraine in February 2022 effectively propelled Finland to discard the non-treaty based alignment strategy in favour of formal and full membership in NATO. The debate about Finland's NATO accession had already intensified prior to Russia's invasion of Ukraine as Russia amassed troops on the Ukrainian borders and demanded NATO preclude all further enlargement. While the Russian demands did not target Finland specifically, they were seen to directly challenge Finland's international room for manoeuvre and its long-standing policy of maintaining the option to apply for NATO membership. In view of the Russian demands, both President Sauli Niinistö and Prime Minister Sanna Marin used their new year's addresses to highlight that Finland would make its own decisions concerning its security policy choices.[44] In retrospect, President Niinistö also described the Russian demands as an important turning point in his own thinking on NATO membership.[45]

However, the real start of the Finnish NATO process was the beginning of the Russian war of aggression in February 2022 and, above all, the resulting shift in Finnish public opinion regarding NATO membership. After decades during which it mostly stood at around 20–25%,[46] support for NATO membership suddenly jumped to 53% in a poll by the Finnish public broadcasting company Yle published on 28 February[47] and continued to rise in subsequent polls. The radical shift in the public's preferences paved the way for parliamentary deliberations in which the implications of the Russian war of aggression against Ukraine on Finnish security, as well as the potential added value of NATO membership, were evaluated. To support these deliberations, the Finnish government also published its own report on the changes caused by Russia's war on Finland's security environment, which did not express an explicit position on the issue of NATO membership.[48]

Two points were particularly important in the discussions about Finnish NATO membership. First, Russia's attempt at a full-scale invasion of Ukraine highlighted the Russian regime's growing appetite to assume military risks as well as its complete disregard for the sovereignty of its neighbour.[49] Due to Finland's geographic location and its history with Russia, this was a particularly strong argument to seek additional security solutions. Second, Russia's use of nuclear coercion, aiming at limiting the level of military support for Ukraine, demonstrated how vulnerable a country could be when not covered by a nuclear umbrella in a war against a nuclear power. This brought home the value of collective (nuclear) deterrence.[50]

Based on the domestic deliberations, a strong consensus emerged on the insufficiency of Finland's deterrence vis-à-vis Russia.[51] While the Russian attack vindicated Finland's long-standing commitment to uphold a capable national defence, investing more in national capabilities was not, in and of itself, considered to be enough to remedy the identified 'deterrence deficit' in Finland's security arrangements. Instead, deepening the international dimension and embeddedness of Finnish defence appeared, from the very beginning, to form an integral part of Finland's efforts to strengthen deterrence and defence. As formulated by the Finnish government, '[i]n response to the changed security situation, Finland will in any case have to strengthen its security and defence capability and intensify long-term cooperation with key partners'.[52]

Regarding military cooperation, two broad options were outlined by the Finnish foreign policy leadership as possible ways to strengthen Finnish security: full membership in NATO or further intensification of non-treaty based cooperation with key partners, above all Sweden and the US.[53] However, the Finnish public's radically changed view on the possibility of Finland's accession to NATO quickly steered the Finnish decision-makers towards the NATO path. The general public was mostly unaware of how deeply Finland had already aligned its defence with the NATO-led Western security system, which is why a further deepening of the non-treaty based relationships with key partners never became a serious alternative to applying for NATO membership. Even President Niinistö himself, careful not to intervene in the parliamentary debates, spoke of NATO membership as the 'most sufficient' option.[54]

Nevertheless, the different bilateral, trilateral and minilateral partnerships that Finland had built since Crimea played a highly visible and important role in the pre-accession phase. Consultations and close coordination with Sweden and the US opened the way for the joint NATO application of Finland and Sweden. The JEF, for its part, constituted an important forum to exchange information and views after the start of the Russian invasion.[55] The UK, as the lead nation of the JEF, was also quick to offer Finland and Sweden security assurances before they submitted their NATO applications. In a joint statement between the UK and Finland in May 2022, the two countries pledged to 'assist each other in a variety of ways, which may include military means' should one of them suffer a disaster or an attack.[56] Informal security assurances were also offered by France and the US.[57] Moreover, NATO allies underlined their commitment to Finnish security by sending forces to Finland for visits or exercises.

Finland's Miliary Cooperation upon Accession to NATO

Less than 11 months after the submission of its membership application to NATO, Finland joined the alliance on 4 April 2023. This doctrinal shift related to NATO membership will result in both immediate and long-term changes to Finland's military cooperation and integration both within and beyond alliance structures.

First and foremost, as an ally, Finland will be integrated into NATO's military structures.[58] More precisely, it will be involved in the new family of regional war plans describing how NATO aims to defend itself against its adversaries, most notably Russia. Finland will also be integrated in the alliance's command and control system. It will additionally earmark troops and capabilities for NATO's ambitious new Force Model. Furthermore, by taking part in the NATO Defence Planning Process, it will contribute to the alliance's force structure—that is the number and types of equipment and organizations that NATO requires to conduct its operations.[59] Lastly, Finland will be incorporated into NATO Integrated Air and Missile Defence, including ballistic missile defence.[60]

Thus, Finland's accession into NATO will not only deepen the scope of Finland's integration into Western defence structures but also introduce a stronger element of advance planning to the relationship between Finland and its allies. Whereas the alignment strategy banked on the emergence of ad hoc coalitions and spontaneous coordination of Finnish and allied efforts in a conflict situation, Finnish NATO membership ensures that the country is also involved in core NATO and allied activities in peacetime. Should a war break out, there would be less need for spontaneity, as Finnish and allied efforts would rely on existing plans and command arrangements.

Finland's accession to NATO will also change the nature of its existing bilateral, trilateral and minilateral defence partnerships. As discussed earlier, since Russia's first invasion of Ukraine in 2014, non-treaty based defence cooperation has constituted an increasingly central element of Finland's defence policy, partly serving as a substitute for NATO membership. With Finland's NATO accession, these diverse cooperation formats will be reoriented towards operationally implementing NATO's deterrence and collective defence in Northern Europe. At the same time, they form an additional layer of cooperation beyond NATO structures, complementing the alliance and serving as a hedge against cases in which NATO, for one reason or other, is unable to respond to a contingency in the Nordic–Baltic region.

Given Finland's and Sweden's accession to NATO, the respective security solutions of the Nordic–Baltic countries are aligned—a historic situation which allows for a significant deepening of cooperation among these nations as well as those allies with security interests in the region.[61] Accordingly, Finland is currently involved in several efforts aiming to bolster military cooperation. The Nordic countries have announced that they will place an increasing emphasis on operational cooperation. In November 2022, Finland, Sweden and Norway updated their trilateral Statement of Intent to strengthen operational planning in areas of common concern, especially in the northern parts of the three nations.[62] This format addresses a specific concern—namely the security of the northern parts of the three nations, which form a shared strategic space between the Norwegian Sea and the Kola Peninsula. Furthermore, in March 2023, another milestone agreement was concluded between the air forces of Denmark, Finland, Norway and Sweden, with the four countries declaring their aim to operate their approximately 250 fighter jets as a joint operational fleet. The four countries will pursue four areas of action: integrated command and control, operational planning and execution; flexible and resilient deployment of their air forces; joint airspace surveillance; and joint education, training and exercises.[63] Neither of the new announcements would have taken place without the Finnish and Swedish NATO bids.

Finland is also intent on deepening defence partnerships with non-Nordic allies. In October 2023, the negotiations with the United States on a new Defence Cooperation Agreement were concluded, paving the way for more intense collaboration between Helsinki and Washington. The aim of the agreement is simple: it provides a legal framework for US forces operating in Finland, thereby facilitating more effective security cooperation between the two allies.[64] Finland—like its fellow frontline allies—sees the US as its primary security guarantor, an actor both able and willing to reinforce them if push comes to shove. A new defence relationship with the US could open entirely new avenues for bilateral cooperation, such as positioning of American equipment in Finland or granting the US the authority to access and use agreed bases.

FINLAND'S APPROACH TO MILITARY COOPERATION

Furthermore, Finland increasingly sees the UK as a security provider in the Northern European security landscape. The government's report released in April 2022 called the UK a 'major military player in Northern Europe and the Baltic Sea'.[65] In May 2022, Finland and the UK released a joint statement reiterating their 'shared desire for ever deeper defence and security cooperation that is fit for any circumstances'.[66] Key areas of bilateral cooperation include training and exercises, exchange of information, and development of interoperability.[67] Participation in the JEF is seen as a key element of the Finnish–UK defence relationship, and the coalition is regarded as an agile responder to military crises, potentially playing a first responder role in a Northern European contingency.

Lastly, Finland's entry into the NATO alliance will enable deeper military cooperation with its southern neighbour, Estonia, which Helsinki has not previously regarded as a central partner. Emergent cooperation will likely evolve around the defence of the Gulf of Finland—a significant maritime bottleneck, providing a gateway from Saint Petersburg to the Baltic Sea and beyond. Potential cooperation efforts could most notably include the integration of Finnish and Estonian coastal defence, which would necessitate joint situational awareness and close information-sharing, for example.[68]

To summarize, with Finland's NATO accession, evolving and deepening military cooperation with allies will, and should, contribute at least to four different tasks:

1. Coordinating, organising, and executing NATO's deterrence and defence activities in the Nordic–Baltic region and beyond.
2. Strengthening and/or fine-tuning the concrete political and military arrangements for receiving and providing military assistance and ensuring security of supply in a conflict scenario.

3. Hedging against situations in which NATO for some reason is too slow or wholly incapable of taking decisions or action.
4. Increasing cost-efficiency through coordination of defence planning, pooling and sharing of military assets, as well as joint development and acquisition of defence materiel.[69]

Crucially, despite NATO membership, the lodestar of Finnish defence cooperation remains the same: Helsinki is seeking to deepen military partnerships with Northern European NATO members as well as militarily capable allies with security interests in the region, most notably with the US and the UK. Finland's military cooperation continues to be strategically informed, focusing on Northern Europe, which is the country's immediate security environment.

Conclusion

This chapter has argued that since 2014 and Russia's first invasion Ukraine, Finland has practiced strategically informed military cooperation in several formats and with various partners. The development of these partnerships has been guided by a simple principle: it should intensify cooperation with nations that, in addition to serious military capabilities, have security interests in Northern Europe. Importantly, the emergence of these sprawling partnerships in the latter half of the 2010s tied Finland to the NATO-centred European security and defence system, creating alignment between Finland and the alliance.

As a reaction to Russia's full-scale invasion of Ukraine in 2022, Finland decided to join the ranks of NATO. It became a full member of the alliance in April 2023. This doctrinal shift from alignment to alliance has led to significant changes in Finland's international military cooperation and integration. As an ally, Finland will contribute to the alliance's collective defence, and it will be fully integrated into NATO's military structures. Importantly, Helsinki will continue to pursue military cooperation within and beyond the NATO framework with increasing vigour. The guiding principle of this cooperation has not changed, however. Rather, NATO membership will allow Finland to take novel steps in defence cooperation, substantially deepening military integration with its fellow allies.

The proliferation of international defence cooperation as well as NATO membership have fundamentally transformed Finland's approach to managing its permanent security dilemma, that is, its proximity to Russia. From the end of the Second World War to the mid-2010s, Finland relied on nationally produced deterrence and considerable reassurance measures in handling the relationship with its big eastern neighbour. From 2014 onwards, Finland has been moving towards an increasingly deterrence-based approach, based not only on national measures but also international military cooperation. NATO membership marks a decisive shift in this respect—Finland's days of sole self-reliance are over.

10

NATO AND THE UKRAINE DEFENSE CONTACT GROUP
FRONTLINE STATES AND FOLLOWERS

Janne Haaland Matlary

The war in Ukraine shows unprecedented Western unity after almost 2 years of fighting. 'The West' in this case also comprises democratic states like Australia, Japan and Korea, making for a *de facto* coalition of democracies. This coalition has delivered weapons, unlike the situation after the annexation of Crimea in 2014–15. It does so in accordance with Article 51 of the UN Charter, a clause that defines self-defence as the right of the attacked to ask for assistance: an age-old ethical principle. It is this clarity of purpose that binds the Western world together in the face of evident aggression.

This chapter analyses the ad hoc Ukraine weapons assistance coalition, asking whether it amounts to 'defence integration', which is the topic of this book. It also assesses the role that NATO plays in relation to the coalition that is assisting Ukraine—is this an example of an 'alliance in the alliance, or an alliance around the US'?

NATO AND THE RUSSIAN WAR IN UKRAINE

NATO is not a direct party to the war, but its role is highly flexible, given its partnership with Ukraine (under the terms of the Partnership for Peace, PfP), which has developed from a small number of cooperation projects to major assistance in intelligence, military and political support. NATO and the Ukraine Defense Contact Group (UDCG), which provides assistance and advice to Ukraine, are also closely aligned: meetings of NATO member states are followed by defence group meetings of the coalition within NATO headquarters.[1] Moreover, NATO Secretary General Jens Stoltenberg plays a very prominent role in speaking in favour of weapons assistance to Ukraine. NATO also provides signals intelligence from satellites and other intelligence to Ukraine, but not lethal aid.

The relationship between the coalition and NATO is thus complementary—NATO deters Russia, but it also assists Ukraine in various non-lethal ways, whereas the coalition can undertake much riskier types of weapons assistance in terms of escalation dangers. Moreover, as most coalition member states are also NATO members, there is an important overlap that allows for deep coordination between the coalition and NATO. Secretary General Stoltenberg participates in all meetings of the coalition, and these meetings take place after North Atlantic Council meetings in NATO.

One can term NATO the shield, in deterring Russia beyond Ukraine, and the coalition the sword, actively assisting the country with lethal arms. This illustrates the advantage and flexibility of such coalitions: they allow for groups of states to act together within the framework of established, permanent multinational organizations when this is useful, but they can also be organized outside of such frameworks or partially consist of members of the EU or NATO, and include non-members too. Coalitions, sometimes ad hoc, can integrate and cooperate more deeply than formal organizations and provide flexibility and versatility. They do not represent the 'mother' organization and do not have to take the views of all members of the latter into consideration. Veto power cannot be used against them, and they may act as 'bridge-heads' for subsequent policy of the organization. The EU has a formal mechanism for groups that want to do this in the security and defence area—called 'Permanent Structured Cooperation'. The EU also conducted consultations with the three great powers, France, the UK and Germany (when the British were still in the EU) as an informal leading group. The euro group (member states that have the euro as their currency) is another example of a coalition in the EU, having the role of an 'advance party' in monetary policy.

Coalitions of like-minded states are increasingly common. As discussed in the introduction, they are not 'competing' with formal multilateral organizations; rather, they seem to complement them.[2]

Before we turn to the analysis of the rationale and potential for this coalition, let us look at the brief history of this coalition in the first year of the war and beyond.

The Ukraine Defense Contact Group: A Case of Converging Strategic Interest?

The large-scale attack on Ukraine by Russia on 24 February 2022 elicited an unprecedented response among Western states, resulting in a coalition called the Ukraine Defense Contact Group (UDCG). Led by the US and the UK, the contact group has organized weapons delivery to Ukraine and the training of Ukrainian troops. Counting some 50 states, the coalition is unprecedented, only rivalled by the coalition to aid Kuwait militarily, which sent troops in 1991, or the large number of states that supported Operation Enduring Freedom in 2001 in Afghanistan.

In terms of European response, the UDCG represents a major change politically. It is no secret that many European states would have preferred to continue their *Ostpolitik*, seeing Russia as a commercial and/or energy partner. This has been the normal situation since 1990, and the supply of arms to Ukraine would normally have been regarded as too provocative.

In my book *Hard Power in Hard Times: Can Europe Act Strategically?*,[3] I found that the annexation of Crimea in 2014 led to a response where European states were reactive and the US assumed the leading position, with the policy response it chose being to use sanctions and political condemnation. France was, at the time, closely aligned with the German position of developing a diplomatic solution to the crisis, and Chancellor Angela Merkel played the leading role in formulating the Minsk agreements. The British were primarily preoccupied with domestic politics, national elections and the Brexit referendum. They did not play their normally leading role in security and defence policy in Europe. Ultimately, the US led and the Europeans followed. Is this the pattern we see again after the invasion of 2022?

At the time of Russia's invasion of Crimea and Donbass in 2014, there was talk of arming Ukraine, launched by American think-tanks and policymakers, notably Strobe Talbott, but this was considered too risky to undertake. There was no serious consideration of military assistance to Ukraine in Europe—Angela Merkel even remarked that this was not an issue on the table at all.[4]

There was even less response from the West some years earlier when the Russians attacked two regions of Georgia in 2008, Abkhazia and South-Ossetia. The Russian attack came in response to NATO's offer of membership to Georgia and Ukraine some months before, at the Bucharest summit of NATO that April. The reaction in Washington to Russia's blatant use of military power was one of great caution: they did not want a conflict with Russia, according to the account by Ron Asmus in his book *The Little War that Shook the World*.[5]

Thus, in the two similar cases preceding the present situation—of occupation and annexation of regions in other states—there was a clear demarcation in Western thinking between military and non-military means. Furthermore, the US played the leading role in both crises, yet opted for a very subdued role with regard to Georgia in 2008, asking the EU president, then Nicolas Sarkozy, to travel to Tbilisi to make a deal for a cease-fire with Russia. In the Crimea case in 2014–15, the US also took the lead, but military assistance was ruled out.

From this, three inferences can be made: first, on the Russian side there was no reason to assume that Western military assistance would happen in the present war in Ukraine, as this was not a seriously considered option for the West before. Second, the coalition that now supplies Ukraine is surprising, both in terms of scope—its membership numbers over 50 states—and in terms of its willingness to also provide heavy weapons. Third, the US leads again, Europe follows.

Given Ukraine and Georgia's geographical proximity to European states, one might have expected more willingness in Europe to arm these states when attacked by Russian forces. But there were no calls for this in 2008 and 2014. One caveat in comparing these cases is that the attack in 2022 was an attempted full-scale invasion, which Russia did not even try to justify in terms of international law. This was especially shocking and probably explains the Western willingness to act. Yet the inaction at previous annexations is perhaps what warrants explanation, as the main principles of the UN Charter were also violated then.

NATO AND THE RUSSIAN WAR IN UKRAINE

The Road to Crisis: US Leadership

Already in 2012 there was training by allied forces in Ukraine, especially by UK and US forces. These two states were key in training Ukrainian army personnel.[6]

Before the invasion itself, the US was the key actor trying to convince its allies that Russia would invade. In a detailed account in the *Washington Post*,[7] we learn of the political reluctance to take American intelligence seriously. The findings of the article are based on some thirty interviews with key officials. Jake Sullivan, the national security advisor, recounted how the administration was alarmed by president Putin's long essay on Ukraine and that defensive weapons worth 60 million dollars were sent to Ukraine in the summer of 2021. The US was already engaged politically from this time, and, as mentioned, present with training programmes in Ukraine from 2012.

As the signs of an impending invasion grew stronger, CIA director William Burns went to Moscow on 2 November 2021, but with no result. He returned stating that the decision to invade might already have been taken. The same month, the US held briefings with allies, who remained skeptical. Yet the UK, Poland and the Baltic states were alarmed and engaged. Note that we see here a 'frontline' group of states around the US, as well as a larger, more reluctant group—a topic to which we will return.

A meeting at deputy defence minister level between Wendy Sherman and Sergei Ryabkov was held in Geneva in January 2022. A Russian ultimatum to NATO was presented in December 2021 demanding the 'Collective West' de-militarize Eastern Europe and accept no new members. The US continued to preposition troops in Eastern Europe at this time—inter alia one helicopter battalion in Poland and paratroopers from the 71st Airborne in the Baltic states. The increase in US troop numbers in Europe went from 74,000 to 100,000 in a few months. The existing four air force fighter squadrons increased to twelve, while the five surface combatant ships routinely deployed were increased to twenty-six. A direct line between the Ukraine high command and the US Europe command was established.

The US decision to publish intelligence on Russian military plans before and during the invasion was unprecedented and very important. The element of surprise was removed from all aspects of Russian plans, and 'false flag' operations were revealed before they could be launched. Also, the detailed Russian deployment around Ukraine was made public: 100 battalion tactical groups with 190,000 troops, field hospitals, support elements and even units of blood to be transported to the frontline. Moreover, the UK and US published intelligence on Russian plans to install a puppet government in Kyiv in late January, a few weeks before the actual *coup de main* was attempted.

In February, the CIA published the operational plan for the attack on the Antonov airport at Hostomel. There were still talks going on, but they were entirely fruitless, as was the meeting between US secretary Anthony Blinken and Russia's foreign minister Sergei Lavrov in Geneva. A flurry of Western diplomatic activity took place at this time—president Macron and chancellor Scholz both went to Moscow and called president Putin several times, to no avail.

Russia recognized Donetsk and Luhansk as 'independent republics' on 21 February 2022.

During this time, the Biden administration consulted widely with allies and with Ukraine, but it was clearly the US that led. Its closest ally was Britain, but this is only to be expected, given the close intelligence sharing between these states.

Arms Aid to Ukraine, 2022–2023

There was little or no discussion of arms aid in Europe. In the US, this has been one of the few issues that was agreed upon across party lines, while Germany shifted its policy position in a so-called '*Zeitenwende*', a total change in its posture towards Russia (see chapter 8).

Some Western governments tried to avoid being laggards: while the Norwegian government was to supply helmets and shrapnel vests, the Germans suddenly decided on anti-tank weapons. And then, that same afternoon, Norway announced the delivery of T-72s. As we shall see, this pattern was visible also later, pointing to the logic of alliance dependence: wanting to be close to the Americans and in the 'right' company, but not wanting to go first and assume risk.

Country after country followed the American and British lead in the matter of weapons to Ukraine. We can see the rapid progression of support by studying the timeline of donations: many countries, such as Norway, Canada and Germany, were initially supposed to stick to 'non-lethal aid', but this quickly changed throughout the spring of 2022. We also find continuous assistance at all levels from the US and the UK for a ten-year period from 2012, notably a discreet 'train, advise, and assist' mission to Ukraine.

As noted, the UDCG comprises a very extensive group of countries; from this, arms aid from Australia and South Korea has been included. This emphasizes that the Ukraine war not only concerns Europe and the United States. Levels of commitment are nevertheless uneven. France is a significant player, although one can get the impression of the opposite in much of the public debate. French arms exports to Ukraine were the most important of all until 2012, and since then a great deal has been given to the Kyiv authorities. At the end of November 2022, for example, long-range French artillery arrived.

The Nordic region is also strongly present, with significant contributions from all the Nordic countries, including Sweden and Finland. In Central Europe, the picture is complex—Poland is heavily involved with both large donations, an increase in its own defence budget and with the transport of almost all materiel into Ukraine. The Baltic countries give very much as a percentage per capita, especially Lithuania, while the Czech Republic is deeply involved on Ukraine's side. Several donations are old Soviet material, which these states are able to have replaced from Germany through the so-called *Ringtausch* or from the United States. Hungary stands out as the only country that does not want to deliver or transport weapons; it only contributes humanitarianly. Romania too provides only 'non-lethal aid'.[8]

In a well-documented article in *The New Yorker*, Yaffa writes about the US, British and Ukrainian military cooperation, which dates back to 2012. The US changed its approach when the Americans saw how solidly Ukraine was fighting: 'The Ukrainians were putting up a good fight, which helped open up the flood-gates for a lot more military assistance'.[9]

If we look more closely at the timeline for arms aid, it is clear that the most engaged countries in the north and east were the earliest to make contributions.[10] The continental powers of Germany and France, which had formerly been considered the natural 'leaders' of Europe, then followed suit.[11]

More significantly, perhaps, for the first time the EU was also supplying weapons for an ongoing war through its European Peace Facility fund, a fund that, despite its name, pays for weapons that member states buy through a 'war chest'. This is a diplomatic revolution; in a very short time, an organization that has always been characterized by non-military means and with a security policy only focused on crisis management and not conventional war or aid for conflicts, there has been a complete change. The initiative has largely been taken by the European

Commission, and the fund is outside the EU budget. The European Commission coordinates purchases and deliveries or finances individual countries' contributions.[12]

Looking at the statistics of weapons deliveries, the US was the absolutely dominant player with a total support equivalent to more than $500 billion in 2022 and more in 2023. Congress has passed package after package of military and humanitarian aid. US aid accounts for about 90% of all arms aid, followed by aid from Britain, Poland and the Baltics. The UK was by far the largest donor in Europe, followed by Poland and the Baltic states if we measure per capita. However, much of this comprised legacy weapons that were already phased out.

Aid from the northern and eastern countries was stepped up in the run-up to the invasion. Poland reinforced NATO in the east early on, while Lithuania sent defensive equipment in December 2021 and in January 2022. The British delivered 2,000 anti-tank weapons and were the first to send armoured vehicles and long-range artillery.

After much hesitation and contradictory political signals, Germany announced it would provide main battle tanks in late January 2023. This was a critical moment in the coalition's short history in which Germany seemed to back out from pledges made earlier. The announcement was only marred by a clarifying statement that it would take up to a year for the vehicles to be made serviceable.

Air power remained a weak point. Ukraine fights an offensive without significant air power, something that is both extremely difficult and rare. The UDCG discussed donations of fighter planes for a very long time, but the US ruled out this weapon system despite its key role in war fighting. Some Europeans pushed for this, however, including Poland, the British, the Balts, the Dutch and the Danes. In late August 2023, the US agreed to allow for the donation of F-16s and the training of pilots. By then, the French had also opted to train pilots on their Rafale plane. This and the F-16 exist in large numbers in Western states and are being phased out. Yet these complex weapon systems depend on much maintenance and availability of spare parts, and it will therefore take around a year or more after the decision was made for them to be operational in Ukraine.

Norway again followed others, announcing the donation of 19 F-16s on Ukraine's national day in August, and Sweden announced that it may give JAS Gripens.

The US has been conservative and cautious in making decisions to donate new weapon systems and had resisted donating very long-range artillery (ATAC-MS) for more than a year, but it finally announced[13] that a few pieces would be given to Ukraine during president Zelensky's visit to the White House in late September 2023. However, these come with the same caveat as other donations—they are not to be used to attack inside Russia. Yet they can reach targets in Crimea, and in sufficient numbers, make for a major change in the war. The Biden offer is only for a few weapon systems of this kind, however.

US–UK Role in Military Planning with Ukraine

In the summer of 2022, the Ukrainians launched two offensives that were successful. The Americans and the British helped Ukraine with planning, munitions supply and weapons. When Russia started to move their most able troops south in order to defend Kherson, 'the Ukrainian military proposed two offensives'.[14] The US, UK and Ukraine assessed the plan, wargaming it, and found that it was possible, provided new materiel came from the US, 'but the plan depended *entirely on size and pace of additional military aid from the US*' (my emphasis).[15]

This 'began to take shape months ago during a series of intense conversations between Ukrainian and US officials ...'.[16]

US National Security Adviser Jake Sullivan spoke with Andriy Yermak, his counterpart in Kyiv, and General Mark Milley, the US defence chief, was in close contact with his Ukrainian counterpart: 'Throughout August, at the behest of the Ukrainians, US officials stepped up feeds of intelligence about the position of the Russian forces, highlighting the weakness in the Russian lines'.[17] This was an ingenious military manoeuvre, for the Russians believed that the attack was coming on Kherson and moved their best forces there. When this happened, the Ukrainians attacked towards Kharkiv.

Again, it was the Americans who led the way and provided the necessary military aid from the United States.[18] The British played a key role, and these two states have, as said, been training Ukrainian soldiers from 2012.

Although the offensive was successful, the front line is long (about 1,000 km), and there are huge areas to be recaptured. A debate about the productive capacity of weapons and ammunition arose at this time. Ammunition was being consumed in staggering quantities in Ukraine, and it is clear that the West's production lines cannot keep up. What has been sent to Ukraine so far is often from stockpiles and legacy weaponry. The West's production of ammunition has been at a low level for the whole post-Cold War period.

In an overview of stockpiles based on public sources, the Center for Strategic and International Studies shows that Javelins, HIMARS, MLRS rockets, Stingers and 155-mm artillery ammunition are thinning in the US, to name the most important items. In November 2022, the United States ordered 100,000 artillery shells from South Korea that we have to assume are going to Ukraine—but that only covers about a month's consumption.[19]

The West has used up stockpiles during the first months of the war, and, due to difficulties in obtaining inputs in time, cannot easily increase production. With a daily consumption of between 5,000 and 10,000 such shells, it is clear that production in the West cannot keep pace unless one wants to escalate to war production. This sensitive issue is important, but not one discussed in detail publicly. Yet in industrial warfare, relative production capacity is a major factor, and this kicked in from the fall of 2022.[20]

This is an issue of relative production capacity, and here the sanctions against Russia come in as an important factor. A much-discussed and very comprehensive study from Yale University shows that sanctions work and that they affect technology needed in weapons production. One source claims that the Russians need to cannibalize household electronics to find semiconductors that can be used in weapons, but this could just as easily be a propaganda story. US political science professor[21] Bruce Jentleson, an expert on sanctions, concludes that 'claims about sanctions driving Putin to economic oblivion and wrecking Putin's war machine don't reflect the full picture'.[22]

There is still a steady flow of weapons to Ukraine from Western countries. The United States has maintained its leading role after the so-called November 2022 midterm elections, which did not yield strong gains for the isolationist wing of the Republican Party. Ukrainian advances in the field are a direct result of Western arms deliveries, and so far none of the countries in the coalition have openly disagreed with the United States on this strategy.

As mentioned, US reservations continued with regard to ATAC-MS long-range artillery (300 km), but Britain supplied Storm Shadow missiles (250-km range). Britain and Poland spear-headed action for supplying what Ukraine needs, and the US seemed to agree after a while. Washington restricted its weapons supply in the beginning, wanting to ensure that the war did not escalate, yet the evolution of the war indicates that Russian reactions to Western arms supplies are largely rhetorical.

In sum, the US continues to lead in supplying arms to Ukraine, and there are no states in the coalition that have opted out of it. Yet the problem of production capacity is rather acute, and there are some signs of deeper cooperation or integration on this score.

During the first year of the war, much old Soviet equipment was sent to Ukraine from Eastern Europe, only to be replaced by Western materiel. As stocks were depleted, however, Western weaponry was sent to Ukraine, and soldiers from Ukraine were given training in these systems at record speed. Artillery ammunition changed from Soviet 122 mm to NATO standard 155 mm. Ukraine is gradually being integrated with NATO systems and NATO standards by virtue of this transfer of military 'know-how' and technology—an unintended yet important aspect of the arms aid.

Furthermore, the weapons delivery effort proves that close multinational cooperation within the Ukraine Defense Contact Group exists. The US has put pressure on the French and the Germans on the supply of, for example, fighting vehicles, such as the Bradley from the US, Marder from Germany and the AMX-10 from France.[23] The supply of these rather heavy weapons in turn led to the supply of main battle tanks. The US put very heavy pressure on Germany to supply Leopard 2A tanks, the result of which is German permission to deliver these from Finland and Poland, when they declared that they would proceed anyway. Eventually Germany itself delivered the tanks. The British offer of 14 Challenger 2 tanks came right before the German permission was given, underscoring the leading role that it plays. The timing was important here—when the US, the UK, Poland and Finland declared their willingness to supply main battle tanks, Germany also followed.

The US is in a position to lead by example but also to apply the necessary pressure. For example, in dire need of more production capacity for artillery ammunition, Norway suddenly announced the construction of major new lines of production for the 155-mm artillery rounds on 13 January 2022. Nammo, the producer, is one of only three in Europe, the others being Rheinmetall in Germany and Nexter in France. The author talked with Nammo representatives only two days prior to this announcement, and they were at that time disappointed that the Norwegian government did not act on their request for a much more modest production line increase (650 million NOK). Then, like a *deus ex machina*, a colossal increase (2.6 billion NOK) was announced. One may surmise that allied requests have played a role here.

In sum, there is a movement towards more integration in the coalition and towards the supply of heavier weapons as the war grinds on. The US has been leading, with Britain, Poland and the Baltic countries as key supporting states. There is also more commitment to the strategy that Ukraine must win on the battlefield as the requirements of warfare itself are more pressing—can a combined arms offensive be launched without air power? Could infantry fighting vehicles be of use without main battle tanks?

What Explains the Coalition?

The question is why so many states have opted for sending weapons to Ukraine, a non-NATO member state. Why not follow the 'script' after 2015; sanctions and condemnation, but no weapons assistance?

One explanation is that where the US leads, others follow—the logic of alliance dependence that is often seen in optional wars, such as International Security Assistance Force in Afghanistan and, before that, the American-led Operation Enduring Freedom in 2001. Countries that rely on security guarantees follow its hegemon, and alliance-dependent states try to achieve reassurance from the state providing security while having to show solidarity when said state expects contributions.[24] Being a good ally is so important that it is actually the title of the Afghanistan report on Norwegian participation there, entitled *A Good Ally*.[25] When the leading NATO states—the US and the UK—take the initiative, most follow suit. In this case, only Hungary refuses to send weapons to Ukraine. Everyone else is on board. Sweden and Finland are also sending weapons, both prior to formal membership. One indicator that alliance dependence explains the coalition is that the European allies followed the US lead in 2014 as well when the reaction against Russia consisted of political condemnation and sanctions, but not arms aid. Prior to this, Europe also agreed with the United States' reaction when Russia invaded two regions in Georgia in 2008 despite the fact that states in Europe disagreed with the United States in offering membership to Georgia and Ukraine.

The counterfactual question when assessing alliance dependence is whether Europe would have provided arms aid to Ukraine if the United States had not done so. After all, the United States is far away from Ukraine and protected by an ocean, while Ukraine is located in the middle of Europe. It is highly possible that the British, Poles and Balts would have provided arms, but highly questionable whether others would have done so. What we do know about European preparation is that there was a refusal to believe that invasion would come till the very last minute, and that this option (of arms supply) was not given any attention for this reason. Since few believed an invasion would occur, countermeasures were not planned and arms aid was simply not discussed in European capitals.[26]

Another explanation is that this aggressive war implies that something extremely important is at stake, namely the UN Charter's prohibition of aggression and fundamental rules of warfare as enshrined in the Geneva Conventions and other *in bello* rules. The war must therefore be countered, lest the rest of Europe be imperiled: the murder of civilians, torture, attacks on civilian targets and massacres are all clear and frightening violations of international law and basic human rights. We have not seen this in Europe since Srebrenica in 1995 and the wars in the Balkans, including the attempts at ethnic cleansing in Kosovo in 1999.

We see evidence of this in the German reaction, where public opinion obviously cannot be neutral in the face of massacres in Ukraine, and the same happened in 1999 when Germany participated in the NATO operation against Serbia despite the lack of a UN mandate and German reluctance to use military force outside its borders. But in general, too, the values at stake are of paramount importance—when President Biden began to label President Putin a war criminal, many diplomats shook their heads, because Biden had thereby made negotiation with Putin impossible. That's true, but what was also true was that massive war crimes have been committed in the invasion attempt. While Western forces are carefully trained to follow the international law of war (Geneva-Hague 'law'), it is clear that Russian forces are not following these universal principles and rules. The warfare in Syria as well as in Chechnya showed the same contempt for civilian lives as in Ukraine. The difference between Russian conduct and the values that apply *in bello* is clear, and all evidence of abuse is systematically denied by Russia.

There is, in addition, the explanation that has to do with the concept of extended deterrence: if Russia can attack Ukraine with impunity, other states such as China will learn the lesson and perhaps attack Taiwan. Others may follow. As Stephen Walt proposes, this is a situation of balance of threat—a need to act because of the threat that the Russian invasion poses to all of Europe and beyond.[27] Walt's criteria include geographical proximity, and here Europe is relevant, but the United States is not. One should therefore expect Europe to act first, not the US. The invasion represents a radical change: Russia invades a neighbouring country without provocation or pretext. This was a shock to everyone in NATO and beyond, and led to the Finnish application for NATO membership, followed by Sweden. Thus, the Finns saw the invasion as such a threat that the country no longer dared to be outside NATO, even with many bilateral agreements, JEF membership and Host Nation Support agreement with NATO—as well as PfP. Another strong indicator that is explained by threat is the German *volte-face* with the acceptance of increasing the defence budget to 2% of GDP. Norway also considered the threat picture to be elevated and entered a new phase in its armed forces' plans from 1 November 2022; the threat was also defined by Prime Minister Støre as 'a vulnerable security situation'. [28]

In general, one can say with certainty that the reaction in Europe was one of shock over the Russian invasion of a neighbouring country and this is clearly different from the previous reaction to the annexation of Crimea in 2014. But in the United States as well, the consequences of allowing Russia to act in this way would entail that the United States abdicate its role as the world's leading power. After World War II, the US assumed the role of the 'world's policeman', but has often wanted to be out of this role, evidenced most recently in a speech Biden gave after the withdrawal from Afghanistan in 2021. There, the main message was that the United States should not enter unnecessary 'wars without end'. But the arms aid to Ukraine is an expression of the opposite, and we must assume that the assessment of China has played a significant role in US strategy.

In sum, while we can assume that alliance dependence explains much of the coalition and the arms aid provided, the important question is why the United States took this step in 2022 but not in 2014 or 2008. The decision on some arms supply to Ukraine was taken long before the invasion—such arms aid began in the summer of 2021. At the same time, the United States deployed more soldiers and materiel to Eastern Europe. The American decision to step up arms and aid to Ukraine was thus logical as it started well in advance of the invasion. US and British training of Ukrainian forces go back to 2012. Yet these measures were well within PfP projects.

This is where the strategic logic comes into play and may explain the resolute policy of organizing major arms supplies after 24 February, for Putin's misjudgment opened a window of opportunity in which Russian conventional power could be weakened without American casualties. When the US saw how motivated and capable Ukrainians were, their own willingness to send weapons increased, a source said.[29] In addition, we must take into account the latest US security strategy where Russia is seen as an 'acute problem' but China is seen as the defining challenge.[30] It is China that is the major threat in this strategy, hence the importance of extended deterrence, and perhaps of weakening Russia, China's ally. Above all, the main principles of sovereignty and non-intervention, human rights and humanitarian law become markers of civilization, 'red lines' in themselves. These values and principles are all contested by both Russia and China and have been so for a long time.

What we know so far about US decision-making supports balance-of-threat theory, although questions of value and principle can also be classified as relevant to threat because the very fact of having autocratic regimes that are also aggressive represents a threat to basic human rights.

The Frontline States and the Pragmatists in the Coalition

The war has arguably changed the balance of power in security policy in Europe: America's closest allies are now Britain and Poland; in Poland there are now US bases with 10,000 US troops and there has been an enormous increase in the national defence budget. Poland is building Europe's largest land power to counter a Russian threat and is ordering more than 1,000 tanks among other things.[31] Poland is one of the NATO states that has responded most dramatically to the war in Ukraine, and it has been and remains invaluable to the United States in transporting weapons into Ukraine. Much the same can be said about the Baltic states as well as Slovakia, the Czech Republic and Romania. With the exception of Hungary, Central Europe has become much more important within the NATO alliance and in relations with the United States than before. Yet these states are dependent on the US more than security providers in their own right, with the exception of Poland.

Finnish and Swedish membership of NATO also strengthens the northern dimension, in which Norway also participates. The Nordic countries discuss integration among themselves as part of NATO, and the key leading state in Northern European defence is Britain. The Nordics are rich countries and can contribute well to NATO if they want to.

The British have strengthened their position in Europe because of their leadership role in Ukraine policy and are now also cooperating well with the EU on other policies. The war has shown that it is the transatlantic relationship that counts, not the intra-European one, and that it is also nations that remain the building blocks of European security.[32,33]

But what about Germany and France, and their joint leadership in the EU? 'Im Osten wächst das Misstrauen gegenüber Berlin und Paris' ('In the East there is growing distrust of Berlin and

Paris'), writes[34] *Die Welt*.[35] For NATO has been strengthened at the expense of the European Union's military plans.[36] Thus, France's room for 'European autonomy' is also limited; its defence role will have to evolve within NATO, not the European Union. France is increasingly displaying this policy with regard to Ukraine, as the latest *Revue strategique* from the French Ministry of Defence emphasizes in its first sentence: 'L'invasion de l'Ukraine par la Russie, le 24 février 2022, représente un glissement stratégique' ('The Russian invasion of Ukraine on 24th February 22 represents a strategic shift').[37]

It remains to be seen, however, whether France will be able to assume a leadership position in Europe alongside Britain, the other great power with military capability for leadership. 'A view is emerging that NATO's centre of gravity is shifting from France and Germany towards the East and North', writes *The Economist*.[38] At the Munich Security Conference in February 2023, French President Macron said negotiations with Russia remain important. He also said that those who think about regime change in Russia do not know their own best interests because any change there will be for the worse. Those who want to attack targets inside Russia (which is perfectly legal and logical for Ukraine) and weaken Russia are on the wrong track, he believes: [39] 'These observers want above all to crush Russia. That has never been France's position and never will be'.[40]

We can assume this is also the German position, but Germany has undermined the little credibility it has as a military actor through its attempt to say no to the important Leopard 2 tank capability.

The implication is therefore that France stands quite alone in its idea of strategic 'autonomy' in Europe with the EU as an actor base. The Franco–German 'engine' in the EU is no longer able to start. Germany is not credible as an actor that can and will use military force—deterrence is a function of both the ability and the will to win the battle if attacked. While France is a strong and strategic player in Europe, along with the British, the value of Germany as a partner is probably weakened in terms of deterrence after the hesitation over the supply of arms, especially Leopard tanks.

Macron and his peers are right that Russia is not going away, that Putin is likely to stay in office long after this war—and that a successor could probably be worse. In international politics, stability in itself is important—the worst-case scenario for Europe is a chaotic and unstable Russia with power struggles without governance. Then nuclear weapons could come into play because control of them might become precarious. The question is whether this implies negotiations sooner than later.

To sum up, it is clear that NATO has been strengthened as a military alliance and that the EU's ambitions to be a military actor are less realistic than before the war. Central Europe looks to the US and the UK, as do the Nordic countries. There is a frontline coalition and a pragmatic group in the UDCG, and the former consists of states that look to Britain and above all, the US, for leadership.

How Durable is the Coalition?

The year 2024 is election year in the US. The president will be extremely concerned about re-election, and his opponent will be Donald Trump, if not another Republican, like Ron DeSantis. Already, Congress's contribution to Ukraine is much debated as Republicans hold a majority in the House of Representatives, and this is a majority that is small and dependent on the Trump wing. We have seen how strong the American leadership is in this war, so whether it disappears or weakens, what is Europe doing?[41]

Commentator Walter Russel Mead puts it bluntly: 'The Continent's hopes rely on GOP votes in Congress'.[42] Europe doesn't care much about Ohio and Florida, he adds, which are some of the places important for continued support for Ukraine: 'Europe is walking on thin ice'.[43]

The German hesitancy to give tanks to Ukraine shows how risk-averse German politicians are. Of course, this makes them even less attractive as a strategic partner for France, which probably has the foremost strategic culture in Europe. It is claimed that President Macron has concluded that NATO must be the scene of French allied policy going forward, not the EU. This is logical, because the leadership of Ukrainian and Russian policy in terms of military means is neither French nor German, but American, British and Polish.[44]

Therefore, the division of labour is now a reality: the EU's power is primarily economic, but also political in terms of enlargement and in relations with Russia and the rest of the world. The diplomatic and economic instruments are of course of enormous importance over a long period of time—the EU is as strong a player as the United States. A united EU will be even more important in shaping China's policy. Here we see contradictions between the US and the EU, and this is nothing new. Many a 'trade war' has been fought between these two over the years. The importance of a united Europe will therefore be even greater in the future.

This contradiction may be said to have been sharpened in the recent past. The German chancellor went to China with a large business delegation in November 2022, the first such visit to China in more than 3 years.[45] The visit was pragmatic when it came to trade, but this is obviously indistinguishable from politics. Following this, came China's state visit to Moscow in March 2023, which led to more cooperation but without direct support from China for the war in Ukraine. Nevertheless, there was still no condemnation of the attack on Ukraine from the Chinese side, but there was a presentation of a twelve-point

219

peace plan.[46] The latter says nothing about who is to blame for the war, and all the points are quite general and generic. The Chinese initiative was dismissed as a kind of 'stunt' by the US to portray China as a neutral peace mediator.[47] Commenting on the move, Jake Sullivan and Secretary of State Blinken said it was meant to provide cover for Chinese support for Russia while portraying China as neutral and willing to mediate.

Nevertheless, President Emmanuel Macron and European Commission chair Ursula von der Leyen travelled to China with a large business delegation in April 2023. Macron was clear that China must use its influence in Moscow, but the host in Beijing did not take part in statements beyond the purely banal.[48,49]

Trade was the main purpose of the journey. The visit resulted in, among other things, the sale of 160 Airbus aircraft to China. In light of the US rejection of the 'peace plan several weeks earlier, there was nothing to indicate that the West would have made any progress towards China. Setting up a major trade delegation trip to China at such a time undermines Western cohesion, as a Politico commentator said.[50] 'China is driving a wedge into Western unity', wrote Time Magazine.[51] Criticism of the trip was strong.[52]

We observe a certain dividing line in the Western camp at the moment—the French state visit to China in April 2023 was heavily criticized by many who believe that it gives China an ability to divide the West and that President Macron was used as a wedge. In an interview after returning from the state visit, he warned against following US policy and advocated for 'strategic autonomy' for Europe. But it is China that decides what happens to Taiwan and that is rearming itself; it is not the United States.[53]

As the war drags on, war weariness sets in and weapons suppliers find their cupboards bare, as Schake points out in chapter 7. The UDCG cannot last for years at this level of war intensity, and the US will be wholly preoccupied with the presidential elections in 2024.

Conclusion

It seems that the frontline states agree to continue cooperation; Britain and Poland stand out in this regard. These states, along with the Baltic states, Finland and perhaps also Norway and Sweden see Russia as a threat that must be deterred. They share strategic threat assessments and can therefore integrate deeper than before. Here one should add that NATO's new Strategic Concept, as discussed by Sweijs and de Klerk, outlines the details of such deterrence. Thus, the frontline states should and can integrate with each other inside the context of NATO.

NATO has been strengthened due to the war, with new members and a renewed emphasis on deterring Russia, and the coalition around British leadership in Northern Europe has been strengthened as well. As chapter 9 on Finland underlines, formal membership and integration in coalitions of the like-minded states go hand in hand.

Thus, the Russian invasion of Ukraine has resulted in a clear strengthening of the formal military alliance—NATO—as both Finland and Sweden rushed to join, concluding that only formal membership in the protection policy of a US nuclear 'umbrella' would suffice. The same applies to Ukraine whose main goal is to join the alliance, not just to have an informal cooperation arrangement. Partnership with NATO is not enough—only membership. But the importance of formal membership does not diminish the usefulness of coalitions; in fact, when all coalition states are also member states of NATO, such coalitions are stronger, as suggested at the outset of this chapter.

The UDCG is a large coalition of states, probably united by the interest in being allies with the US and leading NATO states. It carries a cost to refrain from donating weapons to Ukraine in the sense that the key actor of NATO, the US, expects allies to contribute, and clearly those that do get to cooperate closely with the US. We have seen that the 'frontline states' in the coalition, the US, some Nordic countries, Balts, Poles and the Dutch, have been acting as a spearhead for donating heavy weapons systems to Ukraine. These states in Northern Europe are increasingly integrated, a development spurred by having Russia as a common adversary.

Moreover, taking seriously the need to deter major war in the time ahead will require integration of arms production and procurement. The war has shown how European states have 'thin red lines' in terms of ammunition stocks and production capacity. This can only be remedied with more cooperation and integration among states. Rising defence procurement cost, low if any growth, inflation and the need for much more defence spending brings back the cost factor as a driver of integration.

NOTES

1. INTRODUCTION

1. Bence Nemeth, *How to Achieve Defence Cooperation in Europe? The Subregional Approach* (Bristol University Press, 2022).
2. Ibid.
3. Ibid.
4. At the time of writing Sweden had not yet acceded to NATO, but this was expected to be in October 2023. Finland had joined.
5. Letter of intent, Nordic air forces, 6 April 2023.
6. HM Government, The Integrated Review Refresh 2023, UK, p. 22, https://assets.publishing.service.gov.uk/government/uploads/system/uploads/attachment_data/file/1145586/11857435_NS_IR_Refresh_2023_Supply_AllPages_Revision_7_WEB_PDF.pdf.
7. Press conference after Chief of Defence meeting (meeting of the most senior position of the armed forces in each member country of NATO), Holmenkollen Hotel, 17 September 2023.

2. MULTIDOMAIN INTEGRATION AND MULTIDOMAIN OPERATIONS

1. Dave Johnson, *Shared Problems: The Lessons of AirLand Battle and the 31 Initiatives for Multi-Domain Battle* (Santa Monica, CA: RAND, 2018), https://www.rand.org/pubs/perspectives/PE301.html (Accessed April 2022).

2. Michael Kofman, 'It's Time to Talk About A2/AD: Rethinking the Russian Military Challenge', *War on the Rocks*, 5 September, 2019, https://warontherocks.com/2019/09/its-time-to-talk-about-a2-ad-rethinking-the-russian-military-challenge (accessed April 2022).
3. Frank Hoffman and Michael C. Davies, 'Joint Force 2020 and The Human Domain: Time for A New Conceptual Framework?', *Small Wars Journal*, 2013, https://smallwarsjournal.com/jrnl/art/joint-force-2020-and-the-human-domain-time-for-a-new-conceptual-framework; UK Joint Doctrine Note 4/13 Culture and Human Terrain, https://assets.publishing.service.gov.uk/government/uploads/system/uploads/attachment_data/file/819815/archive_doctrine_uk_culture_human_terrain_jdn_4_13.pdf#:~:text=Joint%20Doctrine%20Publication%20%28JDP%29%2004%2C%20Understandingintroduced%20the%20idea,Doctrine%20Publication%20%28JDP%29%200-01%2C%20British%20Defence%20Doctrine%28BDD%29%2C%204thedition (accessed April 2022).
4. US Army Training and Doctrine Command (TRADOC), 'The US Army in Multi-Domain Operations 2028', 6 December 2018, https://api.army.mil/e2/c/downloads/2021/02/26/b45372c1/20181206-tp525-3-1-the-us-army-in-mdo-2028-final.pdf (accessed April 2022).
5. US Air Force (USAF), 'Air Force Doctrine Note 1-20: USAF Role in Joint All-Domain Operations', 2020, https://www.doctrine.af.mil/Portals/61/documents/Notes/Joint%20All-Domain%20Operations%20Doctrine--CSAF%20signed.pdf (accessed April 2022).
6. Video showing multidomain battle space scenario: https://www.youtube.com/watch?v=car1O_qfkW0 (17 July 2017).
7. See, for example, Tayfun Ozberk, 'Analysis: Chain Of Negligence Caused The Loss Of The Moskva Cruiser', *NavalNews*, 17 April 2022.
8. Justin Bronk, Nick Reynolds and Jack Watling, 'The Russian Air War and Ukrainian Requirements for Air Defence', *JRUSI*, 7 December 2022.

3. THE NATO 2022 STRATEGIC CONCEPT

1. Daniel S. Hamilton and Hans Binnendijk, 'One Plus Four: Charting NATO's Future in an Age of Disruption', NATO Task Force Report, accessed 21 April 2023, https://www.transatlantic.org/wp-content/uploads/2022/02/NATO-TF-SC-final-feb-16-2022.pdf.
2. James Lacey, *Great Strategic Rivalries: From the Classical World to the Cold War* (New York: Oxford University Press, 2016), 511.
3. Kristen Gunness et al., 'Anticipating Chinese Reactions to U.S. Posture Enhancements', Research Reports (RAND Corporation, 2022), https://doi.org/10.7249/RRA1581-1.
4. 'The Godfather' (United States: Paramount Pictures, 1972).
5. Tad A. Schnaufer II, 'The US-NATO Relationship: The Cost of Maintaining Political Pressure on Allies', *Georgetown Journal of International Affairs* (blog), 15 January 2021, https://gjia.georgetown.edu/2021/01/15/the-us-nato-relationship-the-cost-of-maintaining-political-pressure-on-allies/.
6. Jim Garamone, 'NATO Stands Together as Biden Reaffirms U.S. Commitment to Alliance', U.S. Department of Defense, accessed 9 May 2023, https://www.defense.gov/News/News-Stories/Article/Article/2658794/nato-stands-together-as-biden-reaffirms-us-commitment-to-alliance/.
7. The White House, 'National Security Strategy', White Paper (Washington, DC: White House, 2022), https://www.whitehouse.gov/wp-content/uploads/2022/10/Biden-Harris-Administrations-National-Security-Strategy-10.2022.pdf.
8. Beatrice Heuser, *The Evolution of Strategy: Thinking War from Antiquity to the Present* (Cambridge University Press, 2010), 5, https://doi.org/10.1017/CBO9780511762895.
9. Lawrence Freedman, *Strategy: A History* (New York: Oxford University Press, 2013), 498.
10. NATO, 'The Official NATO Terminology Database', NATOTerm, accessed 9 May 2023, https://nso.nato.int/natoterm/Web.mvc.
11. 'NATO Strategic Concept 2022', https://www.nato.int/nato_static_fl2014/assets/pdf/2022/6/pdf/220629-factsheet-strategic-concept-en.pdf, accessed 6 February 2023, https://www.nato.

int/nato_static_fl2014/assets/pdf/2022/6/pdf/220629-factsheet-strategic-concept-en.pdf.
12. Jens Ringsmose and Sten Rynning, 'NATO's New Strategic Concept: A Comprehensive Assessment' (Danish Institute for International Studies, 2011).
13. NATO, Official NATO Website: https://www.nato.int/cps/en/natohq/topics_56626.htm, accessed October 23, 2023.
14. Vasile Cretu, 'NATO Post-Madrid Si Conceptul Strategic 2022: Intre Continuitate Si Schimbare' XIV (September 24, 2022): 15–28.
15. Ismail Erkam Sula and Cagla Luleci, 'Bridging the Gap between Theory and Practice: The Evolution of NATO's Security Agenda', *Turkish Journal of International Relations* 12, no. 2 (2013).
16. Sean Monaghan, 'Resetting NATO's Defense and Deterrence: The Sword and the Shield Redux', 28 June 2022, https://www.csis.org/analysis/resetting-natos-defense-and-deterrence-sword-and-shield-redux.
17. Ezio Pistotti, 'A Report by the Military Committee to the Defence Planning Committee on the Overall Strategic Concept for the Defense of the North Atlantic Treaty Organization Area', NATO Strategy Documents 1949–69 (NATO, 1968), 351.
18. Ismail Erkam Sula and Cagla Luleci, 'Bridging the Gap between Theory and Practice: The Evolution of NATO's Security Agenda'.
19. C.H. Donnelly, 'Note by the Secretary to the North Atlantic Military Committee on the Strategic Concept for the Defense of the North Atlantic Area', Strategic Concept, NATO Strategy Documents 1949–69 (NATO, 1949), 23.
20. C.H. Donnelly, 'Note by the Secretary to the North Atlantic Defense Committee on The Strategic Concept for the Defense of the North Atlantic Treaty', Strategic Concept, NATO Strategy Documents 1949–69 (NATO, 1952), 188.
21. Eugene A. Salet, 'A Report by the Military Committee on the Overall Strategic Concept for the Defense of the North Atlantic Treaty Organization Area', NATO Strategy Documents 1949–69 (NATO, 1957), 293.
22. Ezio Pistotti, 'A Report by the Military Committee to the Defence Planning Committee on the Overall Strategic Concept for the Defense of the North Atlantic Treaty Organization Area'.

23. 'The Alliance's New Strategic Concept', Strategic Concept (NATO, 1991).
24. 'The Alliance's Strategic Concept', Strategic Concept (NATO, 1999).
25. 'Active Engagement, Modern Defence—NATO 2010 Strategic Concept', Strategic Concept (NATO, 2010), https://www.nato.int/cps/en/natohq/official_texts_68580.htm.
26. For a brief but useful introduction, see Michael E. Porter, 'What Is Strategy?', *Harvard Business Review*, 1 November 1996, https://hbr.org/1996/11/what-is-strategy. Michael D. Watkins, 'Demystifying Strategy: The What, Who, How, and Why', *Harvard Business Review*, 10 September 2007, https://hbr.org/2007/09/demystifying-strategy-the-what.
27. 'Scowcroft Center for Strategy and Security', *Atlantic Council* (blog), accessed 3 February 2023, https://www.atlanticcouncil.org/programs/scowcroft-center-for-strategy-and-security/. 'NATO's Strategic Concept: Three Do's and Don'ts', 10 June 2021, https://css.ethz.ch/en/center/CSS-news/2021/06/natos-strategic-concept-three-dos-and-donts.html.
28. NATO, 'NATO 2022—Strategic Concept' (NATO, June 2022), para. 6, https://www.nato.int/strategic-concept/.
29. NATO 2022, para. 8.
30. NATO 2022, para. 13.
31. Bruno Tertrais, 'An Evolutionary, Not Revolutionary, Strategic Concept', in *NATO's New Strategic Concept* (NATO Defense College, 2022).
32. NATO, 'NATO 2022—Strategic Concept', para. 18.
33. 'NATO's New Strategic Concept: What Should We Expect?', Martens Centre, accessed 13 February 2023, https://www.martenscentre.eu/publication/natos-new-strategic-concept-what-should-we-expect/.
34. 'Scowcroft Center for Strategy and Security'.
35. NATO, 'NATO 2022—Strategic Concept', para. 20.
36. Bruno Tertrais, 'An Evolutionary, Not Revolutionary, Strategic Concept', 29.
37. NATO, 'NATO 2022 - Strategic Concept', para. 31.
38. 'Active Engagement, Modern Defence—NATO 2010 Strategic Concept'; Thierry Tardy, 'Six Takeaways from NATO's New Strategic

Concept', in *NATO's New Strategic Concept* (NATO Defense College, 2022), 15, https://frstrategie.org/sites/default/files/documents/publications/autres/2022/NDC_RP_25.pdf.

39. Alessandro Marrone, 'NATO's New Strategic Concept: Novelties and Priorities', Text, IAI Istituto Affari Internazionali, 7 July 2022, https://www.iai.it/en/pubblicazioni/natos-new-strategic-concept-novelties-and-priorities.
40. NATO, 'NATO 2022 - Strategic Concept', para. 41.
41. Sven Biscop, 'The New Force Model: NATO's European Army?', 2022, https://www.egmontinstitute.be/the-new-force-model-natos-european-army/.
42. NATO, 'New NATO Force Model', n.d., https://www.nato.int/nato_static_fl2014/assets/pdf/2022/6/pdf/220629-infographic-new-nato-force-model.pdf.
43. Loic Simonet, 'NATO's 2022 Strategic Concept: Analysis and Implications for Austria', 2023, https://nbn-resolving.org/urn:nbn:de:0168-ssoar-85195-9.
44. Jens Stoltenberg and Joe Biden, 'Remarks by NATO Secretary General Jens Stoltenberg and US President Joe Biden at the Start of the 2022 NATO Summit', NATO, June 2022, https://www.nato.int/cps/en/natohq/opinions_197374.htm.
45. Lieutenant Colonel Jose Diaz de Leon, 'Understanding Multi-Domain Operations in NATO', *The Three Swords Magazine*, 2021.
46. General Philippe Lavigne, 'French Air Force Supreme Allied Commander Transformation' (NATO, n.d.), https://www.jwc.nato.int/application/files/7916/6067/2972/02-Foreword_Supreme_Allied_Commander_Transformation.pdf#:-:text=This%20is%20a%20huge%20task,%2C%20air%2C%20space%20and%20cyberspace.
47. Andrew Tunnicliffe, 'Multi-Domain Operations in the Future Battlespace', *Army Technology* (blog), 12 September 2022, https://www.army-technology.com/features/multi-domain-operations-in-the-future-battlespace/.
48. NATO, 'NATO 2022—Strategic Concept', para. 21.
49. Thierry Tardy, 'Six Takeaways from NATO's New Strategic Concept', 11.

50. North Atlantic Council, 'Madrid Summit Declaration Issued by NATO Heads of State and Government (2022)', Summit Declaration (NATO, 29 June 2022), 18, https://www.nato.int/cps/en/natohq/official_texts_196951.htm.
51. Francisco Proença Garcia, 'NATO's New Strategic Concept', in *The Madrid Summit and NATO's New Strategic Concept*, Idn Brief (Instituto da Defesa Nacional, 2022), 7.
52. Patricia Daehnhardt, 'NATO's Response to the New Confrontational Euro-Atlantic Order', in *Idn Brief: The Madrid Summit and NATO's Strategic Concept*, Idn Brief (Instituto da Defesa Nacional, 2022), https://www.idn.gov.pt/pt/publicacoes/idnbrief/Documents/2022/IDN%20brief%20julho_Ingl%C3%AAs%202022.pdf.
53. Patrick Keller, 'The New Status Quo Concept', NATO's New Strategic Concept (NATO Defense College, 2022), https://www.jstor.org/stable/resrep43425.9.
54. The White House, 'National Security Strategy'.
55. Yascha Mounk and Roberto Stefan Foa, 'The Danger of Deconsolidation: The Democratic Disconnect', *Journal of Democracy* 27 (2016).
56. North Atlantic Council, 'Madrid Summit Declaration Issued by NATO Heads of State and Government (2022)', para. 11.
57. NATO, 'NATO 2022 - Strategic Concept', para. 41.
58. North Atlantic Council, 'Madrid Summit Declaration Issued by NATO Heads of State and Government (2022)', para. 17.
59. North Atlantic Council, para. 14.
60. Thierry Tardy, 'Six Takeaways from NATO's New Strategic Concept'.
61. Daniel S. Hamilton and Hans Binnendijk, 'One Plus Four: Charting NATO's Future in an Age of Disruption', 10.
62. Lauren Speranza, 'More in the Med: How NATO Can Refocus Its Efforts in the South and Italy Can Lead the Charge', *Atlantic Council* (blog), 22 October 2019, https://www.atlanticcouncil.org/in-depth-research-reports/report/more-in-the-med-how-nato-can-refocus-its-efforts-in-the-south-and-italy-can-lead-the-charge/.
63. NATO Public Diplomacy Division, 'Substantial NATO-Georgia Package (SNGP)', Factsheet (NATO), accessed May 12, 2023, https://www.nato.int/nato_static_fl2014/assets/pdf/pdf_2016_02/20160303_160209-factsheet-sngp-full-eng.pdf.

64. Rachel Ellehuus et al., 'NATO's 2030 Reflection Process and the New Strategic Concept' (German Council on Foreign Relations), accessed 5 May 2023, https://dgap.org/sites/default/files/article_pdfs/dgap-report-2022-03-EN_0.pdf.
65. Daniel S. Hamilton and Hans Binnendijk, 'One Plus Four: Charting NATO's Future in an Age of Disruption', 11.
66. Sven Biscop, 'The New Force Model: NATO's European Army?'
67. Ministry of Defence, 'A Stronger Netherlands, a Safer Europe: Investing in a Robust NATO and EU', Defence White Paper (Ministry of Defence, 2022).
68. Markus Kaim, 'Germany and the Madrid NATO Summit', in *The Madrid Summit and NATO's New Strategic Concept*, Idn Brief (Instituto da Defesa Nacional, 2022).
69. 'Why European Strategic Autonomy Matters | EEAS', accessed 12 May 2023, https://www.eeas.europa.eu/eeas/why-european-strategic-autonomy-matters_en.
70. Président de la République, 'Revue nationale stratégique 2022', White Paper (Secrétariat général de la Défense et de la Sécurité nationale), 2022, http://www.sgdsn.gouv.fr/publications/revue-nationale-strategique-2022.
71. Alper Coşkun Ülgen Sinan, 'Political Change and Turkey's Foreign Policy', Carnegie Endowment for International Peace, accessed 12 May 2023, https://carnegieendowment.org/2022/11/14/political-change-and-turkey-s-foreign-policy-pub-88387.
72. Patricia Daehnhardt, 'NATO's Response to the New Confrontational Euro-Atlantic Order.'
73. NATO, 'NATO 2022 - Strategic Concept', para. 14.

4. MARITIME-STRATEGIC INTEGRATION AND INTEROPERABILITY IN NATO

1. Initially the force was called Standing Naval Forces Atlantic, or STANAVFORLANT in NATO jargon, but the name was changed to SNMG1 in 2005.
2. For more on NATO in the maritime domain after the Cold War, including SNMG1, alliance maritime operations and national

perspectives, see Jo G. Gade and Paal Sigurd Hilde, 'NATO and the Maritime Domain,' in *International Order at Sea: How It Is Challenged. How It Is Maintained*, ed. Jo Inge Bekkevold and Geoffrey Till (London: Palgrave Macmillan, 2016); Keith Blount and James Henry Bergeron, 'VII. NATO's Maritime Domain', *Whitehall Papers* 95, no. 1 (2019/01/02 2019), https://doi.org/10.1080/02681307.2019.17312 15, https://doi.org/10.1080/02681307.2019.1731215; John Andreas Olsen, ed., *NATO and the North Atlantic: Revitalising Collective Defence*, vol. 87 (Abingdon: Routledge, 2017); John Andreas Olsen, ed., *Security in Northern Europe: Deterrence, Defence and Dialogue* (Whitehall, London: RUSI, 2018); Luca Bonsignore, 'NATO'S Standing NRF Maritime Group 1 (SNMG1)', *NATO's Nations and Partners for Peace*, no. 2 (2005).
3. NATO, 'Interoperability: connecting forces', 2022, accessed 18.10.2022, https://www.nato.int/cps/en/natohq/topics_84112.htm.
4. Mark Dopitz, 'Indo-Pacific Deployment: Multinational exercises', German Bundeswehr, 2021, accessed 18.10.2022, https://www.bundeswehr.de/en/organization/navy/news/indo-pacific-deployment-multinational-exercises-5223140.
5. NATO, 'Operation Ocean Shield,' accessed 02.12.2022, https://shape.nato.int/missionarchive/operation-ocean-shield.
6. Supreme Headquarters Allied Powers Europe (SHAPE), 13.02.2017, https://www.facebook.com/SHAPE/posts/images-of-nato-exercise-dynamic-guard-which-wrapped-up-yesterday-off-the-coast-o/10154916549353805/.
7. NATO Maritime Command, 'Standing NATO Maritime Group One Visits Trondheim', 2017, accessed 05.12.2022, https://mc.nato.int/media-centre/news/2017/standing-nato-maritime-group-one-visits-trondheim.
8. NATO Maritime Command, 'SNMG1 Concludes Participation in Joint Warrior 17-1', 2017, accessed 05.12.2022, https://mc.nato.int/media-centre/news/2017/snmg1-concludes-participation-in-joint-warrior-171.
9. See for example Standing NATO Maritime Group 1, January-June 2017, https://www.facebook.com/snmg01; Standing NATO Maritime Group 1, August-December 2020, https://www.facebook.

com/snmg01; Standing NATO Maritime Group 1, January-July 2021, https://www.facebook.com/snmg01; Standing NATO Maritime Group 1, January-July 2022, https://www.facebook.com/snmg01.
10. NATO Maritime Command, 'SNMG1 Concludes Baltops 2017', 2017, accessed 05.12.2022, https://mc.nato.int/media-centre/news/2017/snmg1-concludes-exercise-baltops-2017.
11. These ships were not under official SNMG1 command as the force was at least given tactical control of the ships. The sources used for this chapter generally do not address the details of the command-and-control arrangements during such exercises. For simplicity, it is therefore assumed that SNMG1 has command of the ships that are officially part of the force, and tactical control of the additional ships assigned to it during exercises. For the difference between 'command' and 'control', see US Department of Defense, DOD Dictionary of Military and Associated Terms (2021).
12. NATO Maritime Command, 'Dynamic Mongoose 2017', 2017, accessed 15.02.2022, https://mc.nato.int/missions/exercises/dynamic-mongoose-2017.
13. NATO Centre for Maritime Research and Experimentation, 'NRV Alliance participating in Dynamic Mongoose 2017', 2017, accessed 05.12.2022, https://www.cmre.nato.int/rockstories-blog-display/399-nrv-alliance-participating-in-dynamic-mongoose-2017.
14. This semester, Dynamic Guard was merged with Norwegian-led exercise TG 19-1, which meant that the exercise also included training in anti-submarine warfare.
15. NATO, 'Exercise Joint Warrior 2019', 2019, accessed 07.12.2022, https://www.natomultimedia.tv/app/asset/604001.
16. Standing NATO Maritime Group 1, 'ESCORT OF M/V GUTE', 03.06.2019, https://www.facebook.com/snmg01. Standing NATO Maritime Group 1, August-December 2019, https://www.facebook.com/snmg01.
17. Standing NATO Maritime Group 1, August-December 2019, https://www.facebook.com/snmg01.
18. Standing NATO Maritime Group 1, 13.9.2019, https://www.facebook.com/snmg01.

19. NATO Maritime Command, 'NATO Nations Hone Anti-Submarine Warfare Skills During Cutlass Fury 2019,' 2019, accessed 06.12.2022, https://mc.nato.int/media-centre/news/2019/nato-nations-hone-antisubmarine-warfare-skills-during-cutlass-fury-2019-.
20. NATO, Exercise Dynamic Mariner/Flotex 2019 NATO Crisis Response Exercise, (2019). NATO Maritime Command, 08.10.2019, https://www.facebook.com/NATOMaritimeCommand/posts/pfbid0HWEXN6rrmAaPBGqXs5wjfmhLfwokzXbeBZFDmw RXYZcBEvF3oBZ5kqGiv1WcqhG1l.
21. NATO Maritime Command, 'SNMG 1 and SNMCMG 1 in Joint Exercise,' NATO Maritime Command, 2020, accessed 06.09.2022, https://mc.nato.int/media-centre/news/2020/snmg1-and-snmcmg1-in-joint-exercise?fbclid=IwAR3dj2VREumJGZj4ypuIVZJ87t2dvxw2 oN3ABEVKCNFKYl60zN4Ez_DzZn0.
22. NATO Maritime Command, 'Exercise Dynamic Mongoose Underway in High North', NATO Maritime Command, 2020, accessed 06.09.2022, https://mc.nato.int/media-centre/news/2020/exercise-dynamic-mongoose-underway-in-high-north.
23. NATO Maritime Command, 'Standing NATO Maritime Group 1 Takes Part in Joint Warrior', NATO Maritime Command, 2020, accessed 06.09.2022, https://mc.nato.int/media-centre/news/2020/standing-nato-maritime-group-1-takes-part-in-joint-warrior?fbclid =IwAR3obTwdmiiMSsnSkrE402uHImaH9Ypzjb9ItomR4F2zNH9 RVMRhumy_87w; NATO Maritime Command, 'NATO Monitors Russian Ships in English Channel', 2020, accessed 06.09.2022, https://mc.nato.int/media-centre/news/2020/nato-monitors-russian-ships-in-english-channel?fbclid=IwAR16kEZU0EXb8QVGN9BNY6ae2C 7v7YHv4YLVQ17sc5KuuMQMRFOOJNGHkAE; NATO Maritime Command, 'SNMG 1 and SNMCMG 1 in Joint Exercise'; NATO Maritime Command, 'NATO Forces Exercise With French Carrier Group', NATO Maritime Command, 2020, accessed 06.09.2022, https://mc.nato.int/media-centre/news/2020/nato-forces-exercise-with-french-carrier-strike-group?fbclid=IwAR2Tsxw6Pr5uLs4KQ prG8Hx1P7u91GXzGVHfzjoz8C7x8Oh0TZk5nO3wGBA; NATO Maritime Command, 'NATO Forces Exercise with Finland', NATO Maritime Command, 2020, accessed 06.09.2022, https://mc.nato.

int/media-centre/news/2020/nato-forces-exercise-with-finland?fbcli d=IwAR0HX6528BewONT5fXDWM2Jp20d KeoNmPje49WRMe-KbP9RT6lzcaV8POA0; Standing NATO Maritime Group 1, 'Thank you, Sweden!', 24.05.2020, https://www.facebook.com/snmg01/posts/pfbid02UhviFCMf5TojkMtKuYfBPFz5kYVpuMUzW pctjVWyRtMM9AEM5NbWixBE6ySo93K9l; Standing NATO Maritime Group 1, '#BALTOPS 2020 starts TODAY!', 07.06.2020, https://www.facebook.com/watch/?v=1203876363288725.

24. Paragraph based on SNMG1's posts on Facebook: Standing NATO Maritime Group 1, August-December 2020, https://www.facebook.com/snmg01.

25. US 6th Fleet Public Affairs, 'U.K.-Led Exercise Joint Warrior 20-2 Concludes', 2020, accessed 06.09.2022, https://www.navy.mil/Press-Office/News-Stories/Article/2384549/uk-led-exercise-joint-warrior-20-2-concludes/.

26. NATO Maritime Command, 'NATO Ships Train in Exercise Joint Warrior 21-1 with UK Queen Elizabeth Carrier Strike Group', 2021, accessed 06.09.2022, https://mc.nato.int/media-centre/news/2021/nato-ships-train-in-exercise-joint-warrior-211-with-uk-queen-elizabeth-carrier-strike-group; Strike Force NATO, 'Exercise BALTOPS Kicks Off Today', 2021, accessed 06.09.2022, https://sfn.nato.int/newsroom/2021/exercise-baltops-50-kicks-off-today.

27. NATO Maritime Command, 'NATO Ships Train in Exercise Joint Warrior 21-1 with UK Queen Elizabeth Carrier Strike Group'; NATO Maritime Command, 'NATO Standing Naval Forces Participate in the 50th Iteration of Exercise Baltops', 2021, accessed 07.12.2022, https://mc.nato.int/media-centre/news/2021/nato-standing-naval-forces-participate-in-the-50th-iteration-of-exercise-baltops.

28. NATO Maritime Command, 'NATO Completes Exercise Dynamic Guard', 2021, accessed 07.12.2022, https://mc.nato.int/media-centre/news/2022/nato-completes-naval-exercise-dynamic-guard.

29. NATO Maritime Command, 'NATO Exercise Dynamic Mariner and Joint Warrior Begins in the Atlantic', NATO Maritime Command, 2021, accessed 07.09.222, https://mc.nato.int/media-centre/news/2021/nato-exercise-dynamic-mariner-and-joint-warrior-begins-in-the-atlantic; NATO Maritime Command, 'NATO Exercise Dynamic

Mariner/Joint Warrior Concludes in UK', 2021, accessed 09.12.2022, https://mc.nato.int/media-centre/news/2021/nato-exercise-dynamic-marinerjoint-warrior-concludes-in-uk.
30. COM SNMG1 (@NATO_MARCOM and @MarineNationale), 22.09.2021, https://twitter.com/COM_SNMG1/status/1440730947058421772.
31. Standing NATO Maritime Group 1, January-July 2022, https://www.facebook.com/snmg01.
32. Standing NATO Maritime Group 1, 'SNMG1 Kicks off Batlops 2018', 03.06.2018, https://www.facebook.com/snmg01; NATO Maritime Command, 'Standing NATO Maritime Group One Changes Flagship', 2016, accessed 13.12.2022, https://mc.nato.int/media-centre/news/2016/standing-nato-maritime-group-one-changes-flagship.
33. Joshua Tallis, 'NATO's Maritime Vigilance: Optimizing the Standing Naval Force for the Future', *War on the Rocks*, *Texas National Security Review*, 20.12.2022, https://warontherocks.com/2022/12/natos-maritime-vigilance-optimizing-the-standing-naval-force-for-the-future/.
34. For more on this topic, see Paal Sigurd Hilde, 'Lean, Mean Fighting Machine? Institutional Change in NATO and the NATO Command Structure', in *The Future of NATO: Regional Defense and Global Security.*, ed. Andrew A. Michta and Paal Sigurd Hilde (Ann Arbor: University of Michigan Press, 2014); Robert B. McCalla, 'NATO's Persistence After The Cold War,' *Int Org* 50, no. 3 (1996), https://doi.org/10.1017/S0020818300033440; Thomas Risse-Knappe, 'Collective Identity in a Democratic Community: The Case of NATO', in *The Culture of National Security: Norms and Identity in World Politics*, ed. Peter Katzenstein (New York: Columbia University Press, 1996); Celeste A. Wallander, 'Institutional Assets and Adaptability: NATO After the Cold War', *Int Org* 54, no. 4 (2000), https://doi.org/10.1162/002081800551343.
35. Tallis NATO's Maritime Vigilance: Optimizing the Standing Naval Force for the Future.

5. BACK TO THE 1930S?

1. Dutch Ministry of Defence: *Defence Vision 2035* (October 2020).
2. Lydia Wachs & Liviu Horowitz: 'Frankreichs Atomwaffen und Europa', SWP-Aktuell 2023/A 07, (30.01.2023), https://www.swp-berlin.org/10.18449/2023A07/, accessed on 2 April 2023.
3. A realisation that underlay the already-cited bold Dutch defence review of 2020.
4. One must caution straight away that only a part of human societal behaviour is thus recorded. Nevertheless, we do have written evidence—which alone gives us more complex insights into human reasoning—for other parts of the world: China; for some periods, India; the Mediterranean world from about 1500 BC; for South-East Asia at least for the past millennium; Europe in antiquity, and after obscure or even dark patches in the second half of the first millennium and again in the past millennium.
5. The Persians adopted it from Mesopotamian models. It originated in the first Akkadian empire in the third millennium BCE and was expanded and refined as an ideological premise under the Assyrian empire in the ninth to seventh centuries. See Beate Pongratz-Leisten: *Herrschaftswissen in Mesopotamien. Formen der Kommunikation zwischen Gott und König im 2. und 1. Jahrtausend v.Chr.* (Helsinki, 1999); Mario Liverani, Niels Peter Lemche, and Emanuel Pfoh: 'The ideology of the Assyrian empire', in Mario Liverani (ed.): *Historiography, Ideology and Politics in the Ancient Near East and Israel* (Abingdon: Routledge, 2021), pp. 135–54; Seth Richardson: 'Early Mesopotamia: the presumptive state', *Past & Present* Vol. 215 No.1 (2012), pp. 3–49.
6. See the eulogy of Christian Rome by Aurelius Prudentius Clemens (384–c.413), printed in Arthur Herman: *The Idea of Decline in Western History* (New York, the Free Press, 1997), p.18.
7. See for example Ian Morris: *War: What is it Good For? The Role of Conflict in Civilisation, from Primates to Robots* (New York: Profile Books, 2014).
8. 'Discours sur ce que les guerres et divisions sont permises de Dieu pour le chastiement et des prince et du peuple mauvais' (1497–8):

in *Mémoires de Messire Philippe de Commines*, Denis Savvage (ed.), (Iaques Chouët, 1603), ch. 18.

9. Martin Wight: 'The Balance of Power', ch. 7 in *Diplomatic Investigations: Essays in the Theory of International Politics*, ed. by Herbert Butterfield and Martin Wight (Cambridge, Massachusetts: Harvard University Press, 1966), pp. 149–75; and Martin Wight: 'The Balance of Power and International Order', in A. James (ed.): *The Basis of International Order: Essays in Honor of CAW Manning* (New York: Oxford University Press, 1973). pp. 85–115.

10. The five powers included Austria–Hungary, Prussia, Russia, Britain and finally France herself, stripped of the Napoleonic conquests but with its reactionary Bourbon monarchy reinstated.

11. Beatrice Heuser: *Brexit in History: Sovereignty vs European Union* (London: Hurst, 2019).

12. This principle is that of the right to secede from a larger entity (state, empire) if that is the wish of a sub-entity. Oddly, it is precisely the negation of this right over which the American Civil War was fought in 1861–5. Nor does it resolve the problem of a minority within the sub-entity disagreeing with the break-away, and of what should become of them.

13. Vladimir Putin: 'On the historical unity of Russians and Ukrainians', http://en.kremlin.ru/events/president/news/66181 accessed 2 April 2023.

14. *Integrated Review Refresh 2023* (UK, 13 March 2023), https://assets.publishing.service.gov.uk/government/uploads/system/uploads/attachment_data/file/1145586/11857435_NS_IR_Refresh_2023_Supply_AllPages_Revision_7_WEB_PDF.pdf.

15. *Defence Vision 2035* (2020), https://english.defensie.nl/downloads/publications/2020/10/15/defence-vision-2035.

16. 'A Strategic Compass for Security and Defence for a European Union that protects its citizens, values and interests and contributes to international peace and security' (21 March 2022), https://data.consilium.europa.eu/doc/document/ST-7371-2022-INIT/en/pdf, here p.2.

17. https://www.europarl.europa.eu/RegData/etudes/BRIE/2023/739366/EPRS_BRI(2023)739366_EN.pdf accessed on 2 April 2023.

18. Jade McGlynn: 'Do ordinary Russians support Putin's war?', https://unherd.com/2023/02/do-ordinary-russians-support-putins-war/ accessed on 2 April 2023.

6. THE UNITED STATES AND EUROPE

1. The opinions expressed here are those of the author and do not reflect the official policy or position of the George C. Marshall European Center for Security Studies, the US Department of Defense or the US government.
2. Andrew A. Michta, 'Three Decades of Delusion,' *The American Interest*, 4 August 2020, https://www.the-american-interest.com/2020/08/04/three-decades-of-delusion/.
3. Essi Lehto and Mike Stone, 'Finland orders 64 Lockheed F-35 fighter jets for $9.4 bln,' *Reuters*, 10 December 2021, https://www.reuters.com/business/aerospace-defense/lockheed-f-35-jet-wins-finnish-fighter-competition-source-2021-12-10/.
4. Gerard O'Dwyer, 'Nordic nations move to link air forces into 250-strong aircraft fleet,' *Defense News*, 24 March 2023, https://www.defensenews.com/global/europe/2023/03/24/nordic-countries-move-toward-linking-their-air-forces-250-planes/.
5. Matti Pesu and Tuomas Iso-Markku, *Finland as a NATO Ally: First Insights into Finnish Alliance Policy* (Helsinki, FIIA, December 2022), p. 11.
6. Felicia Scwartz, 'Biden vowed to stand by Ukraine for "as long as it takes". But will America?', https://www.ft.com/content/129ba43f-aa4b-4dc3-9273-ff9e64bb923f.
7. Devin Klecan. 'Easternmost Army base in Europe now named after Polish-American hero,' *Dvids*, 30 July 2022, https://www.dvidshub.net/news/426178/easternmost-army-base-europe-now-named-after-polish-american-hero.
8. NATO, 'Strategic Concept 2022,' https://www.nato.int/nato_static_fl2014/assets/pdf/2022/6/pdf/290622-strategic-concept.pdf.
9. NATO, 'Deter and Defend,' https://shape.nato.int/news-archive/2022/deter-and-defend-an-overview.

10. *2019 Army Modernization Strategy: Investing in the Future*, U.S. Army, 2019, https://www.army.mil/e2/downloads/rv7/2019_army_modernization_strategy_final.pdf.
11. Brandi Vincent, 'NATO refining domain-specific "family of plans" to guide allies" cooperation in future contingencie,' Defense Scoop, 27 September 2022, https://defensescoop.com/2022/09/27/nato-refining-domain-specific-family-of-plans-to-guide-allies-cooperation-in-future-contingencies/.
12. Brandi Vincent, 'Air Force leaders eye deeper tech integration with allies earlier in development,' *Defense Scoop*, 20 September 2022, https://defensescoop.com/2022/09/20/air-force-leaders-eye-deeper-tech-integration-with-allies-earlier-into-development/.
13. Henry Foy, Barney Jopson and Guy Chazan, 'Explosives shortage threatens EU drive to arm Ukraine,' *Financial Times*, 19 March 2023, https://www.ft.com/content/aee0e1a1-c464-4af9-a1c8-73fcbc46ed17.
14. Zdfheute, 'Rheinmetall-Chef: Leopard-Panzer frühestens 2024 lieferbar,' 15 January 2023, https://www.zdf.de/nachrichten/politik/leopard-kampfpanzer-ukraine-rheinmetall-krieg-russland-100.html.
15. Charlie Cooper, 'German arms firm Rheinmetall says Leopard tanks can't be ready for Ukraine until 2024,' *Politico*, 15 January 2023, https://www.politico.eu/article/ukraine-war-germany-tanks-rheinmetall-leopard-2024/.
16. Alexander Michael Pearson and William Wilkes, 'Germany's Top Defense Contractor Blames Government for Ammo Shortfalls,' 14 March 2023, https://www.bloomberg.com/news/articles/2023-03-14/rheinmetall-says-europe-must-double-shell-production-for-ukraine?leadSource=uverify%20wall.
17. Reuters, 'German army to procure more than 100 additional Leopard 2 tanks,' *Reuters*, 10 April, 2015, https://www.reuters.com/article/us-germany-defence-tanks-idUSKBN0N11A920150410.
18. Deborah Haynes, 'US general warns British Army no longer top-level fighting force, defence sources reveal,' *Sky News*, https://news.sky.com/story/us-general-warns-british-army-no-longer-top-level-fighting-force-defence-sources-reveal-12798365.

19. Michael Shurkin, *The Abilities of the British, French, and German Armies to Generate and Sustain Armored Brigades in the Baltics* (Santa Monica, CA: RAND, 2017).
20. Alie Peter Neil Galeon, 'Poland Set to Become First Country to Have F-35 Pilots Trained at Fort Smith,' The Defense Post, 16 September 2022, https://www.thedefensepost.com/2022/09/16/poland-train-f35-fort-smith.
21. Alicja Ptak, 'Poland to buy $10 billion in HIMARS rocket launchers and ammunition,' *Notes From Poland*, 8 February 2023, https://notesfrompoland.com/2023/02/08/poland-to-buy-10-billion-in-himars-rocket-launchers-and-ammunition/.
22. Daniel Tilles, 'First Korean tanks and howitzers arrive in Poland,' *Notes From Poland*, 6 December 2022, https://notesfrompoland.com/2022/12/06/first-korean-tanks-and-howitzers-arrive-in-poland/.
23. Iulian Ernst, 'Romania to step up military spending to 2.5% of GDP,' *Intellinews*, 26 October 2022, https://www.intellinews.com/romania-to-step-up-military-spending-to-2-5-of-gdp-260461/.

7. THE THREAT POSED BY RUSSIA AND CHINA AFTER THE UKRAINE WAR

1. Mark Galeotti, quoted in '"Big War Is Back": Five Lessons from Russia's War in Ukraine,' *Financial Times*, 25 December 2022.
2. Mykhaylo Zabrodskyi, Jack Watling, Oleksandr V Danylyuk and Nick Reynolds, 'Preliminary Lessons in Conventional Warfighting from Russia's Invasion of Ukraine: February–July 2022,' *RUSI*.
3. Desertion rates taken from Jason Lyall, How Putin's partial mobilization could backfire, *Washington Post*, September 22, 2022.
4. Germans resolve to support Ukraine despite gas prices as FM visits Kyiv, *Euravtiv*, September 11, 2022.
5. Lawrence Freedman, 'Is Russia Losing?,' https://samf.substack.com/p/is-russia-losing?utm_source=twitter&sd=pf.
6. Alexander B. Downes and Kathryn McNabb Cochran, 'Targeting Civilians to Win? Assessing the Military Effectiveness of Civilian Victimization in Interstate War', in Erica Chenoweth and Adrian

Lawrence, eds., *Rethinking Violence: States and Non-State Actors in Conflict* (MIT Press, 2010).

7. The data and arguments for and against are most clearly laid out in Erik Gartzke and Kristian Skrede Gleditsch, 'Why Democracies May Actually Be Less Reliable Allies,' *American Journal of Political Science* (Vol 48, No. 4, October 2004).

8. Figures as of 3 October 2022 tabulated by the Kiel Institute for World Economy (https://twitter.com/ulrichspeck/status/1607271670355578880/photo/1).

9. Retired General Mick Ryan, 'Learning from the War in Ukraine,' 18 December 2022 (https://mickryan.substack.com/p/learning-from-the-war-in-ukraine?r=1gv0l&utm_campaign=post&utm_medium=web).

10. Ken Dilanian, Dan De Luce and Courtney Kube, 'Why didn't the U.S. and allies provide Ukraine with a better air defense system?' *NBC News*, 23 February 2022.

11. General Mark Milley, quoted in Vladislav Zubok, 'No One Would Win a Long War in Ukraine,' *Foreign Affairs*, 21 December 2022.

12. Zabrodskyi *et al.* 'Preliminary Lessons in Conventional Warfighting from Russia's Invasion of Ukraine: February–July 2022.'

13. Rob A. Lee and Michael Kofman, 'How the Battle for the Donbas Shaped Ukraine's Success,' *Foreign Policy Research Institute*, 23 December 2002.

14. General Mark Milley, quoted in 'Top US General Argues Ukraine May Be In Position of Strength to Negotiate Russian Withdrawal,' *CNN*, 16 November 2022; Alexander Ward, Lara Seligman and Erin Banco 'U.S. Scrambles to Reassure Ukraine After Milley Comments on Negotiations,' *Politico*, 14 November 2022.

15. Lawrence Freedman, 'Is Russia Losing?' (https://samf.substack.com/p/is-russia-losing?utm_source=twitter&sd=pf).

16. John Paul Rathbone and Steff Chávez 'Ilitary Briefing: Is the West Running Out of Ammunition to Supply Ukraine?' *Financial Times*, 10 July 2022.

17. Assessment by former US Army Europe commander Ben Hodges; Jack Maidment, 'British Army 'ran out of ammunition in just eight days of fighting' in simulated 10-day online war exercise, warns ex-

commander of the US Army in Europe,' *Daily Mail*, 7 July 2021; and Mykhaylo Zabrodskyi, Jack Watling, Oleksandr V Danylyuk and Nick Reynolds, 'Preliminary Lessons in Conventional Warfighting from Russia's Invasion of Ukraine: February–July 2022,' *RUSI*.

18. William LaPlante, quoted in 'Military Briefing Ukraine War Exposes 'Hard Reality' of West's Weapons Capacity,' *Financial Times*, 1 December 2022.
19. The idea of industrial warfare returning is by Alex Vershinin, 'The Return of Industrial Warfare,' *RUSI*, 17 June 2022.
20. Bryan Bender and Lara Seligman, '"We Haven't Got This Figured Out Just Yet": Pentagon, Industry Struggle to Arm Ukraine,' *Politico*, 4 December 2022.
21. 'What is the War in Ukraine Teaching Western Armies?' *Economist*, 30 November 2022.
22. 'The Technology of Seeing and Shooting Your Enemies,' *Economist*, 20 January 2022.
23. Jeremy Fleming, 'The head of GCHQ says Vladimir Putin is losing the information war in Ukraine,' *Economist*, 18 August 2022.
24. 'Lessons from Russia's Cyber-War in Ukraine,' *Economist*, 30 November 2022.
25. 'Does the tank have a future?' *Economist*, 15 June 2022.
26. Chris Miller makes this argument in his history of silicon wafers, *Chip War: The Fight for the World's Most Critical Technology*, London: Simon & Schuster, 2022.
27. The phrase is Walter Russell Mead's, from *Special Providence: American Foreign Policy and How It Changed the World* (Routledge, 2002) describing the risk tolerance of American finance in the Hamiltonian tradition.
28. 'China set to expand nuclear arsenal to 1,500 warheads by 2035, US says,' *Financial Times*, 29 November 2022.
29. Caitlin M. Kenney, As Marines' Arms and Gear Flow to Ukraine, Corps Keeps Close Tabs on Its Own Stocks, Commandant Says, *Defense One*, 7 December 2022.
30. Elina Ribakova and Edward Fishman, 'Russia's Economy is Still Working but Sanctions are Starting to Have an Effect,' *NPR*, 27 December 2022.

31. 'The West Must Bridge the Global Divide Over Ukraine', *Bloomberg*, 6 June 2022.
32. 'UK Economy "Not Prepared" For Fallout If China Invades Taiwan,' *The Times*, 27 December 2022.
33. Yimou Lee and David Lague, 'Chinese Spies Have Penetrated Taiwan's Military, Case Documents Reveal,' *Reuters*, 20 December 2021.
34. See, for example, the dueling *Foreign Affairs* articles by Hal Brands and Michael Beckley ('Competition With China Could Be Short and Sharp,' 17 December 2020), and Derek Scissors and Oriana Skylar Mastro (China Hasn't Reached the Peak of Its Power, 22 August 2022).
35. Michael Beckley, 'China's Century? Why America's Edge Will Endure,' *International Security* (Vol 36, No. 3, Winter 2011/12); Dan Blumenthal and Derek Scissors, 'Breaking China's Hold,' *Atlantic*, 23 December 2022.

8. *ZEITENWENDE* OR BUSINESS AS USUAL?

1. Policy statement by Olaf Scholz, Chancellor of the Federal Republic of Germany and Member of the German Bundestag, 27 February 2022, in Berlin.
2. The term *Zeitenwende* was used five times in the speech.
3. Olaf Scholz, 'The Global Zeitenwende—How to Avoid a New Cold War in a Multipolar Era', *Foreign Affairs* (January/February 2023).
4. See for example, Bastian Giegerich and Maximilian Terhalle, *The Responsibility to Defend: Rethinking Germany's Strategic Culture*, vol. 477. Adelphi Series (London: Routledge, 2021); Håkon Lunde Saxi, 'British-German Defence and Security Relations After Brexit: Quo Vadis, "Silent Alliance"?,' in *The United Kingdom's Defence After Brexit: Britain's Alliances, Coalitions, and Partnerships*, ed. Rob Johnson and Janne Haaland Matlary (London: Palgrave Macmillan, 2019), 130–3.
5. Robin Allers, 'The Framework Nation: Can Germany Lead on Security?' *International Affairs*, vol. 92, no. 5 (2016): 1167–87; Håkon Lunde Saxi, 'British and German Initiatives for Defence Cooperation: the Joint Expeditionary Force and the Framework Nations Concept',

Defence Studies, vol. 17, no. 2 (2017): 171–97; Claudia Major, 'NATO's Strategic Adaptation: Germany Is the Backbone for the Alliance's Military Reorganisation', *SWP Comments 16*. Berlin: SWP, March 2015.

6. Edward Lucas, 'Why Germany Has Learned the Wrong Lessons From History', *Foreign Policy*, 27 December 2022.
7. Policy statement, Olaf Scholz, 27 February 2022.
8. NATO Heads of State and Government, *Wales Summit Declaration* (Brussels: NATO, 2014).
9. Håkon Lunde Saxi, 'German Military Strategy: Culture Eats Strategy for Breakfast,' in *Military Strategy in the 21st Century: The Challenge for NATO*, ed. Janne Haaland Matlary and Rob Johnson (London: Hurst, 2020), 396–7; on German defence spending in 2019, see NATO, *The Secretary General's Annual Report 2021* (Brussels: NATO, 2022), 141 (Table 3: Defence expenditure as share of GDP).
10. SPD, Bündnis 90/Die Grünen, Den Freien Demokraten (FDP), *Mehr Fortschritt Wagen: Bündnis für Freiheit, Gerechtigkeit und Nachhaltigkeit* (Berlin: Koalitionsvertrag 2021–2025), 114.
11. Policy statement by Olaf Scholz, 27 February 2022.
12. Policy statement by Olaf Scholz, 27 February 2022.
13. Alexandra Marksteiner, 'Explainer: The Proposed Hike In German Military Spending', *SIPRI Blog*, 25 March 2022, https://www.sipri.org/commentary/blog/2022/explainer-proposed-hike-german-military-spending (accessed 11 April 2023).
14. See NATO, *The Secretary General's Annual Report 2021* (Brussels: NATO, 2022), 43, 141–3.
15. The regular budget for the Federal Ministry of Defence (BMVg)—*Einzelplan 14*—was in fact slightly lower in 2023 compared with 2022. See the digital budget published by the Federal Ministry of Finance (BMF) at https://www.bundeshaushalt.de/DE/Bundeshaushalt-digital/bundeshaushalt-digital.html (accessed 22 September 2023).
16. Policy statement by Olaf Scholz, 27 February 2022.
17. The debt break was enacted in 2009.
18. The vote in the German Bundestag produced 567 votes in favour of the amendment to the Basic Law, 96 against and 20 abstentions. The Bundesrat enacted that same amendment on 6 June 2022. Guy

Chazan, 'Germany approves €100 billion found to modernise its armed forces', *Financial Times*, 3 June 2022.
19. Parliamentary Commissions for the Armed Forces, *Jahresbericht 2022* [Annual report 2022] (Berlin: German Bundestag, 2023), 6.
20. See, for example, Ben Knight, 'What Happened to the German Military's €100 Billion Fund?', *Deutsche Welle*, 28 February 2023, https://www.dw.com/en/what-happened-to-the-german-militarys-100-billion-fund/a-64846571 (accessed 22 September 2023).
21. The so-called *Einzelplan 14*. See the digital budget published by the Federal Ministry of Finance (BMF) at https://www.bundeshaushalt.de/DE/Bundeshaushalt-digital/bundeshaushalt-digital.html (accessed 22 September 2023).
22. German Ministry of Finance, *Haushaltsaufstellung 2023 und Finanzplan des Bundes bis 2026* [Proposed 2023 federal budget and financial plan until 2026] (Berlin: BMF, 2022), 14, 25, Anlage 9.
23. German Ministry of Finance, *Haushaltsaufstellung 2023 und Finanzplan des Bundes bis 2026*.
24. Matthew Karnitschnig, 'The Truth About Germany's Defense Policy Shift', *Politico*, 27 February 2023, https://www.politico.eu/article/germany-zeitenwende-defense-spending-nato-gdp-target-scholz-ukraine-war-russia/ (accessed 22 September 2023).
25. Florian Dorn, Niklas Potrafke and Marcel Schlepper, 'NATO Defense Spending in 2023: Implications One Year After Russia's Invasion of Ukraine', *Econpol Policy Brief*, vol. 7, no. 50, May 2023, 8–9.
26. Marksteiner, 'The Proposed Hike In German Military Spending'.
27. Hans von der Burchard, 'Germany's New Defense Minister Faces "Ticking Time Bombs" In His Armed Forces', *Politico*, 25 February 2023, https://www.politico.eu/article/germany-defense-minister-boris-pistorius-army-forces-military/ (accessed 22 September 2023).
28. Karnitschnig, 'The Truth About Germany's Defense Policy Shift'.
29. The Federal Government, *National Security Strategy: Robust. Resilient. Sustainable. Integrated Security for Germany* (Berlin: Federal Foreign Office, 2023), https://www.nationalesicherheitsstrategie.de/National-Security-Strategy-EN.pdf (accessed 24 September 2023); The Federal Government, 'NATO Summit in Vilnius—A signal of unity and solidarity', 11 July 2023, https://www.bundesregierung.de/

breg-en/news/nato-summit-vilnius-2202172 (accessed 25 September 2023); The Economist, 'Germany's New National Security Strategy Is Strong on Goals, Less so on Means'. *The Economist*, 15 June 2023, https://www.economist.com/europe/2023/06/15/germanys-new-national-security-strategy-is-strong-on-goals-less-so-on-means (accessed 25 September 2023); Peter Wilke, 'Germany U-turns on Commitment to Meet NATO Spending Target Annually', *Politico*, 16 July 2023, https://www.politico.eu/article/germany-defense-change-of-plan-nato-spending/ (accessed 25 September 2023).

30. See the official Twitter (now X) account of Bundeskanzler Olaf Scholz, 26 February 2022.
31. The policy was established in the mid-1960s, and 'areas of tension' was historically to some extent a euphemism for the Middle East. In reality, the policy was often interpreted loosely, and German arms were frequently exported to non-NATO countries. See, for example, Michael H. Creswell and Dieter H. Kollmer, 'Power, Preferences, or Ideas? Explaining West Germany's Armaments Strategy, 1955–1972', *Journal of Cold War Studies*, vol. 15, no. 4 (Fall 2013): 94–5.
32. Tetyana Klug, 'Does Germany Send Weapons to Crisis Regions?', *Deutsche Welle*, 8 February 2022.
33. Patrick Wintour and Philip Oltermann, 'Russia Would Pay "High Price" For Attack on Ukraine, Says German Minister', *The Guardian*, 17 January 2022, https://www.theguardian.com/world/2022/jan/17/russia-ukraine-attack-german-minister-annalena-baerbock (accessed 22 September 2023).
34. Christopher F. Schuetze, 'Germany Draws Mockery for Promising 5,000 Helmets to Help Ukraine Defend Itself', *New York Times*, 27 January 2022.
35. Policy statement by Olaf Scholz, 27 February 2022.
36. Quoted in Loveday Morris, 'After Hesitancy, Germany Greenlights Some Heavy Arms for Ukraine', *Washington Post*, 26 April 2022.
37. Morris, 'After hesitancy...', *Washington Post*, 26 April 2022.
38. Morris, 'After hesitancy...', *Washington Post*, 26 April 2022.
39. Peter Beaumont, 'Leopard 2 Tanks: What Are They and Why Does Ukraine Want Them?', *The Guardian*, 25 January 2023, https://www.theguardian.com/world/2023/jan/25/leopard-2-german-tanks-

40. Quoted in Dan Sabbagh, 'Olaf Scholz Steers Clear of Commitment to Supply of Leopard 2 Tanks to Ukraine', *The Guardian*, 18 January 2023, https://www.theguardian.com/world/2023/jan/18/olaf-scholz-steers-clear-of-pledging-leopard-2-tanks-to-ukraine (accessed 22 September 2023).
41. Dan Sabbagh and Philip Oltermann, 'US and Germany Agree to Send Infantry Fighting Vehicles to Ukraine'. *The Guardian*, 5 January 2023, https://www.theguardian.com/world/2023/jan/05/germany-tanks-ukraine-russia-war (accessed 22 September 2023).
42. Michael R. Godon, Gordon Lubold and Bojan Pancevski, 'U.S., Germany Approve Sending Tanks to Ukraine', *The Wall Street Journal*, 25 January 2023, https://www.wsj.com/articles/germany-agrees-to-send-tanks-to-ukraine-11674643787 (accessed 22 September 2023).
43. See the German Government website: https://www.bundesregierung.de/breg-de/schwerpunkte/krieg-in-der-ukraine/lieferungen-ukraine-2054514 (accessed 22 September 2023).
44. See *IfW Kiel' Ukraine Support Tracker* at: https://www.ifw-kiel.de/topics/war-against-ukraine/ukraine-support-tracker/ (accessed 22 September 2023).
45. *IfW Kiel' Ukraine Support Tracker*.
46. See, for example, Tom Ball and Bruno Waterfield, 'Germany "Breaks Its Promise" To Give Kyiv More Heavy Weapons', *The Times*, 30 May 2022.
47. Reuters, 'German President Says Kyiv Did Not Want Him to Visit', *Reuters*, 12 April 2022.
48. DPA, Reuters, AFP, 'Germany Approves Polish Request to Send Ukraine 5 MIG Jets'. *Deutsche Welle*, 13 April 2023, https://www.dw.com/en/germany-approves-polish-request-to-send-ukraine-5-mig-jets/a-65301536 (accessed 22 September 2023).
49. Policy statement by Olaf Scholz, 27 February 2022.
50. Policy statement by Olaf Scholz, 27 February 2022.
51. Federal Foreign Office, statement by Foreign Minister Annalena Baerbock prior to her departure for the Baltic states, 20 April 2022,

https://www.auswaertiges-amt.de/en/newsroom/news/-/2523142 (accessed 22 September 2023).

52. On the controversy, see Sabine Siebold and Andrius Sytas, 'Lithuania Wants Permanent German Brigade, Germany Says it's "up to NATO"', *Reuters*, 7 March 2023, https://www.reuters.com/world/europe/decision-permanent-troop-deployment-lithuania-up-nato-germany-2023-03-07/ (accessed 23 September 2023); Laura Pitel and Henry Foy, 'Germany Plans "Permanent" Force In Lithuania to Strengthen NATO's Eastern Flank', *Financial Times*, 26 June 2023, https://www.ft.com/content/78f80ec0-6df8-4f8a-902d-f319afb9fe90 (accessed 25 September 2023).

53. Bundeswehr, 'NATO Air Policing im Baltikum', 2 May 2023, https://www.bundeswehr.de/de/einsaetze-bundeswehr/anerkannte-missionen/nato-air-policing-baltikum (accessed 23 September 2023).

54. NATO, 'NATO's Military Presence in The East of the Alliance', 21 December 2022, https://www.nato.int/cps/en/natohq/topics_136388.htm (accessed 23 September 2023).

55. Federal Government, 'NATO Summit Sets Important Course for the Future', 30 June 2022, https://www.bundesregierung.de/breg-en/service/nato-summit-madrid-2058998 (accessed 23 September 2023); Thomas Wiegold, 'Dokumentation—Scholz-Pk nach dem NATO-Gipfel', *Augen geradeaus!*, 30 June 2022, https://augengeradeaus.net/2022/06/dokumentation-scholz-pk-nach-dem-nato-gipfel/ (accessed 23 September 2023); in 2018, Germany had agreed to establish the Joint Support and Enabling Command (JSEC) in Ulm as one of two new NATO headquarters.

56. Bundeswehr, Fleet Commander: 'German Navy Shows Alliance Solidarity', 18 February 2022, https://www.bundeswehr.de/en/organization/navy/news/fleet-commander-german-navy-alliance-solidarity-5357492 (accessed 23 September 2023); Bundeswehr, 'German Navy Objectives for 2035 and Beyond', 20 April 2023, https://www.bundeswehr.de/en/organization/navy/news/german-navy-objectices-2035-plus-5625058 (accessed 23 September 2023); see also Robin Allers, 'Germany and the Nordics—Is NATO's Northern Flank Part of the *Zeitenwende?*', in Katarina Tracz (ed.),

Stronger together—Sweden and Finland on the Road Toward NATO (Stockholm: Stockholm Free World Forum, 2022), 164–6.

57. Julian Borger, 'Nord Stream Attacks Highlight Vulnerability of Undersea Pipelines in West', *The Guardian*, 29 September 2022, https://www.theguardian.com/business/2022/sep/29/nord-stream-attacks-highlight-vulnerability-undersea-pipelines-west (accessed 23 September 2023); Bundeswehr, 'Deutsche Marine beteiligt sich am Schutz der kritischen Infrastruktur Norwegens', 4 November 2022, https://www.bundeswehr.de/de/organisation/marine/aktuelles/schutz-kritischer-infrastruktur-norwegens-5519846 (accessed 23 September 2023).

58. Norwegian government, 'Norwegian Prime Minister and German Chancellor Propose a NATO Surveillance Centre for Subsea Infrastructure', 1 December 2022, https://www.regjeringen.no/en/aktuelt/norwegian-prime-minister-and-german-chancellor-propose-a-nato-surveillance-centre-for-subsea-infrastructure/id2949149/ (accessed 23 September 2023); the initiative resulted in the establishment of a Critical Undersea Infrastructure Coordination Cell at NATO Headquarters led by retired General Lieutenant Hans-Werner Wiermann.

59. Speech by Federal Chancellor Olaf Scholz at the Charles University in Prague, 29 August 2022, https://www.bundesregierung.de/breg-en/news/scholz-speech-prague-charles-university-2080752 (accessed 23 September 2023).

60. Policy statement by Olaf Scholz, 27 February 2022.

61. Douglas Barrie and Bastian Giegerich, 'European Missile Defence - Right Questions, Unclear Answers?' *IISS Military balance Blog*, 10 February 2023, https://www.iiss.org/online-analysis/military-balance/2023/02/european-missile-defence-right-questions-unclear-answers (accessed 23 September 2023).

62. Scholz, 'The Global *Zeitenwende*'.

63. Press conference by Chancelor Olaf Scholz, 24 March 2022, https://www.bundesregierung.de/breg-de/suche/pressekonferenz-von-bundeskanzler-scholz-zur-teilnahme-des-bundeskanzlers-am-nato-treffen-der-staats-und-regierungschefs-am-treffen-der-g7-staats-

-und-regierungschefs-und-am-treffen-des-europaeischen-rats-am-24-maerz-2022-2020396 (accessed 23 September 2023).
64. Scholz in TV interview with German journalist Anne Will, *ARD*, 27 March 2022 (video no longer available on the website).
65. Giegerich and Terhalle, *Responsibility to Defend*, 107–8.
66. Giegerich and Terhalle, *Responsibility to Defend*, 107.
67. Reuters, 'German Army Chief "Fed Up" With Neglect of Country's Military', *Reuters*, 24 February 2022, https://www.reuters.com/world/europe/german-army-chief-fed-up-with-neglect-countrys-military-2022-02-24/ (accessed 23 September 2023); Der Spiegel, 'Ukraine-Invasion: Bundeswehr steht laut Heeresinspekteur "mehr oder weniger blank da"', *Der Spiegel*, 24 Februar 2022, https://www.spiegel.de/politik/deutschland/ukraine-invasion-bundeswehr-steht-laut-heeresinspekteur-mehr-oder-weniger-blank-da-a-e5bdc1f4-e9d3-472f-9ed7-beed5aa02eb0 (accessed 23 September 2023).
68. Policy statement by Olaf Scholz, 27 February 2022.
69. Nicholas Fiorenza, 'Germany Suspends Puma Procurement, Marder to Continue Serving With VJTF', 22 December 2022, https://www.janes.com/defence-news/news-detail/germany-suspends-puma-procurement-marder-to-continue-serving-with-vjtf (accessed 23 September 2023).
70. Ben Knight, 'Germany Seen as Less Reliable Than Before, Survey Says', *DW*, 10 July 2022, https://www.dw.com/en/germany-seen-as-a-less-reliable-international-partner-than-before-survey-says/a-63361181 (accessed 23 September 2023); Lukas Paul Schmelter, 'How Germany Lost the Trust of Eastern Europe', *Internationale Politik Quarterly*, 4 January 2023, https://ip-quarterly.com/en/how-germany-lost-trust-eastern-europe (accessed 23 September 2023).
71. Katrin Bennhold, 'Olaf Scholz of Germany Won't Send Battle Tanks to Ukraine', *The New York Times*, 25 September 2022, https://www.nytimes.com/2022/09/25/world/europe/olaf-scholz-germany-ukraine-war.html (accessed 23 September 2023).
72. Gabriel Rinaldi, 'Germany Can't Fulfill NATO Obligations, Says Army Chief in Leaked Memo', 11 April 2023, https://www.politico.eu/article/germany-nato-leaked-memo-defense-budget-boris-pistorius/ (accessed 23 September 2023); see also Liana Fix, 'On the

Ukraine War, Germany Has a Leadership Problem. Here's Why', *Council on Foreign Relations*, 14 October 2022, https://www.cfr.org/in-brief/ukraine-war-germany-has-leadership-problem-heres-why (accessed 23 September 2023).

73. Philip Oltermann, 'German Thinkers' War of Words Over Ukraine Exposes Generational Divide', *The Guardian*, 6 May 2022, https://www.theguardian.com/world/2022/may/06/german-thinkers-war-of-words-over-ukraine-exposes-generational-divide (accessed 23 September 2023).

74. See, for example, Malte Riemann and Georg Löfflmann (eds.), *Deutschlands Verteidigungspolitik. Nationale Sicherheit nach der Zeitenwende* (Berlin: Kohlhammer, 2023).

75. For a recent study, see Frank A. Stengel, *The Politics of Military Force. Antimilitarism, Ideational Change, and Post-Cold War German Security Discourse* (Ann Arbor: Univ. of Michigan Press, 2020).

76. Robin Allers, 'Are We Doing Enough? Change and Continuity in the German Approach to Crisis Management', *German Politics* 25, no. 4 (2016).

77. Giegerich and Terhalle, *Responsibility to Defend*, 7–8; Hauke Friederichs, *Spielball der Politik. Eine kurze Geschichte der Bundeswehr* (Munich: dtv, 2023), 314–15.

78. Eckart Lohse, 'Scholz: Bei Waffenlieferungen an die Ukraine "nicht treiben lassen"', *Frankfurter Allgemeine Zeitung*, 13 January 2023, https://www.faz.net/aktuell/politik/inland/scholz-bei-waffenlieferungen-an-die-ukraine-nicht-treiben-lassen-18601015.html (accessed 23 September 2023).

79. Corinna Emundts, 'Kampfpanzer für die Ukraine: Druck auf den Kanzler wächst', *Tagesschau.de*, 16 September 2022, https://www.tagesschau.de/inland/innenpolitik/scholz-waffenlieferungen-ukraine-101.html (accessed 23 September 2023).

80. Hans Monath, 'Zeitenwende als Qual: Die Leiden des SPD-Fraktionschefs Rolf Mützenich', *Tagesspiegel.de*, 29 December 2022, https://www.tagesspiegel.de/politik/warum-der-spd-fraktionschef-leidet-russlands-krieg-zehrt-rolf-mutzenich-auf-9095188.html (accessed 23 September 2023).

81. Lars Klingbeil, 'What the Watershed Moment Means for German Foreign Policy', *Internationale Politik Quarterly*, 22 June 2022, https://ip-quarterly.com/en/op-ed-what-watershed-moment-means-german-foreign-policy (accessed 23 September 2023).
82. Karnitschnig, 'The Truth About Germany's Defense Policy Shift'.
83. Bastian Giegerich and Ben Schreer, 'Zeitenwende One Year On', *Survival*, vol. 65, no. 2(2023): 39.
84. Timo Graf, 'Zeitenwende im Sicherheits- und verteidigungspolitischen Meinungsbild. Ergebnisse der ZMSBw-Bevölkerungsbefragung 2022', *ZMSBW Forschungsbericht*, 133 (2022), 1, 4–5.
85. Tagesschau, 'ARD-Deutschland Trend: Mehrheit der Deutschen stimmt Waffenlieferungen zu', *tagesschau.de*, 2 March 2023, https://www.tagesschau.de/inland/deutschlandtrend/deutschlandtrend-3313.htm (accessed 23 September 2023).
86. The Federal Government, *National Security Strategy*, 12.
87. Scholz, 'Global Zeitenwende'.
88. The Economist, 'Germany's New National Security Strategy is Strong on Goals, Less so on Means'; Ulrike Franke, 'Reading Between the Lines of Germany's New National Security Strategy', *Defense News*, 22 June 2023, https://www.defensenews.com/opinion/commentary/2023/06/22/reading-between-the-lines-of-germanys-new-national-security-strategy/ (accessed 25 September 2023).
89. Parliamentary Commissions for the Armed Forces, *Jahresbericht 2022* [Annual report 2022] (Berlin: German Bundestag, 2023), 6.

9. FINLAND'S APPROACH TO MILITARY COOPERATION AND INTEGRATION

1. Henrikki Heikka, 'Republican Realism: Finnish Strategic Culture in Historical Perspective', *Cooperation and Conflict*, vol. 40, no. 1, 2003, 91–119; Bobo Lo, *Russia and the New World Disorder* (London: Chatham House & Washington, D.C, Brooking Institution Press, 2015).
2. Satu Schauman, 'Suomen pysyvä dilemma on Venäjä—"Nato ei ratkaisu suuntaan taikka toiseen"', *Verkkouutiset*, 15 June 2016, https://www.verkkouutiset.fi/a/suomen-pysyva-dilemma-on-

venaja-nato-ei-ratkaisu-suuntaan-taikka-toiseen-37492/#be028e3c. Accessed 14 April 2023.
3. Finnish scholars have increasingly underscored the role of national resilience in Finland's deterrence model. A resilient society resisting malign foreign influence is seen as a critical tool in dissuading a potential aggressor from carrying out hostile measures, including military aggression, against Finland. See, for example, Jan Hanska, 'Pelotetta vai pidäkettä? Deterrenssiteorian käytäntöä pienen valtion näkökulmasta', *Tiede ja ase*, vol. 77, no. 1, 2019, 42–70; Hiski, Haukkala, *Suuren pelin paluu: Suomen turvallisuus kriisien maailmassa* (Helsinki: Otava, 2020).
4. On Finland's two-track approach to Russia, see Charly Salonius-Pasternak 'Finland's Ambiguous Deterrence: Mixing Deterrence by Denial with Ambiguous Extended Deterrence' in Nora Vanaga and Toms Rostoks (eds), *Deterring Russia in Europe Defence Strategies for Neighbouring States* (London: Routledge, 2018).
5. Johan Jörgen Holst, 'Norwegian Security Policy: The Strategic Context', *Cooperation and Conflict,* vol. 1. no. 4, 1966, 64–79; Olof Kronvall and Magnus Petersson, *Svensk säkerhetspolitik i Supermakternas skugga 1945-1991* (Stockholm, Santérus förlag, 2005); Anna Wieslander, '"The Hultqvist doctrine"—Swedish Security and Defence Policy After the Russian Annexation of Crimea', *Defence Studies* vol. 22, no.1, 2022, 35–59.
6. See, for example, Ulrich Kühn, 'Deter and Engage: Making the Case for Harmel 2.0 as NATO's New Strategy 2015', *New Perspectives*, vol. 23, no. 1, 2015, 127–57.
7. Tomas Ries, *Cold Will. The Defence of Finland* (London: Brassey's, 1988), 227–31.
8. Risto E.J. Penttilä, *Finland's Search for Security through Defence, 1944–89* (London: Palgrave Macmillan, 1991).
9. Matti Pesu, *Koskiveneellä kohti valtavirtaa* (Helsinki: the Ministry of Defence of Finland, 2017), 29–31.
10. Charly Salonius Pasternak, 'Finland's Ambiguous Deterrence', 2018.
11. See, for example, Jukka Pesu, *Suomi, rauhanturvaaminen ja kylmä sota 1956–1990: Rauhanturvaaminen osana Suomen ulko- ja turvallisuuspolitikkaa sekä YK-politiikkaa* (Turku: University of Turku, 2020).

12. Pesu, *Koskiveneellä kohti valtavirtaa*.
13. Finnish Government, *Government Report on Finnish Foreign and Security Policy 2016* (Helsinki: Prime Minister's Office), 2016, 11.
14. Finnish government, *Government Report on Finnish Foreign and Security Policy 2020* (Helsinki: Prime Minister's Office, 2020), 21.
15. Speech by President of the Republic Sauli Niinistö at the Ambassador Seminar 25 August 2015, https://www.presidentti.fi/en/speeches/speech-by-president-of-the-republic-sauli-niinisto-at-the-ambassador-seminar-25-august-2015/. Accessed 23 March 2023.
16. Finnish government, *Government Report on Finnish Foreign and Security Policy 2016*, 18.
17. Ibid., 22.
18. Matti Pesu, 'As Finland Watches: From Alignment to Alliance', *War on the Rocks*, 11 February 2022, https://warontherocks.com/2022/02/as-finland-watches-from-alignment-to-alliance/. Accessed 14 April, 2022.
19. Matti Pesu and Tuomas Iso-Markku, 'Finland as a NATO ally: First Insights into Finnish Alliance Policy', *Finnish Foreign Policy Paper*, no. 9 (Helsinki: Finnish Institute of International Affairs, December 2022), 48–50, https://www.fiia.fi/en/publication/finland-as-a-nato-ally. Accessed 14 April 2023.
20. Håkon Lunde Saxi, 'Nordic Defence Cooperation after the Cold War', *Oslo Files on Defence and Security*, no. 1 (Oslo: Norwegian Institute for Defence Studies (IFS), March 2011), https://fhs.brage.unit.no/fhs-xmlui/bitstream/handle/11250/99335/SAXI%2c%20Nordic%20defence%20Cooperation%20after%20the%20Cold%20War%20%282011%29.pdf?sequence=1&isAllowed=y. Accessed 20 March 2023; Tuomas Forsberg, 'The Rise of Nordic Cooperation: A Return To Regionalism?', *International Affairs*, vol. 89, no. 5, 2013, 1161–81.
21. Finnish Government, *Government's Defence Report 2017* (Helsinki, Prime Minister's Office, 2017), 16.
22. Tuomas Iso-Markku and Matti Pesu, 'From Neutrality to Activism: Finland and EU Defence', in Clara Sophie Cramer and Ulrike Franke (eds), *Ambiguous Alliance: Neutrality, Opt-outs, and European defence*, Essay Collection, European Council on Foreign Relations, 28 June

2021, https://ecfr.eu/publication/ambiguous-alliance-neutrality-opt-outs-and-european-defence/. Accessed 20 March 2023.

23. Iltalehti, 'Pääkirjoitus: Liittoumien synty on Niinistön uusi mantra—onko kyseessä ovela viesti Venäjälle?', *Iltalehti*, 10 December 2017, https://www.is.fi/paakirjoitus/art-2000005485222.html. Accessed 23 March 2023.

24. Finnish Government, *Puolustusministeriön tulevaisuuskatsaus: Turvallisuus ja puolustus—suomalaisen hyvinvoinnin kivijalka* (Helsinki: Finnish Government, 2018), 16.

25. Juha Pyykönen, 'Nordic Partners of NATO: How similar are Finland and Sweden within NATO cooperation?', *FIIA Report*, no. 48 (Helsinki: Finnish Institute of International Affairs, October 2016), https://www.fiia.fi/wp-content/uploads/2017/04/report48_finland_sweden_nato.pdf, p. 103.

26. Ministry of Defence of Sweden and Ministry of Defence of Finland, *Action Plan for Deepened Defence Cooperation between Finland and Sweden*, 6 May 2014, https://www.defmin.fi/files/2833/ACTION_PLAN_FOR_DEEPENED_DEFENCE_COOPERATION_BETWEEN_SWEDEN_AND_FINLAND.pdf. Accessed 21 March 2023.

27. Charly Salonius-Pasternak, 'Deeper Defence Cooperation: Finland and Sweden together again?', *FIIA Briefing Paper*, no. 163 (Helsinki: Finnish Institute of International Affairs, 2014), 3, https://www.fiia.fi/wp-content/uploads/2017/01/bp163.pdf. Accessed 21 March 2023.

28. Matti Pesu and Tuomas Iso-Markku, 'The Deepening Finnish-Swedish Security and Defence Relationship: From Operative Cooperation to "Strategic Interoperability"', *FIIA Briefing Paper*, no. 291 (Helsinki: Finnish Institute of International Affairs, October 2020), https://www.fiia.fi/wp-content/uploads/2020/09/bp291_the_finnish-swedish_security_and_defence_relationship.pdf. Accessed 20 March 2023.

29. Mikko Villikari, 'Finnish—Swedish naval co-operation', *Baltic Rim Economies*, 29 May 2019, University of Turku, https://sites.utu.fi/bre/finnish-swedish-naval-co-operation/. Accessed 14 April 2023.

30. Finnish Air Force, 'International Activities Develop Air Force Capability', https://ilmavoimat.fi/en/-/international-co-operation. Accessed 14 April 2023.

31. Charly Salonius-Pasternak, 'Ambiguity and Stability in the Baltic Sea Region: Defence Cooperation Between Finland and Sweden Increases Both', *FIIA Briefing Paper*, no. 241 (Helsinki: Finnish Institute of International Affairs, June 2018), 3, https://www.fiia.fi/wp-content/uploads/2018/06/bp241_ambiguity-and-stability-in-the-baltic-sea-region.pdf. Accessed 21 March 2023.
32. Ministry of Defence, 'Defence Cooperation Cetween Finland and Sweden', https://www.defmin.fi/en/areas_of_expertise/international_defence_cooperation/defence_cooperation_between_finland_and_sweden#0d118960. Accessed 14 April 2023.
33. Pesu & Iso-Markku, 'The Deepening Finnish-Swedish Security and Defence Relationship'.
34. Department of Defence of the United States of America and Ministry of Defence of Finland, *Statement of Intent between the Department of Defence of the United States of America and the Ministry of Defence of the Republic of Finland*, 7 October 2016, https://www.defmin.fi/files/3543/Statement_of_Intent.pdf. Accessed 9 March 2023.
35. Department of Defence of the United States of America, Ministry of Defence of Finland, Ministry of Defence of Sweden, *Trilateral Statement of Intent among the Department of Defence of the United States of America and the Ministry of Defence of the Republic of Finland and the Ministry of Defence of the Kingdom of Sweden*, 8 May 2018, https://www.defmin.fi/files/4231/Trilateral_Statement_of_Intent.pdf. Accessed 9 March 2023.
36. Ministry of Defence of Finland, Ministry of Defence of Norway and Ministry of Defence of Sweden, *Trilateral Statement of Intent on Enhanced Operational Cooperation among the Ministry of Defence of the Republic of Finland, the Ministry of Defence of the Kingdom of Norway and the Ministry of Defence of the Kingdom of Sweden*, 23 September 2020, https://www.defmin.fi/files/4995/FISENO_allekirjoitettu_aiejulistus_23.9.2020.pdf. Accessed 20 March 2023.
37. NORDEFCO, *Nordic Defence Cooperation Vision 2025*, 13 November 2018, https://www.nordefco.org/Files/nordefco-vision-2025-signed.pdf.
38. Matti Pesu, 'Finland', in Björn Fägersten (ed.), *The Nordics and the New European Security Architecture*, (Stockholm: Swedish Institute

of International Affairs, March 2020), 33, https://www.ui.se/globalassets/ui.se-eng/publications/ui-publications/2020/ui-report-no.-3-2020.pdf. Accessed 21 March 2023.
39. Ibid.
40. Sean Monaghan and Ed Arnold, 'Indispensable: NATO's Framework Nations Concept Beyond Madrid', *CSIS Briefs*, Centre for Strategic and International Studies, June 2022, https://www.csis.org/analysis/indispensable-natos-framework-nations-concept-beyond-madrid. Accessed 14 April 2023.
41. Joakim Erma Møller, 'Trilateral Defence Cooperation in The North, An Assessment Of Interoperability Between Norway, Sweden, and Finland', *Defence Studies*, vol. 19, no. 3, 2019, 235–56, https://www.tandfonline.com/doi/abs/10.1080/14702436.2019.1634473.
42. Ministry of Defence of Finland, Ministry of Defence of Norway and Ministry of Defence of Sweden, Trilateral Statement of Intent.
43. Håkon Lunde Saxi, 'Alignment but not Alliance, Nordic Operational Military Cooperation', *Arctic Review on Law and Politics*, vol. 13, 2022, 53–71.
44. President of the Republic of Finland Sauli Niinistö's New Year's Speech on 1 January 2022, https://www.presidentti.fi/en/speeches/president-of-the-republic-of-finland-sauli-niinistos-new-years-speech-on-1-january-2022/. Accessed 14 April, 2023; Finnish Government, Prime Minister Sanna Marin's New Year's Message, 31 December 2021, https://valtioneuvosto.fi/-/10616/paaministeri-sanna-marinin-uudenvuoden-tervehdys-31.12.2021?languageId=en_US. Accessed 14 April, 2023.
45. Olli Waris, Niinistö: Venäjä näki Suomen etupiiriinsä kuuluvana alueena, *Ilta-Sanomat*, 30 April 2022, https://www.is.fi/politiikka/art-2000008782511.html. Accessed 21 March 2023.
46. Sami Metelinen, Nato-jäsenyyden kannatuksessa on tapahtunut hyppäys, *EVA*, 26 October 2021, https://www.eva.fi/blog/2021/10/26/nato-jasenyyden-kannatuksessa-on-tapahtunut-hyppays/. Accessed 22 March 2023.
47. Yle, Ylen kysely: Enemmistö suomalaisista kannattaa Nato-jäsenyyttä, 28 February 2022, https://yle.fi/a/3-12336530. Accessed 22 March 2023.

48. Finnish government, *Government Report on Changes in The Security Environment*, Publications of the Finnish government 2022:20, Helsinki: Finnish Government, 2022).
49. Pesu & Iso-Markku, 'Finland as a NATO Ally', 12.
50. Ibid.
51. Ibid.
52. Finnish government, *Government Report on Changes in the Security Environment*, 14.
53. Richard Milne, 'Finland Warns of "Major Escalation Risk" in Europe Amid NATO Membership Debate', *Financial Times*, 20 March 2022, https://www.ft.com/content/e636c759-aad7-4ee1-b245-f3575dd5ce73. Accessed 4 April 2023.
54. Hanna Hanhinen, Jyrki Hara, Timo-Pekka Heima, 'Presidentti Niinistö Ylen Ykkösaamussa: Nato-jäsenyys olisi "riittävin" turva Suomelle, mutta päätöstä on pohdittava tarkkaan', *Yle Uutiset*, 26 March 2022, https://yle.fi/a/3-12377613. Accessed 4 April 2023.
55. Monaghan and Arnold, 'Indispensable'.
56. Government of the United Kingdom and Government of Finland, *United Kingdom—Finland Statement*, 11 May 2022, https://assets.publishing.service.gov.uk/government/uploads/system/uploads/attachment_data/file/1074242/UNITED_KINGDOM_-_FINLAND_STATEMENT.pdf. Accessed 14 April 2023.
57. Waris, 'Niinistö: Venäjä näki Suomen etupiiriinsä kuuluvana alueena'.
58. See Pesu & Iso-Markku, 'Finland as a NATO Ally'.
59. On NATO's evolving deterrence and defence posture, see the speech by SACEUR Cavoli on 9 January 2023, at Rikskonferensen in Sälen, Sweden, https://shape.nato.int/saceur/saceur-cavoli-remarks-at-rikskonferensen--salen--sweden.
60. Finnish Defence Forces, 'High-Altitude Capability System Now Selected', 5 April 2023, https://puolustusvoimat.fi/en/-/1950813/high-altitude-capability-system-now-selected. Accessed 14 April 2023.
61. Håkon Lunde Saxi and Karsten Friis, 'After Crimea: The Future of Nordic Defence Cooperation', *NUPI Policy Brief* (Oslo: Norwegian Institute of International Affairs, June 2018), https://fhs.brage.unit.no/fhs-xmlui/bitstream/handle/11250/2593726/

SAXI%20and%20FRIIS.%20After%20Crimea.%202018. pdf?sequence=1&isAllowed=y. Accessed 4 September 2023.
62. Ministry of Defence of Finland, Ministry of Defence of Norway and Ministry of Defence of Sweden, *Statement of Intent on Enhanced Operational Cooperation among the Ministry of Defence of Finland, the Ministry of Defence of Norway, and the Ministry of Defence of Sweden*, 22 November 2022, https://www.defmin.fi/files/5539/SENOFI_SOI.pdf. Accessed 20 March 2023.
63. Kati Pohjanpalo and Niklas Rolander, 'Nordic Nations Agree to Jointly Operate Fighter Jet Fleet of 250', *Bloomberg*, 24 March 2023, https://www.bloomberg.com/news/articles/2023-03-24/nordic-nations-agree-to-jointly-operate-fighter-jet-fleet-of-250. Accessed 14 April 2023.
64. Finnish government, 'United States and Finland to open negotiations on an agreement on defence cooperation', 29 September 2022, https://valtioneuvosto.fi/en/-/united-states-and-finland-to-open-negotiations-on-an-agreement-on-defence-cooperation. Accessed 14 April 2023.
65. Finnish government, *Government Report on Changes in the Security Environment*, 23.
66. Government of the United Kingdom and government of Finland, *United Kingdom—Finland Statement*.
67. Finnish government, *Government Report on Changes in The Security Environment*, 23.
68. Lauri Nurmi, 'Viron puolustusministeri Iltalehdelle, Suomen ja Viron ohjuksilla luodaan Suomenlahdelle Nato-sulku', *Iltalehti*, 12 August 2022, https://www.iltalehti.fi/politiikka/a/0932ec99-89e7-4f85-8a6e-e39dbb43da79. Accessed 14 April 2023.
69. Pesu and Iso-Markku, 'Finland as a NATO Ally', 41.

10. NATO AND THE UKRAINE DEFENSE CONTACT GROUP
1. Interviews, NATO HQ, 21–22 March 2023.
2. Bence Nemeth, *How to Achieve Defence Cooperation in Europe? The Subregional Approach* (Bristol: Bristol University Press, 2022).

3. Palgrave Macmillan, 2018.
4. Ibid.
5. Asmus, R. *The Little War that Shook the World*, Palgrave Macmillan: London, 2010.
6. Lawrence Freedman, 'The Battle fir Kherson and Why it Matters', *Comment is Freed*, 27 July 2002.
7. Washington Post, 'Road to War: US Struggled to Convince Allies, and Zelensky, of Risk of Invasion', 16 August 2022.
8. Details of weapon types and donation timing are provided in the Kiel Institute for the World Economy Ukraine Defence Tracker.
9. Yaffa, J, 'Inside the effort to arm Ukraine', *The New Yorker*, 17 October 2022.
10. Forum on the arms trade, https://www.forumarmstrade.org/.
11. WSJ, 'Who is Really Sending Aid to Ukraine?', 16 June 2022.
12. See E Gunnarsdottir, P Rieker and M Riddervold: 'EU Response to Ukraine War and Implications for Norway' in Cheering, T: *War in Ukraine*, Universitetsforlaget, 2023.
13. Courtney Kube, Julie Tsirkin, Monica Alba and Gabe Gutierrez, 'Biden Tells Zelensky That US Will Send Ukraine ATACMS', *NBC News*, 22 September 2023.
14. Ibid.
15. Ibid.
16. Ibid.
17. Ibid.
18. *The New York Times*, 13 September 2022.
19. Cancian, M., 'Is the US Running Out of Weapons to Send to Ukraine?', *CSIS*, 16 September 2022; *The Wall Street Journal*, 'Who is Really Sending Aid to Ukraine?', 16 June 2022.
20. Ryan, M., 'The West Needs to Boost Its Industrial Capacity Fast', *Engelsberg Ideas*, 24 November 2022.
21. Sonnenfeld, J. *et al.*, 'Business Retreats and Sanctions Are Crippling the Russian Economy', *SSRN*, 7 September 2022.
22. Jentleson, B., 'Who's Winning the Sanctions War?', *Foreign Policy*, 18 August 2022.
23. 'Ukraine War: US provides offensive weapons for first time', *Geopolitical Monitor*, 9 January 2023.

24. Snyder, G., 'The security dilemma in alliance politics', *World Politics*, 1984, 36, 4, 461–95.
25. *En god alliert. Norge I Afghanistan, 2002-2014, NOU* 8: 2016.
26. Yaffa, J., 'Inside the Effort to Arm Ukraine', *The New Yorker*, 17 October 2022.
27. Walt, S., *The Origin of Alliances,* Cornell University Press, 1967.
28. Following the invasion, almost half the population changed their opinion in favour of increasing defence spending to 2% of GDP, 'Germany's Era: Too little, too late?', *Geopolitical Monitor*, 15 September 2022.
29. Yaffa, J., 'Inside the Effort to Arm Ukraine'.
30. The US National Security Strategy, 2022.
31. Day, M., 'Poland Builds Europe's Largest Land Force Two Counter Russian Threat', *The Telegraph*, 11 March 2023.
32. Chalmers, M., 'The UK as a European Power', *RUSI*, 24 February 2023.
33. Melvin, N., 'The UK and European Security: Five Lessons from the Ukraine War', *RUSI*, 1 March 2023.
34. Philipp Fritz, 'Im Osten wächst das Misstrauen gegen Berlin und Paris', 1 March 2023.
35. Shurkin M., 'Olaf Scholz and the New, New Europe', blog, 23 January 2023.
36. Coffey, L., 'Nato is Back', *Engelsberg Ideas*, 17 February 2023.
37. Secrétariat général de la Défense et de la Sécurité Nationale (French Ministry of Defence), *Revue Nationale Strategique*, 28 November 2022, 7.
38. 'Ukraine's Fate Will Determine the West's Authority in The World', *The Economist*, 25 February 2023, 6.
39. Sage, A., 'Russian Regime Change Leads To "Worse Options", Says President Macron', *The Sunday Times*, 20 February 2023.
40. Ibid.
41. Robert Kagan, 'For a Free World If You Can Keep It', Foreign *Affairs*, 20.12.2022
42. Walter Russell Mead, 'The Frailty Behind Europe's Triumphalism over the Ukraine War', *The Wall Street Journal*, 24.1.2023.
43. Ibid.

44. James Crisp: 'Emmanuel Macron 'Abandon's EU Army Dreams'', *The Telegraph*, 3.3.2023. This has not been confirmed by the French, but by the Czech president, former general Petr Pavel, whose source was talks with Macron during the Munich Conference this year.
45. Alain Tao, 'Olof Scholz' China Gamble', *The Diplomat*, 22.12.2022.
46. 'China's Position on the Political Settlement of the Ukraine Crisis', Ministry of Foreign Affairs of the Republic of China, 24 February 2023.
47. Kine, P., 'U.S. Dismisses China's Ukraine Peace Proposal as an Attempt to Distract', *Politico*, 24 February 2023.
48. Calcutt, C., 'Macron Fails to Move Xi Jinping Over Russia's War on Ukraine', *Politico*, 6 April 2023.
49. Ibid.
50. Calcutt, C., 'The Warm Embrace and the Cold Shoulder: China Mines Europe's Fractures During Joint Visit', *Politico,* 6 April 2023.
51. 'China's Xi Courts France's Macron in Bid to Drive Wedge Between Europe and U.S.', *Time Magazine*, 5 April 2023.
52. Taroor, I., 'Macron's China Trip Turns into a European Uproar', *Washington Post*, 12 April 2023.
53. 'Macron incite les Européens à ne pas se penser en "suiveurs" des Etats-Unis', interview with President Emmanuel Macron, *Politico*, 9 April 2023.

INDEX

Note: Page numbers followed by "*n*" refer to notes, "*t*" refer to tables, "*f* " refer to figures.

Abkhazia, 120
Abrams, 129
Afghanistan, 23, 31, 35, 36, 134, 136, 199, 211, 214
'AirLand Battle', 29
Akkadian empire, 236*n*5
Alexander I, Tsar, 106
    America, 107, 113, 118
    Russia's learning, 133–9
American F-18 aircraft, 179
American intelligence, 202
American military, 145
AMX-10, 210
'Anschluss', 112
anti-access, area denial (A2AD) defences, 27, 30, 36
Antonov airport, 203
Apotheosis of War, The (Vereshchagin,), 105
Arctic region, 186
Armenia, 36
'Army 2035', 126

Army Civilians, 126
Army Modernization Strategy, 126
Army Reserve, 126
Article (5), 16, 55, 122, 197
Article (51), 197
artificial intelligence (AI), 24–5, 30, 34, 145
    See also internet of things (IoT)
Asia, 10, 42, 105, 135, 147, 149, 150
Assad's regime, 120
ATAC-MS long-range artillery, 209
Atlantic Ocean, 72, 95
AUKUS, 2–4, 31–2
Australia, 2–4, 31, 32, 60, 148, 149, 197, 204
Austro–Prussian War, 106–7
Azerbaijan, 36

Baerbock, Annalena, 160, 163–4
'balance of powers', 106

INDEX

Balkan wars, 169
Balkans, 213
Baltic Air Policing mission, 78, 83, 164
Baltic deployment, 83–35, 84f
Baltic region
Baltic Sea, 62, 76, 90, 91, 121, 122, 127–8, 164, 165, 180, 182–3
   Baltic deployment, 83–5, 84f, 95
   See also Black Sea
Baltic States, 12–13, 56–7, 59, 78, 82, 109, 186, 202, 206, 211, 216, 221
BALTOPS, 76, 83, 85, 90, 91
Basic Law (Germany's constitutional), 157
'battle rhythm', 26
Bauer, Rob, 5
Beijing, 16, 131, 146, 220
Belarus, 113, 124
Belgium, 92
Belt and Road Initiative, 148
Berlin, 154, 156, 160–1, 162, 173, 178
Biden, Joe, 31, 42, 59, 123, 134
   alliance, 211–14
   Biden administration, 147, 167, 203
   Ukraine, arms aid to, 140–2, 204–7
   See also Europe; Ukraine
Black Sea, 58, 122, 124
Blainey, Geoffrey, 141
Blinken, Anthony, 203, 220
'blue force tracker', 29

Bradley (infantry fighting vehicle), 162
Bradley, 210
Brazil, 111
Brexit, 200
Briand-Kellogg Pact, 110–11
Britain, 4, 101–2, 113, 116, 134, 203, 206, 209, 211, 221
   frontline coalition and pragmatic group, 216–18
   Russian military, 139–43
British army, 128
British nuclear weapons, 59
British, 59, 100, 110, 114, 200, 208, 210, 215, 219
British aircraft carriers, 9
British army, 128
British forces, 142
British government, 149
British leadership, 12, 221
   frontline coalition and pragmatic group 216–18
   'refresh' strategy, 4
   Ukraine, arms aid to, 204–7
   See also Europe; United States (US)
Budapest Memorandum, 113
Bulgaria, 126
Bundestag, 122, 170
Bundeswehr, 122, 127–8, 157, 159, 166–7, 170, 171, 173
Burns, William, 202
Bush, George W., 140
   See also United States (US)

Canada, 80, 121, 204
Carthage, 42

INDEX

Cashman, Edward, 78
Catherine the Great, 112
Central African Republic, 139
Central Asia, 105, 108
Central Europe, 12, 17, 205, 216, 218
Central European states, 10, 63, 122, 124
CH-47F Chinook heavy transport helicopters, 158
Chechnya, 120, 133, 213
Chemical, Biological, Radiological and Nuclear materials (CBRN), 52
China, vii, 4, 33, 35, 42–3, 55, 58, 61, 105, 108, 133, 172, 213, 214–15, 236n4
   China's learning, 146–50
   coalition, durablility, 218–20
   EU and, 219–20
   interdependence, 117–20
   Russia's military, 138
   strategic concepts, use and utility, 44–51, 47–9t, 51t
   support, 135
   vs. west, 144–6
   See also North Korea; Russia; Xi Jin Ping
Chinese armed force, 30
Christian, 106
Churchill, Winston, 146
CIA, 203
Close-quarter combat, 37
Cold Response, 82
Cold War, 5, 15, 22, 45–6, 100, 107, 109, 112, 117, 169, 178–9

Multidomain Concept, origins of, 28–31
NATO, weapon systems, 127–9
command and control (C2), 24–5
Common Security and Defence Policy (CSDP), 181, 186
communism, 104, 108
Communist Party, 145
Commynes, Philippe de, 105–6
Concept for Deterrence and Defense of the Euro-Atlantic Area (DDA), viii, 125–7, 130
Conservative Party (CDU/CSU), 156–8, 169–70
Continent of Peace, 116
Coordinated Annual Review on Defence, 186
COVID-19, 82–3, 101, 102
   Baltic deployment, 83–5, 84f
Crimea, 35, 140, 179, 189–90, 197, 200, 201, 207
   Post-Crimea Deterrence Policy, 181–7
   Russia's annexion, 109, 112, 120, 124, 169, 176, 197, 214
Cutlass Fury, 80
Czech Republic, 12, 205, 216

Danish air force, 121
Davis, Michael C., 30
Davos, 161
D-Day, 28
de Klerk, Tara, 7–8
Defence Cooperation Agreement, 192

265

INDEX

Defense Advanced Research Projects Agency (DARPA), 25–6
Delpeche, Therese, 141
Denmark, 92, 106, 121, 192
DeSantis, Ron, 218
Deter and Defend strategy. *See* Concept for Deterrence and Defense of the Euro-Atlantic Area (DDA)
deus ex machina, 211
Die Welt (newspaper), 216–17
Dolchstoßlegende, 120
Donbas (Eastern Ukraine), 8, 99, 200
Donetsk, 124, 203
Dutch Ministry of Defence, 62
Dutch review (2020), 114
Dutch, 62
Dybbøl, Battle of, 106
Dynamic Guard, 76, 85, 91
Dynamic Mariner, 88
Dynamic Mongoose, 78, 82–3, 88, 91
Dynamic Warrior, 91

Eastern Europe, 108, 109, 154, 165, 202, 210, 215
Eastern European states, 63
eastern Ukraine, 112, 176
Economist, The (newspaper), 217
EI2, 186
18 HIMARS rocket launchers, 129
11 September 2001 (terrorist attacks), vii, 46, 169
See also IS (terror group)

Elizabeth (Queen), 85
Emerson, Ralph Waldo, 149
Energiewende, 118
England, 42
English Channel, 83
enhanced Air Policing (eAP), 164
Enhanced Forward Presence (eFP), 164
Estonia, 126, 193
Estonian coastal defence, 193
EU Global Strategy (2016), 186
EU Rapid Deployment Capacity, 114–15
Euro-Atlantic Area, 3, 42–4, 52, 59, 60, 125, 126–7, 130–1
Euro-Atlantic security, 172–3
Europe, 1, 4–6, 9–15, 17, 46, 92, 106–7, 154, 161–2, 165–6, 204, 213
  defence, 99–103
  Germany's policy, 153–5
  interdependence, 117–20
  MDI and MDO, analysis of, 34–9
  MDI, allies and partners, 31–4
  military planning, US–UK role in, 207–11
  multidomain concept, origins of, 28–31
  NATO, burden-transferring, 130–1
  NATO, change, 63–4
  NATO, defence, 62–3
  NATO, internal strengths and weaknesses, 58–60
  NATO, stakeholders, 60–2

INDEX

NATO, Ukraine in, 123–5
NATO, weapon systems, 127–9
polities, relations between, 103–9
Russia's learning, 133–9
strategic concept, 41–4
Ukraine war, European reactions, 113–16
Ukraine, arms aid to, 204–7
war, outcomes, 111–13
See also Brexit; European Union (EU); Finland; Germany; Russia; Sweden; Ukraine
European armed forces, 39
European Central Bank, 100
European Commission, 186, 205–6
European Defence Community, 99
European Defence Fund, 186
European Intervention Initiative (EI2), 186
European Peace Facility fund, 205
European Sky Shield Initiative, 166
European Union (EU), 2, 60, 123, 135, 176, 201, 217
coalition, durablility, 218–20
Europe, defence, 99–103
Finland's bilateral defence cooperation, 181–7
Finland's NATO membership, 187–90
frontline coalition and pragmatic group 216–18
NATO, burden-transferring, 130–1
Russia's learning, 133–9
Ukraine war, European reactions, 113–16
Ukraine, arms aid to, 204–7
war, outcomes, 111–13
Exercise Task Group 17-1, 76

F-16s, 206–7
F-35A combat aircraft, 158
Fascist Italy, 107
Federal Ministry of Finance, 159
Federal Republic, 161
FGS Berlin, 88
financial crisis (2008), 102
Finland, 2, 4, 11–12, 16, 18, 57, 58, 95, 135, 175–7, 194–5, 205, 210, 212, 221
Finland's bilateral defence cooperation, 181–7
Finland's Miliary Cooperation, 190–4
Finnish defence policy, 177–81
NATO membership, 187–90
in NATO, 121–3
See also Nordic Defence Cooperation (NORDEFCO); Norway; Sweden
Finnish air force, 184
Finnish coastal defence, 193
Finnish defence policy, 179
Finnish minelayer, 78
Finnish–Norwegian agenda, 185
Finnish–Russian relationship, 177, 180

INDEX

Finnish–Swedish defence cooperation, 183–4, 187
Finnish–UK defence relationship, 193
Florida, 219
Flotex Silver, 80
FNC, 186
Foreign Affairs (article), 172
Foreign Affairs (journal), 154
14 Challenger 2 tanks, 210
Framework Nations Concept (FNC), 186
France, 4, 31, 42, 54, 62–3, 85, 88, 92, 101, 116, 122–3, 125, 162, 186, 190, 199–200, 204–5, 210–11, 219
    frontline coalition and pragmatic group 216–18
    See also Hitler, Adolf
Freedman, Lawrence, 135–6, 141
French army, 128
French national security, 63
French nuclear weapons, 59

G-20, 135
G-7, 135
Gauck, Joachim, 169
GCHQ, 143
Geneva Conventions, 213
Georgia, 55–6, 58, 61, 109, 120, 201, 202, 203, 212
German Air Force, 164
German Bundesrat, 157
German Bundestag, 153, 157
German defense industry, 128
German Eurofighter combat aircraft, 164
German Ministry of Defence (BMVg), 158
German Navy, 164–5
Germany, 11, 14, 41, 62, 92, 102, 112, 116, 120, 135, 137, 173–4, 186, 199, 204–6, 210–13
    artillery, 32
    defence budget, 155–9
    frontline coalition and pragmatic group 216–18
    to NATO, Germany's commitment, 163–8
    policy changes, 153–5
    security and military power, 168–73
    Ukraine, delivering weapons to, 159–63
    See also Hitler, Adolf; North Atlantic Treaty Organisation (NATO)
Giegerich, Bastian, 166, 170–1
Gleichschaltung, 104
Global Strategy (2016), 113
Global War on Terror, 117, 130
Good Ally, A (Afghanistan report), 212
Gorbachev, Mikhail, 120
GPS (global positioning system), 29
Graduated Response Plans, 72
Grant, Ulysses, 144
Gravelotte, Battles of, 107
Green Party, 164
'grey zone', 33, 40
Gulf of Finland, 193
Gulf War I, 29
Guttenberg, Karl-Theodor zu, 128

INDEX

HDMS Peter Willemoes, 80
Helsinki Final Act, 112
Helsinki, 121, 122, 178, 180–1,
   186–7, 192, 193–4, 195
Herculean effort, 114
Heuser, Beatrice, 10–11
HIMARS, 208
Hitler, Adolf, 29, 112, 120
HMS Northumberland, 80
HNLMS Rotterdam, 88
Hoffman, Frank, 30
Horn of Africa, 72
Host Nation Support agreement,
   214
Hostomel, 203
Howard, Michael, 141
Hungary, 12, 121, 102, 126, 205,
   212, 216

Iceland, 78
imperialist Japan, 107
India, 108, 111, 236*n*4
Indo-Pacific, 60, 64
Integrated Review, 114
international law, 33, 108, 110,
   136, 180, 201, 213
International Monetary Fund
   (IMF), 148
International Security Assistance
   Force (ISAF), 23, 211
internet of things (IoT), 34
Iran, 52, 148
Iraq War II, 117
Iraq War, 110
Iraq, 35, 36, 61, 136, 140, 169
IS (terror group), 169
Islam, 104

Israel, 61
Italy, 112, 137, 162

Japan, 60, 112, 149, 197
   See also World War II
JAS Gripens, 207
Javelins, 208
Jentleson, Bruce, 209
Johnson, Rob, 7
Joint All-Domain Command and
   Control (JADC2), 127
'Joint All-Domain Operations', 31
Joint Expeditionary Force (JEF),
   2, 16, 186, 190, 193, 214
Joint Warrior (17-1), 76
Joint Warrior (20-2), 85
Joint Warrior, 78, 83, 88, 91
Jordan, 61

Kabul, 55
Kaliningrad, 134
Kazakhstan, 113
Kharkiv, 208
Kherson, 8, 207
Kiev, 55
Klingbeil, Lars, 170
Kofman, Michael, 142
Kola Peninsula, 192
Königgrätz/Sadowa, Battle of,
   106–7
Korea, 46, 197
Korean War, 35
Kosovo, 110, 213
Krab, 129
Kremlin. *See* Russia
Kuehnert, Kenvin, 170
Kuwait, 140, 199

269

INDEX

Kyiv, 8, 32, 112, 123, 162–3, 203, 204, 208

Lancaster House agreement, 3
Latvia, 126
Lavigne, Philippe, 57
Lavrov, Sergei, 146, 203
League of Nations, 107, 108–9
Lee, Rob, 142
Leo VI, 45
Leopard 2 tanks, 128, 162, 210, 217
Leopard 2s, 129, 162
Libya, 35
Lithuania, 62, 126, 164, 205, 206
London, 31
Luhansk, 124, 203
Lukashenko, Aleksandr, 124

M1 Abrams, 162
M1A2 sepV3 tanks, 129
M270 MLRS self-propelled rocket artillery, 161
Macron, Emmanuel, 62–3, 101, 203, 217, 219, 220
Madrid Summit, 60
Madrid, 164
Marder (infantry fighting vehicle), 162, 210
Marin, Sanna, 188
Maritime Command (MARCOM), 165
Mariupol, 37
Mead, Walter Russel, 218–19
Mediterranean, 9, 72, 85, 101
Medvedev, Dmitry, 146
Merkel, Angela, 166, 200

Michael Corleone syndrome, 42
Microsoft, 137
Middle East, 31, 55, 61, 102, 120
Mig-29 combat aircraft, 163
Miley, Mark, 141, 208
Minister of Foreign Affairs (Germany), 160
Minsk agreements, 200
MLRS rockets, 208
Morocco, 61
Moscow, 104, 178, 202, 203
    China's visit, 219
multi-domain integration (MDI), 7, 22, 39–40
    allies and partners, incorporating, 31–4
    analysis, 34–9
    definition, 23–8
    origins of, 28–31
multidomain operations (MDOs), 7, 22, 39–40, 57
    analysis, 34–9
    definition, 23–8
    MDI, allies and partners, 31–4
    origins of, 28–31
Multi-Domain Operations Conference (NATO), 57
Munich Security Conference, 169, 217
Muslims, 104
Mussolini, Benito, 107
Mützenich, Rolf, 170

Nammo, 211
Napoleonic Wars, 106
National Guard, 126

INDEX

National Security Strategy, 171–2
NATO Defence Planning Process, 190–1
NATO Integrated Air and Missile Defence, 191
'NATO lake', 121
NATO Maritime Command, 76
NATO Research Vessel, 78
NATO Response Force, 56, 59, 72
NATO, strategic concepts, 65–9*t*
   change, 63–4
   defence, impact, 62–3
   effort, 56–8
   goals, 53–6
   internal strengths and weaknesses, 58–60
   security environment, 52–3
   stakeholders, 60–2
   use and utility, 44–51, 47–9*t*, 51*t*
NATO's Response Force Maritime Component (NRF/M), 80
NATO–EU Joint Declaration, 60–1
Nazi Germany, 42, 107
Nelson, Horatio, 144
Nemeth, Bence, 2
Netherlands, 88, 92, 100–1
New Force Model (NATO), 56–7, 167
'New Russia', 112
New Yorker, The (magazine), 205
New Zealand, 60
Newfoundland, 80
Nexter, 211
Ngorno-Karabagh, 36
Nigeria, 111

Niinistö, Sauli, 180, 182, 188–9
9/11 attacks. *See* 11 September 2001
19 F-16s, 207
Nixon, Richard, 119
Non-Proliferation Treaty, 54–5
Nord Stream 1, 120
Nord Stream 2 pipeline project, 120, 166
Nord Stream pipelines, 120, 165
Nordic Defence Cooperation (NORDEFCO), 4, 16, 181, 185–6
Nordic–Baltic region, 191, 193
North Africa, 55, 61
North Atlantic Council, 198
North Atlantic Ocean, 165
North Atlantic Treaty Organisation (NATO)
   burden-transferring, 130–1
   Europe, defence, 99–103
   Finland's bilateral defence cooperation, 181–7
   Finland's Miliary Cooperation, 190–4
   Finland's NATO membership, 187–90
   German Zeitenwende, 14
   Germany's commitment, 163–8
   interlocking challenges, 125–7
   MDI and MDO, analysis of, 34–9
   MDI, allies and partners, 31–4
   multidomain concept, origins of, 28–31

271

INDEX

NATO Strategic Concept, 7–8, 125
  politics, change in, 103–9
  strategic integration, 1–2
  Sweden and Finland in, 121–3
  weapon systems, 127–9
  See also Minsk agreements
North Atlantic, 15, 91, 186
North Korea, 52, 148
North Sea, 78, 165
Northern Europe, 5, 12, 17, 57, 59, 92, 176, 182, 191, 194, 221–2
Northern Norway, 80, 82, 83
North-West Europe, 28
Norway, 121, 165, 176, 177, 178, 185, 192, 204, 211, 214, 221
  frontline coalition and pragmatic group 216–18
  See also Nordic Defence Cooperation (NORDEFCO), 4, 16, 181, 185–6
Norwegian government, 204
Norwegian oil and gas platforms, 165
Norwegian Sea, 192
Nova Scotia, 80
Novaya Rossiya. *See* 'New Russia'
Nyberg, René, 178

Ohio, 219
189 K2 tanks, 129
155-mm artillery ammunition, 208

155-mm artillery rounds, 211
One Hundred Years War, 42
Operation Enduring Freedom, 199, 211
Operation Ocean Shield, 74
Oslo, 5

Panzerhaubitze 2000, 161
Paris, 4, 31–2
Parliamentary Commissioner for the Armed Forces, 158
Partnership for Peace (PfP), 179, 214, 215
Pax Augusta, 104
Pax Britannica, 104
People's Republic of China. *See* China
Permanent Structured Cooperation projects, 186–7, 199
Persia, 103
Pistorius, Boris, 158–9
plus 32 F-35 aircraft, 129
Poland, 6, 10, 102, 122, 123, 124, 126, 129, 202, 205, 206, 209, 210, 211, 216, 221
  as a leader, 12
PT-91, 129
Puma infantry vehicles, 167
Punic Wars, 42
Putin, Vladimir, 6, 101, 112, 113, 140, 146–7, 166, 202, 203, 213, 215
  China and, 119–20
  Russia's learning, 133–43
  special military operation, 115

INDEX

See also China; India; Minsk agreements; Nord Stream pipelines; Russia; Xi Jin Ping

Rafale plane, 207
Ramstein-contact group, 167
RAND study, 128
Realpolitik, 109
Rear Admiral, 78
reformation, 104–9
Regular Army, 126
Republic of Korea, 60, 129, 204, 208.
Republic of Moldova, 60
return on investment, 26
Rheinmetall, 128, 211
Rhine, 28
Ringtausch, 205
Roman Empire, 103
Romania, 126, 129, 164, 205, 216
Romano-Christian model, 104
Rome, 42
Royal Navy, 85
Royal Netherlands Army, 62
Royal Norwegian Navy, 76
Royal United Services Institute, 141
rules-based international order (RBIO), 110–11, 112, 113
Russia– United States summit (2018), 180
Russia
  China vs. west, 144–6
  China's learning, 146–50
  cyber tools, 143–4
  Europe, defence, 99–103

Finland's bilateral defence cooperation, 181–7
Finland's NATO membership, 187–90
Finnish defence policy, 177–81
Germany's policy, 153–5
interdependence, 117–20
military, 139–43
reformation, 103–9
Russia's learning, 133–9
self-determination, 110–11
SNMG1, 71–4
strategic concept, 41–4
US leadership, 202–3
war, European reactions, 113–16
war, outcomes, 111–13
See also China; Minsk agreements; Putin, Vladimir; Ukraine
Russian armed force, 30
Russkij Mir, 112
Ryabkov, Sergei, 202
Ryan, Mick, 141
Rzeszów-Jasionka, 123

Sahel, 55, 61
Saint Petersburg, 193
Sarkozy, Nicolas, 201
Schelling, Tom, 141
Scholz, Olaf, 122, 156–7, 161, 163, 165, 166–7, 173–4, 203
  Scholz government, 153–5
  security and military power, 168–73
  tweet, 159–60
Zeitenwende speech, 159

INDEX

Schreer, Ben, 170–1
Sedan, Battles of, 107
self-determination, 110–11
Serbia, 110, 213
71st Airborne, 202
Sherman, Wendy, 202
Sino-Russian alliance, 117
Slovakia, 12, 126, 164, 216
Social Democratic Party (SPD), 156–8, 161, 169
Solferino, 106
South Korea. *See* Republic of Korea
South Ossetia, 120
South-East Asia, 236*n*4
Soviet 122 mm, 210
Soviet Union, 112, 113, 116, 119, 134, 177, 178
Spain, 92
Srebrenica, 213
Stalin, Joseph Vissarionovich, 112
Standing NATO Maritime Group 1 (SNMG1), 8–9, 71–4
  Baltic deployment, 83–5, 84*f*
  control, 88
  COVID-19 arrives, 82–3
  lacking contributions, 74–8, 75*f*, 77*f*
  Maritime-Strategic Integration, backbone of, 90–4
  modest contributions, 85–8, 86*f*, 87*f*
  ships, turnover of, 88–90, 89*f*
  US flagship and deployment, 80–1, 81*f*
  US flagship and substantial contributions, 78–9, 79*f*

Standing NATO Mine Countermeasures Group 1 (SNMCMG1), 82
  Baltic deployment, 83–5, 84*f*
Steinmeier, Frank-Walter, 162–3
Stingers, 208
Stockholm, 121, 122
Stoltenberg, Jens, 165, 198
Storm Shadow missiles, 209
Strategic Compass (2022), 113–14
strategic integration, 90–4
strategique, 45
Sub-Sahara, 61
Sullivan, Jake, 202, 208, 220
Supreme Allied Commander Europe (SACEUR), 57, 130
Supreme Headquarters Allied Powers Europe (SHAPE), 126
swarm-control, 34
Sweden, 2, 4, 6, 11–12, 16, 18, 57, 59, 95, 135, 137, 176, 177, 178, 180, 189, 190, 205, 212, 221
  Finland's bilateral defence cooperation, 181–7
  Finland's Miliary Cooperation, 190–4
  Finland's NATO membership, 187–90
  in NATO, 121–3
  See also Nordic Defence Cooperation (NORDEFCO)
Swedish air force, 184
Swedish corvette, 77
Swedish–Finnish Amphibious Task Unit, 184

INDEX

Swedish–Finnish Naval Task Group, 184
Sweijs, Tim, 7–8
Syria, 35, 52, 120, 133, 139, 169

T-72 tanks, 129
T-72s, 204
Taiwan, 145, 147, 149–50, 213, 220
Taktika, 45
Tallinn Pledge, 12–13
Tbilisi, 201
10th Panzer Division, 100
Terhelle, Maximilian, 166
Third Reich, 112
'Third Rome', 104
13th Light Brigade, 100
Time (Magazine), 220
tockholm International Peace Research Institute, 158
Transatlantic Outlook, 62
Trump, Donald, 42, 218
Tunisia, 61
Turkey, 63, 100, 108, 121
Twitter, 159–60
288 K239 Chunmoo rocket artillery launchers, 129
212 K9 self-propelled howitzers, 129

UDCG, 218
UK force, 202
Ukraine Defense Contact Group (UDCG), 198, 199–200, 204, 210, 218, 220, 221
Ukraine
   arms aid to, 204–7

China vs. west, 144–6
China's learning, 146–50
coup de main, 8
Europe, defence, 99–103
Finland's bilateral defence cooperation, 181–7
Finland's NATO membership, 187–90
Germany, security and military power, 168–73
Germany's policy, 153–5
interdependence, 117–20
military planning, US–UK role in, 207–11
in NATO, 123–5
NATO, burden-transferring, 130–1
NATO, weapon systems, 127–9
reformation, 103–9
Russia's learning, 133–9
self-determination, 110–11
SNMG1, 71–4
strategic integration, 1–2
Ukraine Defense Contact Group (UDCG), 199–201
Ukraine, delivering weapons to, 159–63
US leadership, 202–3
war, European reactions, 113–16
war, outcomes, 111–13
western support, 139–43
See also Minsk agreements; Zelenskyy, Volodymyr
Ukrainian military, 139
UN Charter, 11, 110, 197, 201, 212–13

275

INDEX

UN's Security Council, 107, 108–9, 111
United Kingdom (UK), 2–3, 54, 92, 162, 177, 186, 193, 194, 204
   China vs. west, 144–6
   Finland's bilateral defence cooperation, 181–7
   Finland's NATO membership, 187–90
   frontline coalition and pragmatic group 216–18
   Germany, security and military power, 168–73
   Germany's policy, 153–5
   multidomain concept, origins of, 28–31
   NATO, burden-transferring, 130–1
   NATO, burden-transferring, 130–1
   NATO, weapon systems, 127–9
   Russia's learning, 133–9
   Ukraine Defense Contact Group (UDCG), 199–201
   Ukraine, delivering weapons to, 159–63
   US–UK role in, 207–11
   war, outcomes, 111–13
   See also Britain; North Atlantic Treaty Organisation (NATO)
United Nations (UN), 107, 108–9
   See also World Trade Organization (WTO),
United States (US), 2–3, 5–6, 9, 54, 64, 92, 110, 162, 167, 176, 177, 180, 192, 194, 204, 210
   China vs. west, 144–6
   China's learning, 146–50
   coalition, 211–15
   coalition, durablility, 218–20
   Europe, defence, 99–103
   Finland's bilateral defence cooperation, 181–7
   Finland's NATO membership, 187–90
   frontline coalition and pragmatic group 216–18
   Germany, security and military power, 168–73
   interdependence, 117–20
   MDI, allies and partners, 31–4
   NATO, burden-transferring, 130–1
   NATO, Ukraine in, 123–5
   NATO, weapon systems, 127–9
   Russia's learning, 133–9
   Russian military vs., 139–43
   strategic concept, 41–4
   Ukraine war, European reactions, 113–16
   Ukraine, delivering weapons to, 159–63
   US leadership, 202–3
   war, outcomes, 111–13
   See also Biden, Joe; North Atlantic Treaty Organisation (NATO)
University of Prague, 165
US administration, 100
US Air Force, 31
US destroyer, 76–7
US East Coast, 80

INDEX

US force, 202
US Joint Force, 126–7
US military resources, 130
US military, 56–7, 59, 117
US war (2001–21), 136
US war (2003–10), 136
USS Ross, 83
USSR. *See* Soviet Union,
Uyghur population, 105

Vereshchagin, Vassiliy, 105
Very High Readiness Joint Task Force (VJTF), 167
Vilnius, 159
von der Leyen, Ursula, 220

Wales summit, 183
Wales, 156
Wallace, Ben, 12–13
Walt, Stephen, 213–14
Wandel durch Handel, 118
Warsaw Pact, 116, 123
Warsaw Treaty Organisation, 107, 109
Washington Post (newspaper), 202
Washington, 7, 31, 192, 209
Wehrmacht, 29
Weimar Republic, 120
West Germany, 29, 128
Western air campaign, 110

Western Balkans, 59
Western Europe, 107–8, 125
Western European Union, 101
Western Pacific, 102
Wilhelm, 42
Wilson, Thomas Woodrow, 108
World Central Kitchen, 137
World Economic Forum (WEF), 161
World Trade Organization (WTO), 119
World War I, 107
World War II, 99, 106, 107, 112, 160, 179, 195, 214
World War III, 108, 140

Xi Jin Ping, 145

Yale University, 209
Yeltsin, Boris, 120
Yermak, Andriy, 208
Yle, 188
Yugoslav Wars, 100

Zeitenwende, viii, 14, 41, 62, 122, 135, 153–5, 165, 169, 172, 173, 204
  Scholz's speech, 159
Zelenskyy, Volodymyr, 207
Zeven de Provinciën, 88–90, 89*f*